The Temporary
European

The Temporary European

*Lessons and Confessions
of a Professional Traveler*

CAMERON HEWITT

TRAVELERS' TALES
AN IMPRINT OF SOLAS HOUSE, INC.
PALO ALTO

Travelers' Tales and Solas House are trademarks of Solas House, Inc.,
Palo Alto, California
travelerstales.com | solashouse.com

Art Direction and Cover Design: Kimberly Nelson
Interior Design and Page Layout: Howie Severson
Cover Photograph: © Jannes Jacobs
Interior Photographs: All images © Cameron Hewitt

Library of Congress Cataloging-in-Publication Data is available
upon request.

978-1-60952-204-9 (paperback)
978-1-60952-205-6 (ebook)

First Edition
Printed in the United States
10 9 8 7 6 5 4 3 2 1

For Shawna
(of course)
who made possible all of these stories
and so much more

*Usually none of my friends wants to go to the same place
at the same time as I do, so I strike out alone. But I tell
people I am not alone after a taxi driver comes to my
door and takes me to the airport in Columbus, Ohio,
until a taxi driver brings me back to my door.
Interesting people are found all over the world.*

—Mildred C. Scott, *Jams Are Fun*

*I urge you to please notice when you are happy,
and exclaim or murmur or think at some point,
"If this isn't nice, I don't know what is."*

—Kurt Vonnegut, *A Man Without a Country*

Table of Contents

Table of Contents

THE TEMPORARY EUROPEAN

Foreword

by Rick Steves

*I*n 1999, I received a long letter from a recent college graduate in Ohio. I had just returned from a trip to Europe and was working through a two-month-tall stack of mail. This letter was destined for the recycling bin, but something about it grabbed my attention. The writing was lively, thoughtful, and filled with a boundless joy of travel. And it was ballsy. The writer couldn't wait to tell me about his trip to Europe. He described his favorite moments, shared insights that had escaped me, and even offered to write an Eastern Europe guidebook for me. (The nerve!) And before I knew it, I'd read all five pages.

At the end of the letter, the writer mentioned that he was looking for a job and an excuse to relocate to Seattle. So, I called him and asked: Are you serious about coming to work for me? He was. And a few months later, Cameron Hewitt joined the staff of Rick Steves' Europe.

My instincts told me that Cameron might play a key role in the future of my company. And in the two decades since, that's just what he's done. Soon Cameron was updating our guidebooks in Europe and editing them when he was back in the office. And within three years of his arrival, Cameron had written a *Rick Steves Eastern Europe* guidebook—expanding our coverage, for the first time, to include Hungary, Poland, Croatia, and Slovenia.

Cameron was content to spend time in his beloved Eastern Europe. But gradually I nudged him toward the rest of the Continent. To be honest, I needed another generalist to help shoulder the workload. In the years since, Cameron has updated, at one time or another, just about every chapter in every Rick Steves guidebook. And, collaborating with our talented team of researchers, our co-authors, and our editorial staff, Cameron has spearheaded the creation of many new titles, from Greece to Belgium, from Switzerland to Barcelona, from Istanbul to Scotland, from Iceland to Sicily—and he pioneered our cruise port guidebooks, as well. If you've used a Rick Steves guidebook, you've read a lot of Cameron's words, likely without realizing it.

Meanwhile, Cameron also worked for several years as a tour guide—leading Rick Steves bus tours through Eastern Europe—before "retiring" to focus full-time on books. And he's helped me scout, write, and produce several episodes of my public television series. It turns out that kid from Ohio was prolific . . . a travel content dynamo.

A few years ago—as if he weren't busy enough—Cameron started a blog, which I was proud to host on my website. It became the perfect creative outlet for all of the travel tales and observations that just don't fit in the pages of a guidebook. As Cameron's blog gained a loyal following, I found myself looking forward, too, to each new installment.

When the COVID-19 pandemic hit in early 2020, our travel business basically went into hibernation. Cameron—like the rest of us—was grounded. When he said he was considering using that time to gather these writings, and some new ones, into a travel book, I was all for it. What a perfect way to spend those long quarantine months. After helping create so many Rick Steves guidebooks, and with so much travel experience woven into his unpublished essays, he deserved a book of his own. As Cameron headed off on his writing sabbatical, I told him I wanted to be the first person to read it.

Now that I have—and admittedly, I'm biased—I can say it's some of the best travel writing I've read . Reading it during COVID was, for me, the next best thing to a plane ticket. While Cameron hasn't actually led a Rick Steves tour in many years, with *The Temporary European,* he's once again playing tour guide: His book led me through favorite haunts with a fresh perspective and to new places for wonders I didn't even realize Europe had to offer.

I find Cameron's writing vivid, funny, perceptive, intimate, and charged both with a love of travel and a deep sense of humanity. He has a knack for dropping you right down in the middle of places you didn't even realize you wanted to be. His writing inspires me to be a better and more insightful traveler. Cameron travels and writes as I would hope to, if I were 20 years younger. And he does something I cannot: gives voice to the next generation of "Rick Steves travelers."

Travel writing like this isn't exactly in vogue, and hasn't been for many years. But that's a shame. I'm troubled by the state of what passes for "travel content" these days. In our age of bucket lists, Instagram beauty shots, and content-farmed listicles, we've lost sight of authentic, substantial travel writing: stowing away with a great traveler and seeing where the road takes you. And I'm happy that Cameron's book found the right home at Travelers' Tales, which has been publishing just this sort of high-quality, transformative travel content for decades.

It's fitting that this book was, in a roundabout way, a product of the pandemic. Not being able to travel caused many of us to reflect on what got us traveling in the first place. And, to me, Cameron's thoughtful approach perfectly embodies what I hope will be a new ethos of mindful travel as the world opens up again. What better time to simply read, and dream, as a great traveler leads you through the joys of Europe?

Rick Steves
Edmonds, Washington

Preface

Coffee and Ćejf

One morning in Mostar, I met my friend Alma for coffee. Not just coffee—Bosnian coffee.

Alma greeted me with her customary, exaggerated warmth: "Aaaaah, Cah-meh-ron! So goooood to see you, my old friend!"

I first met Alma years ago, when I was leading a tour in Bosnia and she was our local guide. She has a painful personal history and a huge heart, two things that seem to go together. Alma and her husband were living in Mostar with their toddler on May 9, 1993, when they were rocked awake by artillery shells raining down from the mountaintop. They persevered through the next few years as bombardment, siege, and street-by-street warfare ripped their city apart.

"Alma" means benevolent, soulful, wise. And Alma is all of these things in abundance. Anyone who meets her is struck by both her generosity of spirit and her forthrightness. Alma speaks her mind in the way of someone who knows mortal danger first-hand and no longer worries with niceties. And she has mastered the art of giving visitors insight into Bosnian culture.

"Here in Bosnia, we have unfiltered coffee—what you Americans might call 'Turkish coffee,'" Alma said as we walked. "But it's not just a drink. It's a social ritual. A way of life."

We made our way through Mostar toward a café. The streets were cobbled with river stones—round as tennis balls and polished like marble—that threatened to turn our ankles with each step. Finally we reached a cozy caravanserai courtyard that felt very close to the Ottoman trading outpost that Mostar once was.

We settled in at a low table, and the coffee arrived: a small copper tray, hand-hammered with traditional Bosnian designs. A little copper pot, lined with shiny metal and filled with slightly frothy coffee. A dish containing exactly two Turkish delight candies, dusted with powdered sugar. And two small ceramic cups, wrapped in yet more decorative copper.

The server deliberately poured coffee into each cup. I reached for mine too eagerly. Alma stopped me. "Careful!" she said. "Bosnian coffee punishes those who hurry, with a mouthful of grounds."

Patiently, Alma explained the procedure—and the philosophy—of Bosnian coffee. "There's no correct or incorrect way to drink Bosnian coffee. People spend lifetimes perfecting their own

ritual. But one thing we agree on is that coffee isn't just about the caffeine. It's about relaxing. Being with people you enjoy."

Alma paused for effect, then took a deliberate sip. Looking deep into my eyes and smiling a relaxed smile, she continued with a rhythmic, mesmerizing cadence: "*Talk* to your friends. *Listen* to what they have to say. *Learn* about their lives. Then take a sip. If your coffee isn't strong enough, gently swirl your cup. If it's too strong, just wait. Let it settle. That gives you more time to talk anyway."

Looking around the courtyard, sparkling with mellow conversation and gentle laughter, Alma said, "This is a good example of *merak*. *Merak* is one of those words that you cannot directly translate into English. It means, basically, enjoyment. This relaxed atmosphere among friends. Nursing a cup of coffee with nowhere in particular to be—savoring the simple act of passing the time of day."

Taking another slow sip, Alma noted that the Bosnian language is rife with these non-translatable words. Another example: *raja*. "*Raja* is a sense of being one with a community," Alma said. "But it also means frowning on anyone who thinks they're a big shot. It's humility. Everyone knowing their place, and respecting it."

But my favorite Bosnian word is *ćejf* (pronounced "chayf"). *ćejf* is that annoying habit you have that drives your loved ones batty. And yet, it gives you pleasure. Not just pleasure; deep satisfaction. In traditional Bosnian culture, *ćejf* is the way someone spins their worry beads, the way he packs and smokes his pipe, or her exacting procedure for preparing and drinking a cup of coffee.

Even if we don't have a word for it, *ćejf* is universal. Maybe you have a precise coffee order that tastes just right. ("Twelve-ounce oat milk half-caf latte with one Splenda, extra hot.") Or every weekend, you feel compelled to wash and detail your car, or bake a batch of cookies, or mow your lawn in tidy diagonal lines, or prune your hedges just so. My own *ćejf* is the way I tinker with my fantasy football lineup. (Should I start Marvin Jones or Jarvis Landry this week?) Or the way I chew gum when I'm stressed: Extra Polar Ice flavor, always two sticks . . . never just one.

Americans dismiss this behavior as "fussy" or "O.C.D." or simply "annoying." We're expected to check our *ćejf* at the door. But in Bosnia, they just shake their head and say, "What are you gonna do? That's his *ćejf*." You don't have to like someone's *ćejf*. But—as long as it's not hurting anyone—you really ought to accept it. Because everyone has one.

Reaching the bottom of my cup, I noted that the grounds had left no residue at all. "When it's done properly," Alma said triumphantly, "you'll never feel grit between your teeth. If you find a layer of 'mud' in the bottom, it means that someone—either you or the person who made the coffee—was in too much of a hurry."

Setting down her mudless cup, Alma allowed the silence between us to linger for several long moments. She knew I was in a hurry to get back to work. (I am always in a hurry.) But she was determined to slow me down. We waited. And waited. I sat like a dog with a treat on my nose. My mind began to whirr: Is it easier to be soulful, more at peace with idiosyncrasies, when you've survived hardship? Or is this ritual offering a glimpse into a Muslim worldview?

And then, as if pushing through turbulence on the way to blue skies, I felt myself calming. My pulse abated. I sensed the *merak* percolating around me. I tuned in to the details flowing in the background behind Alma's smiling face. It's the first time that having coffee has slowed me down rather than revved me up.

Finally, sensing my peace, Alma took a deep breath and spoke: "Good. Shall we move on? What's next?"

* * *

Alma is just one of the countless Europeans I've gotten to know over two and a half decades of exploring Europe. During and after college, I traveled around Europe on my own. And since 2000, I've worked for Rick Steves' Europe, one of North America's most respected authorities on travel. For most of that time, I've been an editor, researcher, and author of our bestselling guidebook series. And I've also guided tours, scouted and produced television shows, and much more.

I spend at least three months each year on the road—typically six weeks in the spring and six weeks in the fall. That's a grand total of over five years in more than 35 European countries (which— let's be honest—is more than I once thought Europe even had). And over all those years of spending time with Europeans, I've come to feel like a "temporary European" myself.

Being a travel writer sounds exotic. It's a job that sparks people's imaginations. I get more than my share of strangers gushing, "You have my dream job!" The reality is far less romantic—but even more interesting—than people suspect.

Like any job, most of it grows mundane: fourteen-hour work days, overwhelming to-do lists, meticulous note-taking, marathon walking, and asking a million people a million questions. And then you get up tomorrow and do it all over again. This book pulls back the curtain on that reality, offering a look at "how the sausage gets made" in the travel business. I tell the story of how I got my start, and I describe what it's like to research guidebooks, guide tours, make travel TV, and work with a famous travel guru and his merry band of travelers.

But even the busiest work trip is more than work. And this book is much more than just film shoots and bus tours gone bad. It's a chronicle of travel tales about people, places, and experiences from my 25-plus years of exploring Europe. Along the way, you'll gain some insight into how a travel writer thinks about

Europe—what's going through my mind as I shape the content that shapes your travels.

Of course, Europe is a big place, and this book can only hint at what it has to offer. But having the opportunity to go back again and again feels like slowly, over a lifetime, creating an Impressionist painting of Europe in my mind: Each brushstroke contains its own beauty and nuance; zooming out, a complete, if fuzzy, vision begins to coalesce.

In my first years on the job, I was consumed by my work. But as I grew more efficient, I began to pull my head out of my notes and travel more mindfully. Risa Laib, who apprenticed me, suggested that I find something each day to enjoy just for me. For her, it was pausing to listen to church bells chime. For me, it's the stories you'll find in this book. These are usually not the things I go to Europe to write about. But they're the things that stick with me long after I've come home . . . ringing in my ears like church bells. After all those trips, I've learned an important lesson: When Europe is telling you to slow down and enjoy . . . slow down and enjoy.

These stories, and my travel philosophy, have been shaped by the many Europeans I meet on the road—people like Alma. And they've been shaped by Rick, Risa, and my other well-traveled colleagues. But our spiritual guide on this journey is my wife's Great-Great-Aunt Mildred.

Well into her 70s, Mildred Scott traveled the world by herself, in an era when such a thing was unheard of. Late in life, she wrote a memoir with a title that has become my travel motto: *Jams Are Fun*. Mildred understood that the best memories are created when a trip goes sideways, and the most beautiful moments arrive in the space between the stops on a busy itinerary. She reminds me to slow down and savor those church-bell moments. And when things refuse to go according to plan—as invariably happens—she whispers in my ear, "Jams are fun!"

Obviously, my travels are shaped by who I am: a white, straight, affluent, fortysomething American man. In short, I am ridiculously privileged—and now, to top it off, I get paid to travel for a living. I recognize that my perspective and my experiences on the road will differ from yours. But I hope you'll take these writings as a celebration of the universal joy of traveling in Europe.

When I read Aunt Mildred's words, I'm struck by how her travels—as an arthritic septuagenarian in the 1960s—resonate with my own. The details are different, but the spirit is the same. Regardless of your life story, I hope you'll discover a familiarity in these pages.

While we may approach on different paths, we travelers all wind up on the same road, united by the wonder we find far from home. We travel because we love how it feels to be out in the world, and the people we meet there. We can't explain exactly why we're so driven. But we know good travel when we see it.

The Temporary European is a collection of travel stories, as far-ranging (both geographically and thematically) as my last 25 years of travels. In a few cases, I've simplified events or combined elements of different trips for better storytelling, and I've changed a few of the names. But everything described in these pages really happened.

Some of the chapters are light anecdotes, humorous and just for fun. Others share cultural insights. Still others delve into practical topics, such as how to find good gelato, or how to survive the experience of driving in Sicily. And a few ponder bigger questions: What is the impact of tourism on a fragile place and its people? What can we learn from Europe—about immigration, for example—that might illuminate our own challenges? What makes us like a place, or *not* like a place?

As you read these stories, you may feel like the three blind men pondering an elephant: One touches the trunk and thinks it's a snake; another grabs the tail and believes it's a rope; another feels the leg and decides it's a tree trunk.

This hodgepodge quality feels just right for a travel book. After all, every trip is a loose collection of impactful moments. Sometimes, in retrospect, they come together in perfect harmony; other times they're discordant, with the horn section doing something cheerful over here while the strings weep over there. This is even more the case for a professional traveler, whose itinerary is dictated less by their own interests than by the needs of their employer. (My travel agent answers my phone calls by asking, "All right, which crazy combination of cities are you connecting this time?")

That said, I have organized the stories thematically, juxtaposing ones that, in retrospect, were in conversation all along. You may choose to flip around within these pages, skipping to the places and topics that appeal to you. But if you read cover-to-cover, I hope the shape of a complete elephant emerges.

That "elephant" is a sort-of-memoir about half a lifetime spent exploring Europe. It's my meandering answer to a question I'm frequently asked: "What's it like to be a travel writer for a living?"

*For some reason we Yankees
seem to look different from the
Europeans, and they spot us.*

—Mildred C. Scott,
  Jams Are Fun

PART ONE

The Temporary European

*T*ina Hiti, who lives near Slovenia's Lake Bled, is one of my closest European friends. We became tour guides around the same time, and we quickly hit it off. Although we grew up a world apart—she in socialist Yugoslavia, me in Reagan-era, small-town Ohio—we're a matched set. I'm shy around new people; Tina is the instant life of the party. I tend to be a thinker; Tina is a feeler. Tina dresses with a tasteful blend of fashion and practicality, and has a new hairstyle every time I see her. I am utterly unfashionable, buy most of my clothes in bulk at big box stores, and have had the same haircut since college. And yet, Tina and I see eye-to-eye on what really matters: Our travel philosophies align perfectly. And we both adore Slovenia.

Tina is always trying to better understand her American tour members. And that's probably another reason we get along so well, because I'm just as obsessed with unraveling the mysteries of Europe.

One summer, Tina brought her partner, Sašo, and their two young boys on a road trip across the western United States. They stayed with my wife and me in Seattle for a few days. The boys loved going up the Space Needle, watching the fish-throwers at Pike Place Market, and digging into my famous cedar-plank salmon with corn on the cob. And, of course, we took them to a baseball game. At the seventh-inning stretch, the entire stadium stood up and sang "Take Me Out to the Ball Game." Tina's eyes grew wide and her mouth dropped open. She said, "I cannot believe, after spending months of my life with Americans for the last 20 years, I have never once heard this song that, apparently, *everyone* knows by heart."

Recently, Tina and I were having another of our many conversations about the differences between Europe and the USA. ("What is this word 'washrooms' that some people use?" Tina wonders. "Is it the same as 'bathrooms'?") As we spoke, I kept referring to "we Americans" and "you Europeans." Tina stopped me. "Wait just one minute, Cameron," she said, playfully stern. "Come on. You are a European."

I was flattered. But that's not quite right. Yes, I've been fortunate to have an experience with Europe that's both broad and deep. And yet, I always keep one foot planted squarely in the USA, and America will always be my home. What I think Tina has tuned in to is this: When I cross the Atlantic, I suspend my American-ness and open myself up to wherever I'm visiting—aspiring to become a temporary European.

While this is easier for a professional traveler, I believe anyone can travel with the same goal in mind. It means becoming part of the European ecosystem—not just passively consuming Europe, but actively participating in it. Rick Steves describes this as being a "cultural chameleon"—adopting the customs and daily rhythms of wherever you may go. In England, you might caffeinate with a cup of midafternoon tea; in Italy or France, you slam down a tiny mug of espresso standing at a busy counter; and in Bosnia-Herzegovina, as we've learned from Alma, you deliberately nurse a copper-clad cup of unfiltered coffee while chatting with friends.

The temporary European is empathetic: They assume that other people's ways make sense to them, and they try to understand why. If you barge into a French shop without saying *Bonjour, Madame!* and find the shopkeeper unfriendly, imagine how you'd feel if someone did the same in your living room. If you're in Croatia and people are cranky, trust them when they explain that the muggy Jugo wind puts everyone in a foul mood. If Germans are standing in the pouring rain, with not a car in sight, waiting for the light to change, wait with them while contemplating why rule-following is important to their notion of a successful society. And if an Italian barista grows agitated when you try to order a cappuccino after lunchtime, consider how having so much milk late in the day might be bad for your digestion.

We're primed by both nature and culture to impose our pre-conceptions on anything new. Even for experts, it requires concerted effort to fight those twinges of judgment and travel with curiosity. It's simple in concept, difficult in execution. The goal is to discover, and appreciate, those little quirks that make sense to Europeans just as "Take Me Out to the Ball Game" makes sense to American baseball fans.

The next few chapters begin to explore this "temporary European" mindset. In Kraków, Poland, I battle jet lag while seeking that moment when you know you're back in Europe. Island-hopping along Croatia's Dalmatian Coast, I drop in on old friends and take the pulse of an increasingly popular destination where change is routine. In Tuscany, we consider how so much of Europe approaches every aspect of life with an artisanal zeal. And finally, we flash back to my travel "origin story": my epic post-college trip across Europe, which led to meeting Rick Steves and set me on the path to becoming a professional traveler and a temporary European.

Kraków, Poland

Hey! I'm in Europe!

ulture shock is very real, even for those of us who should
have an acquired immunity.

Flying from Seattle to Kraków, I land in the place in
Europe where I feel most at home. And yet, I still have to ease
myself into Europe.

From the baggage claim, sliding glass doors admit me to
Poland. Out at the stanchions is the usual scrum: Well-dressed
chauffeurs holding placards with the names of strangers. Grubbier-
looking cabbies hoping to snare some impromptu business. And
families—some literally bouncing with excitement—awaiting the
arrival of a loved one.

At the end of a redeye journey, this sea of faces always makes
me jealous. I have an ethic of riding public transportation into
town, so I can explain it to my readers. But I've been to Kraków
more times than I can count. I know exactly where the train
departs from, how long it takes, and how much it costs. So I've
treated myself to an easier arrival.

"Cah-meh-ron!" shouts a familiar voice—enunciating my name
phonetically, with three syllables, in that distinctly European way.

Striding up to me, with a huge grin, is Andrzej—or, as he insists
to Americans, Andrew. He wraps me up in a bear hug, gripping me
like a handshake that's desperate to impress. "Welcome home!"

Andrew has been driving my readers around Poland since I first recommended him in my guidebook many years ago. He has white hair, keen eyes, and a kind face. Andrew, who lived for a few years in Chicago, speaks flawless American English and is a generous conversationalist.

About ten years ago, I took my own advice and hired Andrew to explore the pig-farming villages where my great-grandparents were born, about 40 miles east of Kraków. Some relatives from the Chicago suburbs even flew in for the occasion. Andrew was intrepid. He drove us to remote towns we'd found scrawled in Grandpa's chickenscratch, chatted up the old timers hanging out in front of the general store, and charmed the priest of the village church in a quest for family records. Within minutes we were knocking on the doors of Dąbrowskis and Łucarzes with whom we shared a few distant strands of DNA. After that trip, he became Cousin Andrew.

He grabs my bag and ushers me out to his car. On the short drive downtown, we catch up on each other's lives since we last met a year ago. Andrew is at an age where this consists mainly of a rehearsal of recent health scares. But his spirit is as buoyant as ever.

Andrew drops me off at my hotel and envelops me in another fierce hug, naming all of the relatives I'm instructed to convey his greetings to. We confirm plans to meet up in a few days for some day-tripping. Then he drives off, and I collapse on the bed for a few minutes.

On that first afternoon in Europe, giving in to the seduction of sleep is tempting . . . so very tempting. But if I'm to have any prayer of being productive the next few days, I must stay awake until a reasonable local bedtime. I take a shower—that wakes me up for all of five minutes—and head out to walk until I drop.

I'm also looking for something: a "Hey! I'm in Europe!" moment. It's that epiphany where sleep deprivation gives way to euphoria, and you realize that, yes, being awake for more than

20 hours does have a payoff. I never know exactly when this will happen. But it always happens.

Walking toward Kraków's Main Market Square, trying to get my European sea legs, my head swirls with new/old surroundings: I hear horse hooves pounding against cobbles; I smell dill, beets, garlic, and simmering pork fat wafting out of restaurants; and I feel a moist breeze cut through the hot late-summer air, tinged with smog. I subconsciously alter my route to walk past Dąbrowskiego—a men's dress shirt store that shares my Grandpa's name. Cousin Andrew was right: I am home.

Just a few more steps take me into Kraków's Main Market Square. And just like every other time I've been here, that first look takes my breath away. There's something cinematic about this space—the way it opens up with an insistent magnificence as you approach, like Dorothy opening the door to Oz or Harry Potter arriving at Hogwarts.

The vast Square is ringed by colorful mansions and townhomes. The centerpiece is the canary-yellow Cloth Hall, whose frilly Renaissance balustrades furnish the Square with gentility. Always lively, today the Square's bustle is cranked up. It's a sunny weekend in early September, and everyone is out, as if obligated by natural law, celebrating the last hurrah of summer.

Just as I'm admiring the mismatched twin towers of St. Mary's Church, which rise up from one corner of the Square, the church bells clang. And then, with the final tone still resonating in the air, a window at the top of the taller tower opens and the sun glints off the brass bell of a bugle. The trumpeter begins playing the *hejnał*, just as he does at the top of each hour. This simple tune commemorates the 13th-century town watchman who sounded the alarm upon spotting Tatar invaders on the horizon. According to legend, before he could finish, an arrow pierced his throat— which is why the *hejnał* stops abruptly midway through.

And just like that . . . Hey! I'm in Europe!

The *hejnał* cuts off, the trumpeter waves to a smattering of applause, and life resumes.

Suddenly, I'm overtaken by nostalgia, recalling the first time I stood on this spot. It was 1999, and I'd just arrived at the end of an absurdly long journey from England that required a ferry crossing, 30 hours riding the rails, and two successive night trains. Back then, the colors were muted by layers of soot and neglect, and the Square felt far less alive. But you couldn't miss the majesty of the space.

Iconic places create outsized first impressions. These are so vivid, they become tinged with nostalgia even as they occur: Stepping out of Santa Lucia station, on Venice's Grand Canal, and seeing a chaotic swirl of watercraft plying the green-brown water and the languid lagoon air. Laying eyes on the Eiffel Tower, even bigger than you'd imagined—rising shamelessly high above everything else in Paris. Stepping into Red Square, which bends along the Kremlin wall as if with the curvature of the earth toward the fairy-tale domes of St. Basil's, and feeling very, very small.

If you're lucky enough to deepen your familiarity with a place, at a certain point you stop noticing those flamboyant landmarks. You build up a resistance to the majesty; like turning the ring on your camera lens, the grandiosity fades out of focus. And that's when you get to the good stuff: It frees you up to zoom in on details, explore as a temporary local, and begin to assemble the most useful vestiges of those first impressions into a routine of everyday life.

Doing a few lazy laps around the Square, I tune in to the little landmarks, unnoticed by most, that signal my return to Europe: The old hand pumps, caked with thick layers of dark-green paint, still used by the flower vendors under their yellow canopies. The civic donation box, shaped like a shield and marked with the crowned-K city seal. The babushki who sit behind their boxy, blue, aquarium-like stands, filled with fresh-baked dough rings called *obwarzanki*.

Leaving the Square and walking up wide pedestrian streets, I feel my mental map of Kraków lighting up. I spot shortcuts that locals use to slip unnoticed while evading tourists and traffic. I pass my favorite cheap diners and convenience stores to stop in and buy a Prince Polo chocolate-dipped wafer bar, or a pack of Delicje jelly cookies. If a building gets restored or a fence gets painted or a flower bed gets replanted, I notice.

That's the trick to becoming a temporary European: You have to push yourself beyond those big, delicious first impressions. Until you can let go of the "big stuff," you won't have the bandwidth to absorb the "little stuff." The Square will still be there, as spectacular as ever. You just need to train yourself to zoom back out when you pass through at a particularly beautiful moment. Slow down, take a breath, and bottle it up for future daydreams.

After an hour or so of stumbling around town, I find my way back to the Square for exactly one of those moments. In the cool of the evening, under a dreamy purple sky, the monuments glow in decadent floodlights. Cinderella horse carriages line up in front of St. Mary's, the bright lights under their running boards attracting customers like bugs to a zapper. A young mom brings her toddler over to pet a horse.

Soaking in the magic, I become aware that, on my personal list of Kraków icons, something's missing. During one of my earliest visits, back in the early 2000s, I heard clapping to the beat of a tinny boombox. Following the music, I spotted some pre-teens breakdancing on a big piece of cardboard. I mean, full-on, 1984-vintage, Electric Boogaloo *break*dancing. They could barely hold a handstand for more than a second . . . but they were determined. There was something so hopelessly unhip, so disarmingly earnest about it all.

I got used to seeing those breakdancers with each return visit. But not this time. Making my final pass through the Square, I ease myself into the likelihood that, surely, they are old enough by now to have real jobs, families, obligations, and happy memories of breakdancing on the Square.

Just then, Gloria Estefan's "Conga" begins to play. A crowd gathers. Making my way over, I see those same kids—now ripped, bearded, and balding—executing flawless windmills and hand glides and headspins under St. Mary's towers. Their sound system is better, as are their moves. But it's definitely them.

Tossing a few zlotys into the hat, I fight a too-wide smile and head back to my hotel. It has been a long day—two, actually— since I got on that plane in Seattle. But I'm back home in Europe. I laugh to myself at the unlikely longevity of those breakdancers. They created their own weird little European niche, and they filled it. And, I guess, so have I.

The Permanent Residents of Vacationland

*T*he air in Dalmatia is hot and sticky. It smells like the sea, and sunscreen, and grilling fish, and knock-off body spray, and the distinctly perfumed cleaning solution used throughout Croatia. A nice day in Dalmatia shatters your momentum—inviting you to perch on a rock and gaze out over the Adriatic, which reflects back a blaze of sunshine that hurts your eyes. Occasionally, a blast of icy wind screams down the mountain slopes to the sea, waking everybody up, banging wooden window frames against limestone lintels, and interrupting flights and boat departures. And then the lazy, muggy southerly winds pick up again, sending everyone back to the beach.

The Dalmatian Coast is Central Europe's Vacationland, and Dubrovnik is its touristic capital. This is where Germans, Austrians, Czechs, Hungarians, Slovenes, and many others head for fun in the Mediterranean sun. And now, thanks to its status as a major cruise port and a filming location for *Game of Thrones*, Dubrovnik is increasingly known to North American travelers, too.

Over twenty or so visits in about as many years, I've been fortunate to become friends with many Dalmatians—the permanent residents of Vacationland. They help me gauge how the constant changes in this region affect their lives.

Waking up on my first morning in Dubrovnik, I waste no time slipping into my daily routine: coffee at the no-name café at the bottom end of the Stradun, the Old City's central pedestrian drag.

I'm warmly greeted by two guys named Pero and a couple of their friends, who invite me to pull up a chair. The gang used to call this café, where they catch up on each other's lives, "The Sitting Room." But a few years ago, they rechristened it "Facebook."

I order a *bijela kava*—"white coffee," the poetic Croatian name for a caffe latte. Sipping our drinks and chatting, we look out at the promenade. The daily onslaught of visitors has not yet commenced. When it's empty, the Stradun's surface is a mirror—polished to a high gloss by centuries of sailors, spice traders, and cruise passengers. The yellow of the stone, the green of the window frames, the orange of the roof tiles, the blue of the sky, and the white of the clouds are all reflected in the shiny street.

It's a small miracle that this Croatian coffee klatsch tradition has survived. Sitting on what may be the best people-watching real estate in Europe, here's a table full of native-born locals. They grew up playing in Dubrovnik's skinny, steep streets before the town was famous. They lived through the 1991-1992 siege that devastated their city—some of them huddled in the medieval walls, others shooting back from the hillsides above. And in recent years, they've held on for dear life as their hometown has become a tourism superstar.

The two Peros both rent rooms on the stepped lane that climbs up the hill just over my shoulder. I met the first Pero in 2003, when I was writing our new Eastern Europe guidebook. I was determined to sniff out some central, family-run B&Bs as an alternative to the characterless, communist-era conference hotels on Dubrovnik's outskirts. Back then, good accommodations were

hard to find; I had to ask around, anybody and everybody. The tourist office wasn't allowed to recommend specific businesses, but the guy at the desk took pity on me. Glancing around as if about to sell me pure heroin, he whispered, "I know a guy. I'll call him."

When I arrived at Pero's doorstep, he didn't know what to make of me. But he showed me around his restored townhouse: comfortable, affordable, and perfectly located in the Old City. I put it straight in the book. And by the time I came back the next year, his B&B was a hit with my readers.

Soon, Pero couldn't handle the demand. He introduced me to his neighbor across the lane, also named Pero, who had his own stable of rooms. They've dubbed themselves "Pero #1" and "Pero #2." (I call Pero #2 "The Deuce.") My Croatia guidebook mentions at least three other Peros, plus a Pepo and a Petar. Apparently if you want in my book, it really helps to be named "Peter."

When The Deuce's rooms also began to fill up, the Peros introduced me to another neighbor: sisters Anita and Ivana, who rent a few simple but tidy rooms next door. (I've met each sister several times but can't, for the life of me, remember which is which.) The result is a pod of stone houses, facing each other across a narrow lane at the top of town, populated almost entirely by Rick Steves readers. The Peros have nicknamed the street "Rickova ulica."

This morning at breakfast, the gang is recovering from a long, grueling, abnormally hot summer. Peak season is cresting—things should quiet down, gradually, from here on out. Anita (or Ivana), who works at a gift shop just up the main drag, looks exhausted. Squinting into the sun, she takes a drag from her cigarette. "It's been too busy, and too hot, this summer. You would not believe how demanding tourists can be."

Also joining us is Željko, one of the rare Dubrovnik residents who doesn't work directly in tourism. He recently retired after more than 40 years as an air-traffic controller. Sipping his coffee, he jokes, "Now I work with the Peros: publicity and public relations."

Our café sits kitty-corner from the town's bell tower. This medieval belfry is tall, skinny, and square, like a double-high Jenga tower. Midway up the tower is a "digital" readout showing the minutes (to the nearest five). And up at the top, a pair of bronze bell-ringers, Maro and Baro, swing their hammers to mark each hour. I remark how this reminds me of the famous clocktower on St. Mark's Square, in Venice.

Simultaneously, all four of them recoil. The Deuce smiles politely as he informs me I'm full of shit: "Aha! Yes, you are astute. But did you know this tower was built many years before Venice's? If one is a copy of another, then *they* copied *us*." If my goal was to spark a lively conversation at the mention of Dubrovnik's rival Adriatic city-state—which it was—then I've succeeded.

Pero #1's phone rings, and he chats for a few moments in mellow Croatian. He finishes the call using a refrain you overhear again and again in Dalmatia: "*Ajde. Ajde. Ajde. Ajde, Bog. Ajde, Bog. Bog. Bog bog bog.*" Both of these words are filler: *ajde* is "yep," and *bog* is "bye." The words don't matter; Dalmatians just savor the musicality of connection.

We resume chatting and grousing and laughing together. In a town so mobbed by tourists that locals become invisible, these people link me to the real community of Dubrovnik. Every few passersby, the Peros nod or give a subtle wave, revealing a fellow native. They teach me a few pointers: Men carrying cameras are tourists. Men carrying handbags are locals. Men wearing shorts are tourists. Men wearing long pants in the hot sun are locals. Men wearing capri pants are probably Germans.

This café is one of several eateries in Dubrovnik that offer a (semi-secret) 30 percent discount to local residents. But it's a losing battle. In recent years, fewer and fewer natives live inside the Old City—most have converted their residences into tourist apartments. Parking prices near the Old City have skyrocketed even for locals, who now pay a hefty hourly fee to visit their own hometown. The "Facebook" crew has gradually shed members. These days they're lucky if a quorum shows up for morning coffee.

By the time our cups are filled only with brown foam, and Maro and Baro clang their bell nine times, the Stradun is getting crowded. As the sun intensifies, the neighboring shop cranks open their striped awning. I gather my things, head out for a day's work, and wave goodbye to the Peros, Željko, and Ivana (or Anita). I'll be back tomorrow. And so will they.

When I'm doing guidebook research, Dubrovnik is the only place where I need to budget extra time just to socialize. Everyone loves to catch up.

Jadranka rents apartments inside her home on the hillside above Dubrovnik's walled Old City. I always block off at least an hour when I visit her—for a guidebook-updating task that should take ten minutes—simply because I enjoy her company. From the congested chaos of bus stops and tourist agencies just outside the main gate, a steep lane leads up into a peaceful breeze. Ringing Jadranka's doorbell, I step onto a chirpy garden terrace with views over red rooftops, medieval forts, and the distant Adriatic. She remarks how I've lost weight, or gained it, then brings me a cup of coffee and a plate of cookies. We sit together under grape vines and chat. I ask after her son, who was a teenager when I first met the family and is now raising his own kids next door.

On this visit, Jadranka asks me how old Rick Steves is. Turns out they are about the same age. "That explains it," she says. She reminds me that when Rick (then age 50) first listed her place in our guidebook, he described Jadranka and her husband as "a young professional couple." The next year, I (then age 30) came to update Jadranka's listing, and the description changed to "a *middle-aged* professional couple." "I'm just hoping you don't decide to send somebody in their 20s," she jokes. "I'm not ready to be 'an old professional couple' yet."

Tour guide Roberto de Lorenzo is blessed with an unusual gift for sharing his passion for his hometown. His walking tours challenge visitors to see Dubrovnik's recent popularity as one more chapter in the story of a trading post that opens its gates to the world.

Roberto relishes the opportunity to get to know travelers from around the globe, many of whom become friends. On this visit, Roberto is bursting with excitement about his recent trip with his mother to Pennington, New Jersey. They had hit it off with some visitors, who, after returning home, repeatedly invited them to come stateside for a visit. Finally, they made the trip.

Roberto describes stepping out of what he calls "Pennsylvania Station" and into the heart of New York City. "Coming from a Mediterranean city, I expected New York to feel busy and impersonal and cold," he says. "But quite the contrary! People are so friendly, and there is a real sense of community. It could be a Mediterranean city itself."

When it's time to leave town, I hitch a ride with Pepo, a professional driver I met purely by chance many years ago. I liked him, mentioned him in my book, and since then, he's taken hundreds of my readers on day trips.

Trying to reconcile the different viewpoints that have sat in his passenger seat, Pepo quizzes me about politics stateside. Quickly it becomes clear that Pepo's just playing dumb. He listens to NPR at breakfast, reads the *New York Times,* and is better informed about American politics than many of his American clients. He just enjoys listening to the opinions of visitors, without sharing his own or passing judgement.

"You're very wise," I say.

"I'm not wise!" Pepo shoots back. "I've just talked to a million people." (But isn't that the same thing?)

Pepo took up arms to defend his hometown during the siege of Dubrovnik. Several years ago, he drove me to the half-destroyed fortress on the hilltop above town. Exploring the abandoned building, first he showed me the *Saturday Night Fever*–style, light-up disco floor from his carefree adolescence. And then, in a grotesque contrast, we ascended to the rooftop and he described his military service just a few years later: trying to hold this fortress with just a few other local boys with hunting rifles, knowing that the town's hope for freedom resided in them.

I think back on my first-ever visit to Dubrovnik, in 2003. It was about a decade removed from that war, and the city had repaired itself admirably. But tourists were still scarce, and the streets were eerily empty. Locals stood bored in doorways, wishing for customers. There was a sense of desperation—an urgency to restart tourism. Today many tell me that they're weirdly nostalgic for those lazy days, when Dubrovnik was no longer war-torn but still theirs alone.

As I'm updating his details for the book, Pepo suggests that it's time to retire his description as "a veteran of the Yugoslav Wars." This used to be a selling point. But now, he says that visitors just aren't that focused on the war anymore, and he wouldn't mind moving on, too. I see this as a very positive change.

I ask Pepo why I find it so easy to build connections with people in Dubrovnik. He believes it's a product of their unique history. Like Venice, Dubrovnik was an independent city-state. Unlike Venice, it was entirely surrounded by potentially hostile empires, rivals, and pirates. Rather than tucked in a protective lagoon in the crook of the Adriatic, Dubrovnik just sits out there, exposed. (This is also why it surrounded itself with the stoutest city walls in Europe.)

These circumstances forced Dubrovnik to become adept at welcoming outsiders and building alliances. Through this approach, trade increased and tributes decreased. The siege of the 1990s reminded them how fragile their way of life is, and re-motivated them to be good ambassadors for their city.

"It's too bad that so many people come to Dubrovnik in a hurry," I say. "Cruise passengers in town for just a few hours will probably never experience the intimate, community side of Dubrovnik that I enjoy so much."

"Not necessarily," Pepo says. "People in Dubrovnik want to connect. But they have to see that you want it, too. If you're rushing through town, they'll get out of your way. But if they notice you relaxing, lingering, and enjoying, they'll want to join you. It *is* possible."

Based on my experience, Pepo is right on. Europeans are astute: They can spot the difference between the bucket-list tourist and the listen-to-the-church bells traveler. When you're open to Dubrovnik, Dubrovnik is open in return.

Just up the Dalmatian Coast from Dubrovnik is the island of Hvar. Once a sleepy fishing community, Hvar has been discovered by affluent jet-setters. Celebrities make the circuit of Hvar's posh nightclubs and rent out entire nearby islets to moor their mega-yachts. Comparisons to Ibiza or Mykonos used to feel like a stretch. But on this visit, I can see it. Late one evening, walking along the cocktail bar–lined harbor, dodging drunk and rowdy American backpackers, I come this close to just giving up on the island and taking it out of my book.

But then Siniša saves Hvar.

Siniša runs an off-road tour company that takes visitors into the scruffy wilds of Hvar's interior. Meeting up late one afternoon, we grouse at each other for a few minutes, a pair of budding curmudgeons: "Would you believe they had to put up big signs to prohibit picnicking on the main square?" he rants. "People were getting a takeout pizza and a three-liter bottle of cheap beer, and then lying around, getting drunk in front of the cathedral!" *"Right?!"* I agree vigorously. "Kids today! I tell ya!"

With that out of our systems, Siniša gently reminds me that there's more to Hvar than the few congested blocks around its main square. To prove his point, he drives me deep into the island's interior, past rugged stone igloos, scrubby lavender bushes, and distant sea views over golden vineyards.

As we drive, Siniša explains how, as his community plays host to ever more visitors, it's facing an existential tug-of-war. Most Hvaranins are simply riding the beast. They're like contestants in a money booth: Cash swirls around them in a vortex; they flail their arms, grasping wildly into the wind, dropping as much as they're grabbing. The problem is, if the wind turns off, you're left with only what happens to be in your hands. That's why a vocal minority is trying to introduce sustainable tourism.

Siniša sees signs that Dubrovnik, where I just came from, is doing things right. The city strictly limits the number of cruise ships that can dock at any one time. And there's a new no-tolerance ban on loud music in the Old City: If authorities hear a peep after midnight, they pull your permit for outdoor tables. Of course, this irritates bar owners and drives away partiers, which hurts in the short term. But the status quo was scaring off a more thoughtful (and, frankly, wealthier) breed of traveler, which would have led to even more dire consequences. Essentially, Dubrovnik saw itself becoming Hvar, and put a stop to it.

"Here's another example," Siniša says. "I'd love to extend our tourist season into the winter." I couldn't agree more. Croatian seaside resorts close down in mid-October, going into hibernation until the middle of May. Early on, I mistimed some of my research trips—arriving in late April, when it was bright and sunny, but everything was still locked up tight.

"You know, even the winters can be balmy," Siniša continues. "I collect vintage postcards of Hvar. Some are many decades old, written by German tourists enjoying the island well into the winter months. The problem is, people here work so hard in the summer, they think they need a break all winter. What they don't see is that, if we could spread the demand throughout the year, they might not need so much recovery time."

Hvar is at a crossroads. Once a place no longer has to scramble for visitors, it earns the right to choose what kind of destination it's going to become. Siniša sees what few of his neighbors do: The Hvaranins have a say in the matter. The policies Hvar pursues today will shape its long-term identity and viability.

Finally, Siniša turns down a gravel driveway barely wider than his car. We step out into the cool twilight air and feel a gentle sea breeze—a world away from the glaring heat of Hvar's marbled main square. Walking to the outdoor tables of a country *konoba*, we hear only crickets.

"You know about 'zero-kilometer' and 'locally sourced,' and all that foodie stuff?" Siniša says. "This place has always made their food that way. They have no clue they're so trendy."

The restaurant is run by the Pavičić clan, who source most of their ingredients on the premises: They raise lambs, cultivate a prolific produce garden, cure their own prosciutto, make and age sheep's-milk cheeses, and hunt wild boar in the surrounding hills.

"Do you like boar?" Siniša asks. "Don't laugh, but the specialty here is what they call 'boar burgers.'"

We pass the grilling time with some prosciutto and an array of pungent cheeses. Before long, a big platter hits our table, piled high with grilled vegetables, fries, and char-grilled patties of perfectly seasoned boar.

Biting into the most flavorful chunk of meat I can recall eating, I picture all the travelers jammed into Hvar's steamy town center, eating overpriced and overcooked pasta, not even aware that this alternative exists. And I appreciate how Siniša—and people like him, who want to responsibly and respectfully share this island's traditions—give me hope for the future of Hvar. Maybe not all of his ideas will be accepted, but at least he's forcing the conversation.

From Hvar, a catamaran zips me in less than an hour to Split, Croatia's gritty second city. Split's skyline isn't romantic limestone walls and orange terra cotta roofs, as in Dubrovnik or Hvar; it's ten- and twelve-story concrete apartment blocks, weatherbeaten since the Tito years. While small-town Dalmatian ports bob with ramshackle fishing boats, tacky tourist vessels, and angular yachts, all of those get lost in the muscular industriousness of Split's main harbor.

The catamaran drops me off in the heart of the old city center. There's a unique sound to Split's harborfront: Waves, alternating big and small, roll in from the islands and slap against the rigid right angles of the stone embankment. When the swells increase, boats bounce up and down, straining against their ties, creating an irregular and echoing drumbeat that plays jazz with the splash of the surf: *Thump . . . slap . . . thump-thump . . . slap . . . thump-thump . . . slap-slap . . . thump . . .*

Enjoying this soundtrack, I think back on my first visit to Split in 2003. At that time, most travelers considered the city a necessary evil—an ugly transfer point one must endure to reach the Dalmatian Islands. To my surprise, I fell in love with Split, for many of the same reasons that some visitors hated it: Split has substance. It's the real-world antidote to the pithy effervescence of Vacationland's countless beach towns.

My travel writer's sixth sense told me Split had a bright future. And that future is now. At first, Split's discovery as a tourist destination was almost accidental: Cruise lines needed a handy place to divert overflow when Dubrovnik was full. This coincided with the urban beautification that comes as any place gains affluence. And as more people came to Split, more people liked it. Now the city faces an identity crisis: Some residents are all-in on tourism, while others still think of Split as a hardworking port first.

Arriving in Split in the late afternoon, I drop my bags at my B&B and rush out to join the lazy people-parade on the Riva, the broad, palm tree-lined promenade that runs along the harbor. The sun hangs low over the Adriatic, focusing a blazing spotlight on the Riva—making it somehow both hotter, with the concentrated sun, and cooler, with the increasing breeze, than midday.

On the far horizon, beyond the busy harbor, two mammoth cruise ships trundle toward the setting sun. And throughout Split, sunburned beachgoers are back in their rented rooms, resting and showering as they prepare for a night on the town. It's a rare moment when the Riva is, once again, mostly local.

Split's families are out socializing. Some are licking ice-cream cones. Others are camped out on hard marble benches under palm trees. Still others have rented a shaded café chair for the price of an espresso. They've mastered the art of sitting in silence next to a friend, people-watching and squinting into the sun, perfectly at home in the long, empty spaces between conversations.

Most people are simply promenading. I join them and stroll along the front of Diocletian's Palace, the onetime retirement home of the third-century Roman emperor who was born not far from here. The Rutherford B. Hayes of Roman emperors, Diocletian's legacy is a forgettable and mixed one; he's best known for being one of the last emperors to torture and execute Christians, not long before their religion became the religion of the empire.

After his reign, Diocletian returned to his native Dalmatia and built a gigantic and lavish residence, spanning many city blocks. Later, with the fall of Rome, Diocletian's Palace was cannibalized by local residents. The halls of the palace became the narrow lanes of Split's Old Town. The grand foyers and drawing rooms became piazzas. And Diocletian's mausoleum became a Catholic cathedral. Today commoners wander through Diocletian's halls, many not realizing that they're inside some of the best-preserved Roman ruins anywhere.

I carry on down the Riva, pausing at the fishing harbor called Matejuška. I love how, when they renovated this marina a few years back, they didn't replace the old fish-cleaning tables with yacht moorings—they replaced them with modern fish-cleaning tables, carved from an elegant marble-like stone.

Along the coastline past Matejuška rises a towering black box that mars the otherwise idyllic tableau of wooded hillsides and bobbing fishing boats. This is the Hotel Marjan, where the Croatian Tourist Board put me up on that first guidebook-scouting trip, in 2003. At that time, the Marjan had tumbled from its reputation as the city's top business-class hotel. During the Yugoslav Wars, it housed refugees from Croatia's battle-scarred interior; in the intervening decade, a few of its many floors were lightly refurbished and reopened as a hotel. The Marjan was a white elephant, barely remaining open for business, if only because that was simpler than closing it.

One day I returned to my hotel room to find water dripping through the bathroom light fixture, running down the wall, and leaving a rusty brown trail as it trickled toward the drain in the middle of the floor. I reported it to the front desk clerk, who momentarily feigned surprise. "You don't say?" she said. "Hm. Sounds like someone should look into that." Then she idly doodled on a notepad until I retreated to my soggy room. I always suspected that I was the hotel's very last guest.

In those days, the city had "great bones," but the economy remained anemic. It was challenging to find reliably good hotels and restaurants to recommend in my book. The next year, Rick Steves passed through Split to update and improve on my work. Like me, he wished there were better restaurants, and was determined to find one. And he did, or thought he did: a characteristic *konoba* overlooking Matejuška port. He wrote it up lavishly: "This is your cheap, dream-come-true fish joint, where a colorful local crowd shares rough wood tables and the waitstaff seems cold until you crack them up. Their tiny menu is ignored as Zlatko (the charming-as-a-cartoon waiter) tells you what's available today— dictated by what they found at the market. If you ask, they'll grill your fish rather than fry it, and bring a little plate of chopped garlic to doll up your bread with oil."

This sounded fantastic. And on my next visit, I wasted no time in going there for dinner. But when I sat down, something felt . . . off. The fabled Zlatko—tall and slender, with short black hair, an oversized moustache that more than covered his entire mouth, and very tired eyes—seemed harried and grumpy. If he was a cartoon, he was more Droopy Dog than Bugs Bunny, and far from charming.

"What's good today?" I asked Zlatko, raising my eyebrows playfully.

He couldn't possibly have been less interested. Rolling his eyes and exhaling heavily, he said, "Fish. Fish is good. Fried fish."

"Sounds good. I wonder, can I get it grilled instead of fried?"

A glimmer of recognition. Zlatko's eyes became suspicious slits, and his face turned slightly red. "Aha. Grilled."

"Yes, please. And maybe . . . "

"Lemme guess," Zlatko said, mockingly, and with a hint of menace. "You wanna leetle plate of garlic and oil, too?"

"Well, I guess . . . "

"It's OK. It's OK." He stomped off, cursing under his breath. It was clear: At some point in the previous year, Zlatko had become flooded with American tourists. And every single one of them wanted the same off-menu order . . . which, one presumes, was off-menu for a reason.

Zlatko's listing—much to his relief, I'm sure—came back down to earth in the next edition. Gone was the mention of grilled fish and garlic. And Rick and I both learned a lesson about the perils of wishful thinking and inflating expectations.

Over time, very gradually, Split began to transform. Things got better; innovative new businesses—boutique hotels and quality restaurants that didn't view diners as a curse from God—opened up. And each time I was able to upgrade and delete a mediocre hotel or restaurant (the "well, we gotta list *something*" choices), I breathed a sigh of relief.

Back in the present day, I watch the sun dip into the watery horizon. Then I head into the Old Town, winding my way through the warren of skinny alleys to the very center of Diocletian's Palace: the main square, called the Peristyle. The floodlit cathedral bell tower pops against the darkening sky—like an exclamation point celebrating Christianity's final triumph over Diocletian. There are few places in Europe where the layers of history are so easy to grasp; they're literally stacked right there in front of you.

The square resembles a sunken living rom. While fully out-doors, it feels indoors. Its glassy stone floor is surrounded on three sides by steps leading to other parts of the palace. And scattered on those steps are maroon velvet cushions that belong to a café.

I take a seat on one of those cushions, lean back against the limestone step—ignoring its hard edge digging into my back—and gaze up at the tower. Gentle music plays, and a few couples begin dancing, sharing an incredibly romantic twilight moment in Diocletian's entry hall. Having been trained by the Peros to know who's who, I notice several locals sitting on their own cushions, enjoying the scene just as much.

Tourism is an enchanting industry, and a maddening one. As a travel writer, I consider myself "tourism-adjacent"—both an observer/critic and a participant. Wearing both hats, it's clear to me how important tourism is to a destination like Dalmatia. It's in the people's DNA; it's the natural inheritance of living in a place of such astonishing beauty; and, like it or not, it's an irreplaceable source of income. But it can also be draining and exasperating. When they lost tourism during the Yugoslav Wars, Dalmatians feared that visitors would never return. Now that we have, many wish we'd just go home again.

To be honest, my takeaways as a "temporary permanent resident" of Vacationland are confusing. Maybe the answer begins with setting proper expectations on both sides. The Dalmatians would do well to accept that success breeds hard work breeds success; just because you've worked *really hard* for five months solid, you don't necessarily get the next seven months off. For our part, just because a tourist has traveled halfway around the world to find magic in Croatia, that doesn't oblige Croatia to provide it—at least, not on the tourist's terms. I wish I could put Zlatko and Siniša in a room together to duke it out; I promise I'll agree to whatever consensus they can reach.

But there are moments when all of that complexity fades into serenity, like the clear air after a thunderstorm. Sitting here on Split's incredibly old, unspeakably beautiful square, watching happy people create memories on the polished floor of an emperor's foyer, I sense the shared appreciation that all of us—visitors and residents—have for this moment.

My Dalmatian friends never seem to grow immune to the beauty that surrounds them. When they meet up each morning at their "Facebook" café, they compare notes on how gorgeous last night's sunset was. Ultimately, living in a stunning place—being a permanent resident of Vacationland—is both a blessing and a curse.

The Artisanal Life

On my first visit to the Tuscan countryside, I secretly hoped I wouldn't like it. Because falling head-over-heels for Tuscany is so . . . predicable. Certainly, someone who'd seen so much of Europe could hold their own against Tuscany's charms. Certainly, I was mistaken.

Now, a decade of visits later, I'm a convert—another tiresome Tuscany zealot. When I'm in the bucolic heart of Tuscany, I have trouble getting to sleep. My head spins with the sublime experiences of today, and my pulse quickens thinking about tomorrow. I feel like I'm on some sort of globetrotting drug, freebasing the essence of peak travel.

In Tuscany, I have many "dealers." One of them is Roberto Bechi, a tour guide who lives with his American wife and children in the countryside. From their property, you can see the stone towers of one of Italy's most inviting small cities, Siena.

Showing me around his farm, Roberto walked out through an olive grove to a deteriorating stone wall, which he supposes dates back to the Middle Ages, perhaps with Roman foundations. He described some changes he was considering—new crops over there, maybe an outbuilding here—and I could sense his anxiety rising.

Roberto paused and confessed that he feels tremendous generational pressure around creating a beautiful life. He owes it to his ancestors to carry on their legacy—to write a fitting new chapter in the story of Tuscany. Anytime he plants a tree or renovates a house, he asks himself whether it's good enough, *Tuscan* enough. This is a place where everyone is an uncompromising artisan, and life itself is their art.

You find this perfectionism in the Renaissance greats like Michelangelo, da Vinci, Donatello. And you find it on the streets of every town in Tuscany, including my favorite hill town, Montepulciano. From the main piazza, a wide pedestrian lane snakes steeply down through town. Strolling just a few hundred yards, you can drop in on four different artists—each with a fierce passion for doing just one thing at the highest possible level.

My first stop, on the downhill slope of the square, is a wine cellar called Cantina Contucci. I'm greeted with fanfare by Adamo, an elderly gentleman who's worked here most of his life. I ask Adamo what's new. He answers with the polished timing of a Catskills comic: "Last year, I finally retired . . . but they still let me come to work every day."

This town is famous for its robust red wine, Vino Nobile di Montepulciano. The grapes are grown in the surrounding hillsides, but it's here, in a warren of cellars beneath the town center, that they become Vino Nobile. Tidy rows of gigantic wine casks age beneath Gothic vaults.

As we walk among the truck-sized barrels, Adamo's animated chatter crescendos and echoes. My Italian is rusty, but Adamo's exuberance is a universal language. For emphasis, from time to time he reaches out and excitedly grips my arm. Fixing me with an intense gaze, Adamo explains that a good wine has three essential qualities. He points to his eyes, his nose, and his mouth: color, bouquet, and taste.

Finally, Adamo pops a cork and pours a sample in my glass. He won't let me leave until he's certain that I fully appreciate his life's work.

I step from Adamo's dank cellars into the bright sun. Wandering a few steps downhill, I'm drawn to the clang of metal against metal, like the ringing of an out-of-tune bell. Peeking into a cluttered time-warp of a workshop, I see a coppersmith named Cesare, clad in a heavy leather apron and hunched over an anvil—an actual anvil, like in the Roadrunner cartoons.

Cesare, even older than Adamo, still crafts his copper vessels the way he was taught as a boy. He invites me in to see his finely detailed, hammered-copper pots. Like Adamo, Cesare needs no English to convey his devotion to his craft. Proud as a new papa pulling snapshots out of his wallet, Cesare shows me a photograph of the weathervane he created for Siena's cathedral.

Flattered by my interest, Cesare declares that he will make me a gift. He pulls out a set of tools that he inherited from his father,

who inherited them from his father, and so on, dating back to 1857. He lays a copper circle on his anvil and arranges his antique stencils. Dotingly, he dents the disc with floral patterns, my wife's initials, and our wedding date. He refuses payment. Instead, he shows me a scrapbook of photos and postcards from past visitors. At his age, sharing his love for his craft, and connecting with curious people from around the world, is all that matters.

A few doors farther down the same street is a lively restaurant. The lunch rush is on, but I squeeze behind a tiny table in the corner and scan the menu, scrawled in blue pen on a heavy sheet of burnt-yellow paper.

Giulio, the owner, is a tall, balding, lanky artist with a pencil sticking out of his gray ponytail. He's more "aging hippie" than "Italian grandpa," but just like his neighbors, he's fully devoted to his craft: grilling the perfect steak.

First things first: steaming plates of handmade pasta perfectly coated in rich sauce. (While considered *primi*—"starters"—one of these could easily be an entire meal.) Then a rustic salad, with a few top-quality ingredients tossed together in olive oil and *balsamico*.

Giulio makes his rounds through the crowded restaurant. The place is loose and casual, but he enacts a practiced ritual that's mostly for show: At each table, he pulls up a chair and talks his customers into ordering a giant steak. To seal the deal, he pulls the pencil from his ponytail and scratches the price on the paper tablecloth.

When they agree, Guilio hops up and takes two giant strides up the seven steps at the back of the restaurant, where a monstrous slab of Chianina beef rests on a butcher block. First, Giulio gently saws his way through the soft flesh. Then he hacks the sinews with a cleaver. He slaps the five-pound T-bone on a sheet of paper, descends the stairs, and shows it to the customer for their final approval.

There's no asking how you'd like it done. Giulio knows how it's done: Back up the stairs, he places the steak on a grill and pushes it into a wood-fired oven. Five minutes on one side, five minutes on the other, then sprinkled with coarse sea salt. *That's how it's done.*

When Giulio delivers the still-bleeding steak to his customers, the response is always the same: Eyes wide at the giant slab of meat, and protests that they simply can't eat so much—especially after that pasta! And yet, somehow, they manage.

After this feast, I waddle down the steep, twisty main drag. Near the bottom of town, and the gateway to the real world, stands Montepulciano's best *gelateria*, owned by Nicola. I deem this a rare occasion when I won't give in to the temptation.

But as I walk past the door, I hear a familiar voice shout, "*Buona sera!* Hello!" Nicola has spotted me—and even though we've met only once, a year or two earlier, he recognizes me. Sheepishly, I backtrack into Nicola's shop, where I'm handed a half-dozen plastic spoons of free samples.

Nicola is younger than his uptown neighbors—perhaps around 30—but every bit as consumed by a love for what he does. He explains that, after apprenticing at a renowned London restaurant, he returned to Tuscany and opened a *laboratorio*—determined to make his mark on the culinary world.

In those early days, his first product was jam made from fruit and berries foraged on the grounds of posh villas. Nicola had only a bicycle, which he'd ride through the Tuscan countryside to assemble a network of producers: truffle hunter, vintner, olive oil presser, and so on. (While intended as a sad-sack tale of humble beginnings, this experience sounds nothing short of amazing.)

Slowly Nicola transformed his preserves business into a *gelateria*. And he is the very best kind of gelato snob: He makes his gelato from scratch each morning, so it's not available until around noon. On busy days, it sells out in a few hours.

Initially, Nicola made only two flavors each day. Locals came in and asked for flavors they'd seen elsewhere. Unapologetically, he'd steer them to the ones on hand, re-training them to go for what's fresh. On this visit, his creamy basil tastes like an herb garden. On other trips, I've enjoyed carrot-ginger, kiwi-spinach, custard with raspberry jam, and orange-ginger.

From collecting his plums from a local orchard, to shipping in top-quality pistachios from Sicily, hazelnuts from Piedmont, or lemons from Puglia, Nicola obsesses over quality. And the base of his gelato—the milk—is delivered fresh three times each week from a local dairy farm. Not only does this taste better; Nicola explains that, in good Italian fashion, it also *digests* better than processed gelato.

Whether it's gelato, steak, copper, or wine, there's something profoundly inspiring about someone who's completely devoted to their life's work. In Montepulciano, you meet people who can't stop working just because they've retired. People for whom appreciation is better payment than money. People who find their niche in life and fill it proudly.

Tuscany may be the place where this is most keenly expressed, but a similar sensibility pervades much of Europe: The French *boulangère* who devotes her life to baking the perfect *baguette rustique*. The Croatian fisherman who ties his knots just so. The Portuguese artist who hand-paints delicate patterns on tiles. Back home, "artisanal" is trendy, pretentious, and priced at a premium. In Europe, it's simply how things are done, when things are done correctly.

Europe, 1999

My Travel Origin Story

*O*n a visit to my parents' house, I was watching a documentary about the eventful year of 1968, when protest and political discord gripped America. Passing through the living room, my mom said, "Oh, we heard that was really something. But we missed it. We were in North England."

I hit the jackpot by being born into a family that loved to travel and had the wherewithal to do it. Before I was born, my parents spent four years abroad for graduate school, in Durham, England, and Basel, Switzerland. At that time, intercontinental phone calls were so expensive that they'd save up to talk to their parents just twice a year, Christmas and Mother's Day. Otherwise it was letters written on crinkly, blue-and-red-fringed paper. Back then, "living abroad" required a deep cultural immersion that sent you home with a funny accent. (Returning to small-town USA, my parents were informed that they had started talking like Brits.)

As a result, my sister and I grew up thinking things like a cowbell by the fireplace, fondue at Christmas, and *Bircher Muesli* for breakfast were normal. And yet, strangely, I had to be dragged to Europe kicking and screaming. When I was eight or nine, my parents—excited to share the places that meant so much to them—announced that it was time for a family trip overseas. My temper tantrum brought that conversation to an abrupt and definitive conclusion. I don't remember exactly what terrified me so much about going to Europe. I guess it all just seemed so . . . unfamiliar.

When I was in high school, my dad set up a language-study program for his graduate students in Oaxaca, Mexico. He invited me to tag along. Sensing that this was an alternative to getting a summer job, I said, "Sure." I was just adventurous enough to go, yet clueless about how transformative the experience would be.

Oaxaca gobbled me up whole. My wonderful host family took me in as one of their own, and I discovered a passion for experiencing the world beyond my borders. I returned to Oaxaca each of the next two summers, polishing my Spanish and cultivating an affinity for the everyday adventure of travel. My sepia-toned world had been colorized.

I came home from that first Oaxaca summer completely changed. And yet, the rest of my world was exactly the same. I assumed everyone would be dying to hear about my adventures. I imagined friends hanging on my every word. In reality, they politely feigned interest, then changed the subject. They moved on. But I was stuck in Mexico.

I learned a powerful lesson about traveler's narcissism. Subconsciously, I believed all those things I'd experienced only mattered if validated by other people. But of course, travel is intensely personal. What each traveler takes home from each trip is unique. All these years later, I'm still telling travel tales—but now I'm motivated by the simple joy of sharing my passion. And I respect that my listeners may draw their own conclusions.

When it was time for college, I attended Ohio Wesleyan University, in my hometown of Delaware, Ohio. My junior year, I signed up for our semester abroad program in Salamanca, Spain. More than a decade after I'd blown up my parents' family trip overseas, I finally made it to Europe. Returning home, I completed my studies and graduated with honors. Clearly, I had the world by the tail!

Except . . . I truly did not. Quite the contrary, I had no earthly idea what to do next. I had spent too much time striving for straight A's, and not nearly enough time considering what to do with that unblemished transcript.

Thus began what I think of as "The Wilderness Years." As if to scream to the world just how rudderless I felt, I grew an unfortunate scraggly beard. Feeling drawn to the Pacific Northwest—where I have many relatives—I drove cross-country to the Oregon Coast. Upon arriving, I realized I had no clue what to do out there, either. So I drove home to Ohio, moved in with my parents, and got a job at the local movie theater. Thinking I might want to become a teacher, I did some substitute teaching—but that wasn't for me, either. A lone bright spot came when I got a gig writing weekly movie reviews for my hometown newspaper, at $25 a pop. I considered going to film school, because undoubtedly another $100,000 in debt and another marginally useful degree would be the answer to my prayers.

Obviously, I was searching for something—anything—to inspire me. And what do you do when you can't figure out what else to do? You travel.

My high school sweetheart, Shawna, suggested we take a trip to Great Britain. And then, I figured, I could stick around and do some solo backpacking around Europe. But there was one problem: We had no idea how to begin planning an itinerary.

Around this time, the local public TV affiliate was airing a show called *Travels in Europe with Rick Steves*. It became my family's dinnertime tradition to watch this chipper American, in his leather jacket and aviator glasses, dork his way around Europe. Rick was so upbeat—his enthusiasm for Europe was infectious. He made it all seem so . . . possible. We even subscribed to his free travel newsletter, 64 Xeroxed pages of packing tips and travel tales.

I suggested to Shawna that she check out Rick's guidebooks. A couple of days later, she called to say, "I got that Rick Steves book. And now I know exactly what to do on our trip." (Shawna was very astute. But I must have been even more astute, because I wound up marrying her.)

Even with Rick's guidance, I was unbelievably green. I went to the home of a childhood friend for a crash course in budget travel: "Tell me, Chad, what is a . . . rail . . . pass? And those [checks notes] youth hostels—how do those work, exactly?" One of Chad's tips was to bring along a clothesline, so I jammed a bright-blue nylon cord into my backpack. The first time I did laundry, it left blue stripes across all of my clothes.

Shawna and I had a wonderful time in Britain. We still speak fondly of the just-right places and memorable experiences Rick led us to: The foul-tasting "therapeutic" waters at the Pump Room in Bath. The "chirpy attic room" in Keswick and the sunset cruise on Derwentwater. At the Edinburgh train station, the left-luggage clerk with a brogue so thick, we couldn't understand a word.

At the end of our 10-day loop through Britain, Shawna flew home (for, you see, she actually *had a job*). I was left alone in England . . . again rudderless.

I regrouped and strategized. My friend Trevor, who had joined the Peace Corps after college, was stationed in Slovakia. His sister Abby was coming for a visit, and they invited me to join them on a trip through Eastern Europe, starting in Poland. Talking on the phone from Dartmoor, where I was staying with family friends, I agreed to meet them on Kraków's main square in a couple of days at 8 a.m.

I figured out an absurdly complex, Rube Goldberg connection that made maximum use of my rail pass. The next 48 hours are a blur: It began with a ride to the Exeter train station, then a train to Plymouth. From there, a ferry took me across the English

Channel to Roscoff, where I hopped a train to Paris, arriving just in time for a night train to Munich.

On that night train—my first ever—I hadn't bothered to reserve a *couchette* bunk. My penance was spending a mostly sleepless night sitting up in a three-facing-three compartment, jockeying for position with five other sets of huge, hairy legs. The Teutonic he-men sharing my compartment probably weren't the Austrian national weightlifting squad. But they could have been.

I spent the day sightseeing in Munich, then took an afternoon express train to Berlin, where I hopped on my second consecutive night train to Kraków. I'd learned enough from the previous night to book a *couchette* in a sleeper compartment, which I shared with a very frightened elderly Polish couple.

Chugging into the Kraków station, I found my way through the foggy dawn to the Main Market Square and dozed off on a bench. As St. Mary's bell tower began to clang eight times, I caught sight of a familiar figure entering the far side of the square. Trevor slowly made his way across the vast space until we were face to face.

"Hey, Hewitt!" he said, surveying my Wilderness Years beard. "You're a hairy monster! Welcome to Poland."

That moment did it for me. I had set out on an absurdly complex journey from the moors of Devonshire to the plains of Poland. I made every rookie mistake in the book. I was as far from my comfort zone, and as alone, as I could ever remember being. And yet, I loved every second. And that's when I thought: I could get used to this travel thing.

Together with Trevor and Abby, I got to know places that, before this trip, I never would have imagined visiting. From Kraków, we rode the train to Dresden, in the former East Germany, then Prague. Walking through Prague's Old Town, I read passages

from the Rick Steves guidebook aloud to Trevor and Abby, unde-terred by their teasing. In spite of our shared Gen X cynicism, even they—begrudgingly—appreciated Rick's insights and tips. In fact, when we moved on to other places, not covered in Rick's book, Trevor began prodding me: "You gotta write a guidebook on Eastern Europe for twentysomethings, Cameron. It'll be great. Why not? You need a job anyway. What else are you doing?"

Trevor was on to something. Central and Eastern Europe got under my skin. The region would become the main pillar of my career, and of a lifetime of travels. Even to this day, I'm not sure exactly why those places appeal to me so much. Maybe it's my part-Slavic roots. Maybe it's the immediacy of the history, having traveled there just a decade removed from the fall of communism. Maybe it's the underdog appeal of a place that's often overlooked— squeezed between the powerhouses of Western Europe and Russia. For whatever reason, those countries set their hook in me, deep.

Eventually, I split off from Trevor and Abby, diverted west, and hopscotched across Austria, Germany, and Switzerland for a few more weeks. By this point, I'd hit my stride. To stretch my budget, I employed every trick in the backpacker's handbook. I maximized each "flexi-day" of my rail pass by squeezing in as many miles as possible. I took night trains to avoid paying for accommodations. I hauled around a huge jar of Nutella and a sheath of cardboard-like Wasa crackers for emergency picnics. I got 15 free minutes online at a fancy new Internet café, then came back the next day for 15 more free minutes to finish my email home.

Since I slept poorly in youth hostels, my standard operating procedure was to identify Rick's cheapest guesthouse in each town that had a single room with a bathroom down the hall. In retrospect, this probably helped me have a more "local" experience than bunking with a dorm full of fellow Americans. And I certainly wound up meeting more sweet Germanic grannies than they did.

I got word that the German teacher at my hometown high school had quit suddenly, and they were seeking a mid-year replacement. I had a series of job interviews with the principal, standing in a phone booth in a tidy Swiss park, feeding giant five-franc coins into the slot. (I decided to stay in Europe, which in almost any other outcome would have been the less-wise career move.)

Eventually I made my way back to England, then Ireland. In Dingle, I got so excited listening to the trad music in a pub that I called Shawna on a payphone and held it up to the music until her answering machine cut me off. Once again, I just had to share that joy of travel with someone.

A few days later, I ran out of money in Dublin and flew home.

Back in Ohio, I returned to the throes of The Wilderness Years. But something was different. I was more at peace, while also more excited. I had glimpsed a world that felt like it would become important to me. I just had to figure out how.

But first, I decided I should write a thank-you note to Rick Steves. That missive ballooned to several pages, as I waxed poetic about the glories of Eastern Europe that he'd missed in his guidebooks. C'mon, Rick, I chided—why no Budapest? No Kraków?!

I figured I might as well mention that I was looking for a job, and I threw in my resume just in case. I dropped the letter in the mail and got right back to the important business of being underemployed. Somewhere in there, my mom said, "You've got to figure out what you want to do with your life. Take some initiative. It's not like Rick Steves is just going to call you up and offer you a job!"

A couple of days later, the phone rang. A familiar voice said: "Hi, is this Cameron? This is Rick Steves."

After an embarrassing exchange in which Rick repeatedly assured me that he was *actually Rick Steves*, and not my friend Andy, we had a great conversation. He liked my letter. He agreed that he could do better in Eastern Europe. And, by the way, was I serious about coming to work for him?

It was November—the slowest time of year in the travel business—and Rick wasn't hiring just then. But if I was ever in the Seattle area, he said, I should drop in to meet him. The moment I hung up the phone, I called my grandma in Oregon to say I was coming for a visit.

I flew out to the Pacific Northwest and made the rounds with my relatives, couch-surfing my way north toward Seattle. A few days out, I called Rick to tell him that I was on my way to see him.

There was a long, awkward pause. "Um, *who* is this again?"

You know—Cameron Hewitt. That guy from Ohio. The one who wrote you a letter. You said I should come meet you . . . ?

Rick ended the call with an agonizingly noncommittal, "Well, I still have no idea who you are. But if you want to come to my office, I guess I'll talk to you."

I could have—probably should have—hung my head and flown home. But I'd come this far . . . and, frankly, I was entirely lacking in other prospects. So I made the lonely drive north up I-5 to Seattle and showed up on Rick's doorstep.

At first, Rick eyed me suspiciously. But I recapped our previous conversation until he remembered. We hit it off; our travel styles were perfectly in sync. He said they might be hiring the following spring, and took me to meet the HR manager. She had just arrived at her desk for the day—still wearing her jacket and holding her car keys—and she looked at us like a deer in headlights.

A few months later, they were indeed hiring—and I got the job. In March of 2000, I moved to Seattle and started working at Rick's Travel Center, advising travelers on their itineraries and selling guidebooks and backpacks in our retail store. I worked hard there for two years, and when an editorial position came open in our book department, I became a guidebook editor and researcher. The next summer, Rick sent me to write a new guidebook chapter on Dresden. And the year after that, I realized Trevor's wild dream when Rick accepted my proposal to write the first edition of our Eastern Europe guidebook.

In retrospect, it's easy to view my 1999 journey as a pretty conventional backpacking trip for a privileged kid from Middle America. If anything, it could be accused of being callow and clichéd. The more experienced a traveler becomes, the easier it is to look down our noses at people who are behind us on the learning curve—including, and especially, our younger selves.

But the wonder of new travels is vivid, precious, and transformative; it should be celebrated, not diminished. I went from being a kid who pitched a fit to avoid crossing the Atlantic to someone who feels at home just about anywhere in Europe. And it all goes back to that bumbling backpacking trip, that ludicrous two-day journey from England to Poland, and that letter I wrote to Rick Steves.

Jams Are Fun

When Travel Plans
Go Sideways

*After seeing "forty-'leven" temples, I'm not very interested in
seeing any more for a while. Two or three times I stayed in the bus
while the group went to visit another temple. I think I sometimes
saw more interesting things while I waited.*

—Mildred C. Scott, *Jams Are Fun*

On the express train from Warsaw to Kraków, I shared a compartment with two middle-aged American couples. They were
weary and flustered, having rushed to get on the train just before
it pulled out. As they settled in, I remarked how light they were
packing—each one had only a small day bag.

"Oh, we used the luggage check service," they said.

"The . . . luggage check . . . service?" I'd never heard of such
a thing. Either I was about to get a great tip for my book, or they
had made a terrible mistake.

"Yeah. You know, that desk where you give them your bags
and tell them which train you're taking, and they deliver them to
you at the other end."

My heart sank. They looked so exhausted . . . yet happy. They
had dived into Poland headfirst and were making a go of it. And
we were just a few minutes into a non-stop, three-hour train ride.
But they deserved to know.

Gently as I could, I explained that the service they had availed themselves of was a *left*-luggage desk. When they got to Kraków, their bags would be waiting for them . . . back in Warsaw.

They took the news admirably and spent the rest of the trip debating who would be heading back to Warsaw that evening. While that was a very long day for one of them, I like to imagine that this has become one of their favorite travel tales, told with relish anytime someone broaches the topic of "good trips gone bad."

In other words, it was a classic example of my travel motto: Jams are fun.

My wife's Great-Great-Aunt Mildred was a remarkable soul. Around age 60, when most of her peers were gardening and singing in the church choir, Mildred Scott began traveling. Back in the 1950s, such a thing was unheard of for an unmarried woman. No matter. Over the next 15 years, Mildred spent month after month on the road, visiting every continent on earth. And in her final years, after seeing more of our planet than everyone else in her Ohio hometown combined, she penned a travelogue. The title: *Jams Are Fun.*

After all those adventures, what stuck with Mildred wasn't the castles and cathedrals; it wasn't the museums and the monuments; it wasn't the grand spectacles or the gourmet meals or the "forty-'leven temples" she was taken to see. It was those times when she paused to reflect on where she was, without an agenda. It was the people she crossed paths with, both locals and fellow travelers, who made an impression. And most of all, it was those moments when trips went sideways—memorable snags in perfectly laid plans that forced her to scramble for creative solutions, or simply accept whatever life presented her with.

I never met Aunt Mildred. But recently, I finally read her book. It's a slim volume, hardbound with gold lettering embossed on the front cover: *Jams Are Fun: A Book of Travels.* Mildred is concise, devoting as many sentences to a logistical headache as she does to entire continents. Her inner strength, no-nonsense attitude, keen personality, and drive to experience the world are evident throughout. Having grown up surrounded and shaped by strong Ohio women like Mildred, I feel like I know her well.

Mildred was born in 1898—the same year as René Magritte and Bertold Brecht. Growing up, Mildred had severe anemia, which was eventually treated. She attended Miami University in Oxford, Ohio, and became a teacher. When her parents passed away, her two brothers inherited farms while she inherited money. She wrote, "I have taken my girlhood in different form later in life by seeing the world."

Mildred began traveling in earnest in 1958, when she went to Africa. "I was green," she reports, "but how I learned!" On arriving in Johannesburg, "I was confused when it seemed to me that everyone was driving on the wrong side of the street and the sun was in the wrong side of the sky." Mildred goes on safari, visits Victoria Falls, finds herself stranded by her airline in Sudan, travels to Timbuktu, and completes her journey in Egypt.

Clearly this trip transformed Mildred, who issues a *Walden*-like mission statement: "By the time I was 65 I thought I must see some other places on this wonderful earth before I got too old."

In South America, Mildred climbs Machu Pichu, cruises the Amazon, "collects waterfalls" at Iguazu and Angel Falls, and eats the best fish of her life at a beach on Easter Island. She tours the Canadian Rockies and sails to Alaska to see the midnight sun at the summer solstice ("even though my brother said it's the same sun we see here"). Another odyssey takes her to Oceania, then hopscotching across Asia from Japan to India. She takes a transatlantic cruise via Iceland to Nordkapp, Norway—at the northern tip of Europe—before visiting the Nordic capitals, Leningrad, and Amsterdam. Somewhere in there, Mildred even cruises to Antarctica, because "I had always hoped I could see penguins in their natural habitat."

Reading Mildred's stories, I imagine her a kind of intercontinental Forrest Gump. In Amsterdam, she bumps into Queen Julianna of the Netherlands at a harp concert. In the middle of Africa, the president of Liberia and his entourage—on their way home from a gathering of dignitaries—board her plane and take over the first-class cabin.

Travel was different then: interminably long flights with frequent "refueling stops" and overnights in random cities; trip coupons that were traded for boarding passes, taxi transfers, and hotel stays; and complaint letters written on carbon paper. But things were changing. "This was my first trip on a 747," Mildred writes, "and I thought when the planes and the crowds get any bigger I'm going to stay at home!"

Mildred dispenses advice that still feels relevant to today's travelers: "Tourists in foreign countries where other languages are spoken need always to carry a card of their hotel or ship. As one guide once said, 'Taxi drivers can't be expected to know all the languages of the world.'"

And, upon getting lost in Stockholm: "It had been said, 'If you need help, ask a hippie.' Finally it was a young man with hair to his shoulders who directed me aright." (I like to imagine this was a young Rick Steves.)

In my favorite bit of advice, Mildred quotes a college professor who was prepping students for a lengthy road trip: "You'll have to be the kind of a person who, if you don't have a clean handkerchief, you can use your dirty one."

Throughout, Mildred is respectful, curious, and complimentary of foreign cultures. ("I found the Africans a great people, very friendly, gracious, jolly, and a great handshaking people.") Any ire she reserves for fellow Americans . . . and for airline representatives. ("I should have known better because I have been lied to in the offices of that airline all over the world. This was the second time they had dumped me out in the middle of the night in the middle of Africa.")

Most of all, Mildred speaks with a full heart of the many "life savers" she encountered in her travels: kind strangers who offered assistance to an arthritic senior citizen determined to see her planet. And, of course, Mildred relishes reporting misadventures—her own and others'.

In the 119 pages of *Jams Are Fun*, Mildred never articulates what drives her to see so many places, rather than stay home, playing euchre and piano, like other spinster retirees of her time. It's presented as a given: She must go, for as long as her aging body will take her.

Mildred wraps up her book with these words: "One person gave me a left-handed compliment, saying, 'People think a person doing all that traveling has money.' But as Stuart Chase said, 'It's not money that makes the mare go; it's oats.'"

When I encounter fellow travelers on the road, the ones who impress me most share Mildred's "Jams Are Fun" philosophy. They are driven to travel for reasons they don't fully understand. They're less interested in the stops on an itinerary than they are in chance encounters or lingering over a beautiful sunset. And they come alive as they describe a missed connection, or a canceled reservation, or an unplanned layover, or getting hopelessly lost. A good traveler treasures these "catastrophic" events as the centerpiece of their storytelling for years to come. A bad traveler takes the same as an excuse never to travel there—or, perhaps, anywhere—ever again.

This whole "good traveler"/"bad traveler" business is, I'll admit, controversial. I have a close colleague who bristles when I talk about "good travelers." To her, it feels elitist. That's because, as she readily admits, she is not a good traveler. She plans every last iota of her trip; she panics when something deviates from that plan; and she's on edge until she's home and it's all behind her. She travels infrequently, and unhappily. She prefers having traveled to actually traveling.

A good traveler—a "Jams Are Fun" traveler—a Mildred—understands that not being at home is precisely the point of travel: foregoing the predictable rhythms of your life and throwing yourself into a different reality. Problems aren't problems. They're opportunities to create memories. This is most easily appreciated in retrospect; bonus points if you can do it in real-time.

Look at it this way: Memories are the biggest return on any investment you make in a trip. And challenges overcome make for the most memorable memories. So in terms of bang for your buck, a jam is solid gold.

By now, good travelers are replaying all of their own favorite jams in their minds. (And bad travelers have thrown this book in the trash.) Here are a few of mine; several others appear throughout this book.

On a road trip through Provence, my wife Shawna and I followed our GPS to our countryside B&B. As we turned off from wide roads to narrow ones to gravel ones, we began to wonder if we were being steered wrong. Eventually we found ourselves on dirt service roads, driving on hard-packed mud between neat rows of grapevines. After fording a small stream, we came up a rise and—lo and behold—popped out on the front lawn of our B&B. Not sure what else to do, we drove across the grass and parked by the front door. When I went inside to check in, the receptionist, startled by our dramatic arrival, said, "*Oui, Monsieur.* But zere is a car on ze terrace!"

In the Bohemian town of Český Krumlov, family friends took their dirty clothes to a launderette and explained that they'd be back to pick them up that afternoon. Or at least, they thought they had. When they showed up just before closing time, they found the shop locked up tight, with no way to contact the proprietor. They had booked a nonrefundable, early-morning transfer before the launderette opened. What else could they do? They left their clothes behind, bought a new wardrobe in Vienna, packed very light for the rest of their trip, and did lots of laundry in the sink. And they never did see those clothes again.

I arrived at the Naples train station about 10 minutes before my 500-mile express train to Milan. I located my track and sauntered all the way down the platform to my assigned seat—in wagon #1 out of 11. I pressed the "door open" button, and . . . nothing happened. I pressed more buttons and banged on windows until the conductor appeared. She gestured frantically toward the opposite side of the train: I had walked 200 yards down the wrong platform. I was tempted to hop down onto the tracks in front of the locomotive, then climb up the platform on the other side. But, not wanting to spend the night in a Neapolitan jail cell, my only viable option was to run the entire length of the train, in three minutes, with my full rucksack on my back. By the time I'd rounded the end of the platform, hopped on the last car of the train with seconds to spare, then trudged all the way back up to the front of the crowded train to my seat, I was a fountain of sweat.

My wife and I parked our car just outside the Croatian coastal town of Rovinj for a few days. When I went back to get it, the parking lot had become a staging ground for the annual celebration of the town's patron saint. Watching a rickety tilt-a-whirl spinning in the space where I'd left my car, I protested to the parking attendant that I'd had no idea this was going to happen. No worries, he said—they'd simply moved offending vehicles out of the way. (He pantomimed a crane picking up my car and gently depositing it on a flatbed truck.) Following his instructions, I walked about a half-mile along the beach to the overflow lot and started pressing the unlock button on my key fob until I saw the car's lights flash.

I drove back into town to pick up Shawna and our bags. She said, "What took so long?"

"Oh, you know," I said with a wink and a shrug. "Jams are fun."

I've Been in Your Hotel Room

A Day in the Life of a Guidebook Writer

I've been in your hotel room.

While you were out sightseeing, the receptionist let me in. I saw which guidebooks and brochures you had on the desk. I saw that you left the air-conditioning on, full-blast. I saw the mess, or the lack of mess. Some of you arrange your toiletries by size next to the sink and organize your bedside reading into a neat stack. Most of you leave the room looking like a dirty bomb exploded inside your suitcase.

I'm not snooping for a perverse thrill. I'm inspecting your hotel to make sure it's as we describe it in our guidebook. Is it still "nicely appointed" and "well-maintained"? Is it "a bit dumpy" or can it be upgraded to "sharp"? There's only one way to find out.

I have seen thousands upon thousands of hotel rooms, all across Europe. Most are freshly cleaned and ready for check-in. Quite a few, I visit during that odiferous window between check-out and cleaning, when bedclothes are strewn about, a nighttime's worth of garlic breath and stale farts mingle in the humid air, and the toilet bowl is in a state that might cause a veteran housekeeper to retire on the spot. And some rooms are currently occupied, but the occupants have stepped out.

I respect a hotelier who says, "Sorry, we can't show you a guest's room." But, if I'm being honest, I get a kick out of the ones who just don't care—they walk down the hall, lightly knocking then throwing open each door.

And sometimes, while I'm judging someone's choice of tooth-paste or deodorant, or marveling at how many different surfaces upon which travelers can drape wet laundry to dry, or appreci-ating how Germans all seem to fold their pajamas neatly on the pillow—surely this must be taught in schools—I think about how surreal it is to write a guidebook. And also, how much less glamor-ous it is than everyone thinks.

When people find out I write guidebooks, their imaginations run wild. What a life! Perched at a café on a sun-dappled square, sub-sumed in the happy hum of Europe, sipping a cappuccino or a glass of wine. Periodically you take out a leatherbound notebook and jot down some notes—maybe compose a poem—before returning to your people-watching.

This is, I cannot stress enough, the opposite of my reality. While I don't expect one iota of sympathy, I suspect most people would resign in tears if they tried my job. Researching a guide-book—and doing it well—demands fourteen-hour days, chasing down a perpetually growing list of items to check. Then you head back to your hotel, spend a few hours typing up your notes, finally pass out from sheer exhaustion, and wake up the next day to do it all over again. The book is due at the office in four days, after all, and the editors are growing restless.

These days, few guidebook publishers routinely update their material in person. And, to be frank, you can tell. I believe one reason Rick Steves guidebooks are bestsellers is that our research-ers actually go to Europe for each new edition. When I update a chapter, I visit every single listing: each hotel, restaurant, museum, launderette, tourist information office, bus station, and so on. Having done this for several months each of the last 20 years, I can attest that ours are the most lovingly produced guidebooks on the planet.

It's grueling, yes. But there's nothing more gratifying than seeing all that hard work in print and knowing how many trips it will improve. Our job is to anticipate what a traveler needs to know, moments before they need to know it. And we try to do it with personality, a spirit of fun, and—most important—a love of travel.

Most of the stories in this book are not "about" guidebooks. But this chapter explains what I'm doing while all those other stories are happening.

In the spring of 2001, Rick Steves and I walked into a Frankfurt brothel. We were on a mission: to update a guidebook.

The Eros Towers rise up from the gritty urban zone in front of Frankfurt's train station. They're eight stories of sex workers, each one standing in the doorway of a sparsely furnished room: a bed with rubber sheets and a sink.

Rick and I were traveling around Germany so he could apprentice me to research guidebooks. This was a job I'd longed for since my first backpacking trip. And now here I was, living my dream. In a futuristic bordello.

We tiptoed down the hallway together, a pair of bookish, sweetly smiling, bespectacled American dudes—one of us in his mid-20s, the other in his mid-40s. We must have looked like father and son, more at home at a Boy Scout jamboree than being propositioned by a hallway of women.

After 30 seconds that felt like an hour, Rick flipped open his guidebook and scanned the page. He nodded as he mentally ticked off a few points. "OK," he said, "just one more thing to check . . . " His voice trailed off as he pointed to the text: "S&F, 30 DM." The "DM" stood for "Deutschmarks," which was still the currency in Germany at the time. The "S&F" stood for a service provided here that is still unprintable, two decades later.

Rick scanned the hallway for the most approachable-looking sex worker and sidled up to her. She smiled and muttered something in a garbled hybrid of English and German. While her words were indecipherable, her intent was unmistakable.

"Mmmm-hmmm. *Und wieviel kostet das?*" Rick asked, shimmying a bit to get into character as he clicked into information-gathering mode.

"*Dreissig Marken,*" she said with a wink and a shimmy of her own. Thirty Marks.

"OK, *danke! Das ist gut.*" Rick said. "*Später vielleicht.*" "Maybe later"—the perfect, noncommittal-yet-polite way to extract yourself from a conversation once you've gotten the information you came for.

Work done, Rick and I put our heads down and scurried out to the curb. Rick opened his tattered guidebook, made a big show of ticking a checkmark on the page, and tucked it away again. We headed down the street to our next stop, a budget hotel a block away. As we walked, I pulled out my little bottle of hand sanitizer, squirted some into my palm, and began rubbing my hands together furiously. Sheepishly, Rick said, "Can I have some?"

Rick had taken me to a brothel to make a point, in the most vivid way possible: A guidebook researcher must check every last detail. In this case, our book presented the Eros Towers as an opportunity for curious American travelers to better understand (but presumably not partake in) Europe's pragmatic attitude toward legal, safe sex work. And part of our responsibility in introducing readers to these slices of Europe is ensuring that they are precisely as we describe them. (The "S&F" was a tongue-in-cheek inside joke—this is a guidebook listing, after all, so we should list the price—but even jokes must be up-to-date.)

This is an extreme example. But it illustrates the truth of writing a guidebook: You have to walk the walk.

* * *

These days, when I'm training new recruits, I don't take them to brothels. But I do tell them that researching a guidebook means asking a million people a million questions. Obviously, this is hyperbole. Still, when you consider that I've been doing this work several weeks each year for over 20 years, and that each day I visit 50 or 60 businesses, and that each one might involve ten or twelve questions, I probably have asked around one million questions over my career. (And a significant percentage of those questions would be, "Closed Mondays?")

Sometimes I'm writing up brand-new destinations; other times, I'm updating existing material. Either one requires gathering detailed information about dozens upon dozens of listings, and thinking critically about that information.

Over breakfast, I get organized, skimming the chapter and drawing an empty box in the margin next to anything that requires my attention. On a separate sheet, I sketch out a list of every item in geographical order, so I can sweep through town systematically and minimize backtracking. As I make my rounds, I scribble changes directly into the narrow margins of my guidebook. If I run out of space, I pull out a small notebook and carry on there, or I scrawl notes on the back of a business card. When I'm done with an item, I fill that box with a satisfying checkmark and move on to the next one.

My purpose is twofold: First, to verify "data points"—highly changeable details such as prices, hours, phone numbers, and so on. And second, to engage thoughtfully with the descriptions, weighing whether each one is both accurate and helpful. Does the museum still display the same pieces, in the same order? Does the restaurant still offer the dishes we mention? Even the self-guided walks must be carefully followed: "Turn left at the green building" is unhelpful if they've painted it red.

Guidebook researchers are experts who have to think like novices. Even as we infuse our copy with a local savvy, everything needs to be simple and clear to someone who's just stepped off the plane. They're standing on a street corner—jet-lagged, culture-shocked, surrounded by buzzing *motorini*—and they need advice.

At hotels, I confirm details at the front desk and ask to see a standard double room. I'm usually in and out in about 10 minutes. How could I possibly evaluate a hotel so quickly? Consider this: How much of your overall impression of a hotel room is formed within the first few minutes? We all have our little checking-in rituals: peek into the bathroom and the closet, open the drapes to check out the view, and make a quick—even subconscious— assessment of whether the room meets expectations.

That's essentially what I do with those precious few minutes in a room. And I know just what to look for: How tidy are hard-to-clean areas, like the bathroom grout or under the furniture? How's the soundproofing and lightproofing on the windows? Is there heavy wear-and-tear on the carpet, or chipped and scuffed paint on the wall behind the luggage rack? All of these are subtle indicators of whether the management is putting money back into the hotel, or letting it slowly fall apart while using it as a cash cow.

Most important is something Rick taught me on that trip to Germany: the sniff test. Upon entering a room, I take a big whiff. Does it smell musty? Smoky? Stale? Or—potentially even more dire—overly perfumed, to cover something up? Tracking that faint, vaguely "off" odor to its source, I might discover a thriving colony of mildew on the ceiling above the shower, or that the drapes haven't been cleaned since Franco died.

Does the hotel know who I am? Sometimes. Other times— especially if we've received complaints—I "go incognito": I walk in off the street, ask to see a room, and only after my inspection do I reveal myself. When Rick taught me this trick, I assumed the receptionists of Europe would be furious. Having done it hundreds of times, however, I've almost never received pushback. Many hoteliers even get a kick out of it. (One winked and said, "Aha! Espionage.")

Following a visit, I consider changes to our description. A few years after a renovation, "fresh" may become "dated." A "friendly" front desk staff or a claim of "clean" (or even "spotless") must earn its keep, edition after edition.

At museums, I update details at the information desk. And then, if I have time, I ask permission to quickly zip through the collection—and I mean quickly. Once I needed to assess an obscure history museum in Zagreb, Croatia, that sprawled through an old mansion with parquet floors. My shoes squeaked as I walked at a cantering pace from room to room to room. The museum attendant—whose job was to follow museum-goers around, turning lights on and off—struggled to keep up. After sprinting through ten rooms in about five minutes (and seeing not much of note), I gave her an apologetic smile to convey, "Sorry if I've disrespected your lovely museum by seeing it so quickly." She returned my smile with a chuckle and said, "Express!"

At a restaurant, first I review the posted menu and hours, then I step inside and snoop. I take in the vibe (what Rick calls the "eating energy"), scope out what's on the plates, and scan for characteristic details. ("At the *Stammtisch* in the corner, regulars nurse their beers under droopy fishnets.") This lasts for however long it takes a server to ask if I need anything. I verify the details and, if they're not too busy, quiz them about their culinary philosophy. Sometimes they have useful tips to share: "In nice weather, reserve ahead for the sunny patio."

I'm mindful not to push readers too hard toward anyplace in particular. Rather, my duty is to give them a basis for distinguishing among their options. Some of our readers want a memorable splurge; others want a solid, midrange value without pretense; others are seeking a big personality or a big view. We're careful to keep superlatives to a minimum. Our guidebooks don't promote; they inform.

This makes us rare in the world of travel content, which is dominated by breathless raves (often sponsored). Our judgment can afford to be candid because businesses don't pay to be listed; all of our selections and descriptions are based solely on our researchers' judgment about what's best for our readers. We do accept "freebies"—a comped meal at a restaurant, for example— not as a bribe, but as an opportunity for assessment (or re-assessment). In fact, I'm just as likely to downgrade (or even remove) a hotel after a free stay as I am to pump up the listing.

I'm often asked: "Do you have favorite restaurants in each town that you save just for yourself?" While some writers might do this, it strikes me as a deeply selfish act. That would be like a professional football coach, in the playoff hunt, saving a few trick plays for his kid's pee wee league. My philosophy is to leave it all out on the field—I hold back nothing. Family friends often email to say, "I'm going to Berlin. Any tips?" I'm tempted to write back: Just read the guidebook. It's all right there.

So, what am I looking for, exactly? What makes a hotel or a restaurant "good enough" to recommend?

Simply put, I'm looking for a place that's better than it has to be. Tourism, like life, is not a level playing field. Some businesses are born with advantages: a priceless location, a rent-controlled property, an inherited reputation for quality. A café with a privileged position on the main square can get away with charging exorbitant prices for terrible food and service. Cynical entrepreneurs master the art of adjusting those sliders up and down to maximize profit.

Conversely, I just love a place that delivers high-quality food at low prices, even if they could make a killing by doing the opposite. Usually this comes down to conscientious ownership:

someone who loves what they do, even more than they love the income they derive from it. These are the hoteliers who spring for super-soundproofed windows on the rooms facing the busy piazza, or the restaurateurs who source quality ingredients from local producers. They share a wisdom that transcends profit models: If their customers are happy, that happiness begets more customers.

The phrase "hospitality industry" implies that hospitality means "making money from travelers." It should be "making travelers happy." I look for proprietors who obsess over helping each traveler make the most of their trip. People who work in tourism would do well to adopt the Muslim belief that every guest is a gift from God. If they can't do that, they may be in the wrong business. And they certainly don't belong in our guidebook.

Another thing I look for is maintenance. Maintenance is expensive, invisible, and terribly unsexy. But it demonstrates that a business owner is reinvesting their profits in their guests' experience. I've been wowed by many brand-new hotels in Europe. But I reserve judgment until a few years in, when I return to see whether they're touching up paint, replacing carpet, and fixing all those small things that break through normal wear-and-tear.

It requires some sleuthing to find places worth recommending. The vast majority of any day I spend in Europe is devoted to kissing frogs. But that's not a waste of time: Determining that a place doesn't deserve to be in our book is at least as valuable as determining that it does.

Here's an example of what I look for when evaluating restaurants: On my first night in the town of Amalfi, on Italy's south coast, I just wanted an easy dinner. I wandered past a row of interchangeable eateries near the main drag, with matching menus: Pasta with clams. Seafood risotto. Spaghetti bolognese. Because this was the Amalfi Coast, maybe they threw in some lemon here and there. Only the place's name changed.

I eventually settled on a *trattoria* facing a relaxed neighbor-hood piazza. You know the place: red-and-white checkerboard tablecloth; melting candlesticks. I couldn't tell whether I was in Italy, or in Little Italy.

The pasta was solid, with stewed tomatoes, roasted eggplant, and gooey mozzarella. But the "mixed salad" consisted of greens on the verge of wilting, flavorless tomatoes, a few tough kernels of corn from a can, and a half-dozen rubbery olives. I sprinkled on more and more salt and *balsamico* trying to tease out some flavor. I failed. At one point the owner peered into my bowl and said, "You'd better eat those olives! I paid for them!"

I spent my meal listening to the owner chatting up passersby: "Hey! Where you from? You want a good meal? Very cheap 'cause we're not on the main square. Come on! I promise you like it!" Entertaining as it was to watch him set his hook in a family of four from Vancouver, then reel them in, it distracted—and detracted—from my dining experience.

The next night, I was determined to find something better. I had asked a local guide, who leads food tours in a neighboring town, where she eats when she's in Amalfi. Her answer led me to an easy-to-miss taverna tucked around the side of the cathedral's grand staircase. My soundtrack was mellow jazz rather than desperate sales pitches, and the service was astute and warm; when the table in front of me opened up, the server suggested I scoot up for a better view.

The menu was thoughtful, curated, even educational—for example, pasta with anchovies and walnuts. The salad was a revelation: ripe cherry tomatoes, shaved fennel, hand-torn basil, and a few flecks of raw garlic. The pasta was hand-cut ziti with a sauce I'd never heard of, *genovese napoletana*: meat sauce with slow-simmered onions and celery, giving each bite a caramelized sweetness. All in all, it was a memorable meal. I can still taste it.

I paid about the same at each of those restaurants, which had approximately the same number of guests. But only one place's customers leave very happy. My mission is helping readers find that place.

My wife Shawna was tagging along with me on a guidebook research trip. It was an autumn evening in Dubrovnik, under a hazy pink twilight sky, and we were enjoying a quiet, romantic dinner on a back lane. Five minutes in, two boisterous American couples were seated a few feet away.

Soon they began chatting us up, completely missing our signs that we preferred to dine alone. When meeting fellow travelers in Europe, I make a snap judgment whether to "out" myself as a travel writer—depending on the mood I'm in and, frankly, whether they seem worth getting to know. In this case, after they flat-out asked, for the third time, what we were doing on our trip, I committed the tragic error of saying that I was updating a guidebook.

Usually this sparks a lively conversation. But for this gang, it glanced off their windshield. "Guidebooks, huh?" they said. "Yeah, I guess some people still use those. We don't bother. Have you heard of TripAdvisor? That's all we need! Our rule is to always stay at the number one hotel on TripAdvisor, and only eat at restaurants in the top five."

And then, unsolicited, they rattled off horror stories from their trip. At a rental apartment, they'd come home one afternoon to find the proprietor's father making himself at home, watching TV on their couch. They reported unimpressive, overpriced meals with unfriendly service. They'd wasted time and money on over-hyped activities while completely missing beautiful little experiences between the tourist traps. They were about to leave Croatia disappointed and unimpressed.

It took every fiber of my being not to connect the dots for them. But why bother? They already had all the answers. My wife and I finished our meal as quickly as possible, skipped dessert, and disappeared into the once-again-sleepy back lanes of Dubrovnik.

Crowdsourced review sites like TripAdvisor, Booking.com, and Yelp have become a juggernaut on the travel information landscape. European businesses are both impressed and horrified by how powerful they've become. One flustered French hotelier told me, "I don't like those sites. The commissions have gotten so high. But I can't just refuse to work with them. After all, you have to be in the supermarket."

Railing against review sites is as futile as complaining about the weather. But let's consider how they relate to the work I've been doing for 20-plus years.

I wouldn't blame you for thinking that guidebooks—with information *printed on paper*—are old-fashioned and hopelessly out of touch. But guidebooks have the advantage of being carefully assembled by experts rather than an anonymous panel of amateurs.

A tourist-driven review site reflects the collected opinions of people who've been on vacation in a given place for just a few days. They can report only what they personally experienced, without the benefit of comparison. A guidebook researcher is trained to assess and describe a wide cross-section of options. We're curators, not tourists. Frankly, I don't put much weight in the opinion of someone who had ice cream once during their trip and then raves, "The best gelato in Italy!"

All of that said, I do refer to these sites when researching guidebooks. A pattern of terrible reviews is cause for extra scrutiny when I visit. And if a new business is getting raves, I may be more inclined to check it out. But everything is independently evaluated, in person, by a trained researcher.

And that's how I suggest travelers use crowdsourced review sites: Take their "advice" with a grain of salt, and supplement it with other types of information.

A few pro tips: In general, hotel ratings are more reliable than restaurant ratings. Regardless, don't just skim star ratings; delve into details. Learn how to read between the lines. On a site with a mix of local and tourist reviews, put more weight in the former. If people rave about the business *owner* with suspiciously few details about the business itself, they were charmed by the personality but, perhaps, disappointed with the rest of the experience. And if something in particular matters to you—for example, noise at a hotel, or vegetarian options at a restaurant—search within the reviews to isolate the relevant ones.

No matter how good a review site is, a trusted local is always better. For example, in small towns in Great Britain, nobody has a better handle on the restaurant scene than a B&B host. They welcome a steady stream of guests looking for dinner recommendations—and then, the next morning, they spend breakfast debriefing their guinea pigs. If a place is slipping, they'll hear about it. If there's a hot new table in town, they're on it. If the town has four seemingly interchangeable curry houses, they know which one is cheap, which one is the best quality, and which one you should avoid. Busy as I am, I'll lavish time on getting the restaurant scoop from a B&B owner even if it means I have to scramble the rest of the day.

Much of this sounds procedural, dry, even boring. But the human element sparks my work with enjoyment—and, sometimes, frustration. On every trip, I spend weeks appealing to the kindness of strangers, entreating them to spend a few moments answering questions that, I am well aware, are irritatingly precise. (If you are not a "detail person," this could be classified as torture.)

Early on, I figured out that swagger has no place in gathering information. Sometimes, if I was rushed or flustered, I'd exude an air of "I'm a writer for a *very important* guidebook and I require your assistance." Oh, how quickly I learned how counter-productive that was.

So instead, I make a point to be faultlessly polite and humble. In fact, to grease the skids, I've perfected the "dumb American" routine. It's an art to pretend that you are terrifically stupid: overwhelmed by life, perplexed by the simplest information, maybe even on the verge of losing your job and becoming destitute unless you can figure out the exact opening times for this museum. This involves a lot of smiles, puppy-dog eyes, and apologies. (And I'm one-quarter Canadian, so I already apologize at least 25 percent more than the average American).

Is this manipulative? Maybe. But it works. And it grows from a kernel of honesty: I truly depend on people's help. It feels good to help someone, and if they're a mouth-breathing simpleton, it feels even better.

A silver lining of my work is how it buoys my faith in humanity. If you ever wonder whether people are fundamentally good, spend a few weeks incessantly asking strangers about mundane details. The vast majority of people are at least tolerant, and often kind. Quite a few even seem to enjoy the experience of helping somebody out.

And then there are the assholes. I have been met with sneers, snorts, eye rolls, and hands thrown in the air. I have spent several minutes convincing someone to answer my questions, only to have the questioning itself last a fraction of that time. And some people grow so infuriated by my temerity for updating their basic information—for the sin of *recommending their business*—that they insist on being removed from our guidebook. (I am more than happy to oblige.)

It's unhelpful to generalize about entire nationalities. But—based on years of experience—it's clear to me that some countries are better at fielding clueless questions than others. Great Britain and Scandinavia, to name two places, are a dream for the American guidebook writer. Not only is there no language barrier, but these cultures are characterized by hospitality and conscientiousness.

Other places are a mixed bag. In Italy, people typically bend over backwards to help, but often have a less definitive command of those critical details. Portugal is the same, but even more so on both counts. Germany is a special case: They have precisely the information you require—in fact, they take it even more seriously than you do—but, frankly, they're not thrilled with the way you're framing the question or attempting to simplify things, and oh by the way I'm so terribly busy will this take much longer?

A few places make a national pastime of tormenting guidebook writers. In one country, I had to institute a metric called the "asshole quotient," which, once exceeded, requires the offender's business to be purged from the pages of my book forever. This highly subjective, but unforgiving, measurement originated on a challenging day when, for whatever reason, one of my favorite towns was teeming with assholes. (Fortunately, in the ten-plus years of its existence, I have only had to invoke this rule a handful of times.)

And there is another country where I all but refuse to do guidebook research anymore. In this place, being asked an innocent question is akin to insulting the memory of one's ancestors—an invitation to an abusive verbal tussle. I would rather not say which country this is. But it rhymes with "pain."

Some of the most challenging places to get solid information are the biggest, most popular, most famous sights—the ones overrun by tourists, and the ones where our advice is the most important.

In Milan, stepping into the ticket office for Leonardo da Vinci's *Last Supper*, I skim our many paragraphs explaining that reserving ahead is both mandatory and complicated. My job is to confirm every last detail with the woman at the information desk.

She greets me with a permanent snarl, close-cropped, dyed-blonde hair, and tired, cruel eyes. Before I even open my mouth, she doesn't like me. (I don't take it personally. She doesn't like anyone.) After I explain that I'm updating a guidebook, she allows me to continue talking, which I take as a sign of tacit approval.

"So, we say here that you need a reservation."

"Yes, that's correct. You can call or go on our website."

"And we say that you can make a reservation three months ahead."

"It depends."

As a guidebook researcher, sadly, it's my job to probe the nuances of "depends." So I ask: "What does it depend on?"

She sighs theatrically. "On our website, you can reserve three months ahead. At our call center, you can reserve, maybe, ten days ahead."

"So—tickets are available online three months before, but by phone only ten days before?"

"Well, you can get tickets anytime you want."

"Yes, but if someone wants to book very early, they can try three months before?"

"On our website."

"Not by calling?"

"No! Of course, they can get a ticket by calling. Ten days before."

That's good enough. I press on: "OK, so we also explain that if you don't have a reservation and really want to see the *Last Supper*, you can try to ask if there are cancellations."

"No! Not possible."

"Oh, OK. So you . . . "

"Reservations are mandatory!" She holds up a small sign that reads *Reservations are mandatory*, and gestures to it with a flourish of her other hand.

"Yes, I understand that. But what I'm saying is, let's say someone did *not* make a reservation. And now they are in Milan and they really want to see the *Last Supper*. We say that sometimes there may be a few cancellations . . . "

"No! You must reserve." She eyes me with suspicion, and her voice lowers. "Huh. Did you write in your book that you don't need a reservation?"

"No! Absolutely not. In fact, we make it very clear that people *do* need a reservation." I show her the several paragraphs explaining said reservation policy. "However, we also say that, in case you don't have one, *sometimes* it's possible . . . "

She interrupts me. "It's never possible!" Until now, her temper has been held back by a failing dam. Trickles have become torrents. And in this moment, it explodes. "People come here, all day, and complain to me because they do not have a reservation! *And you are telling them to do this in your book!*"

"But I . . . no, wait, look. It's the opposite. I'm trying to help people understand how this works. I want to make it very clear so they are not disappointed."

"I don't care! People come here all day and are disappointed anyway, so what does it matter what you say in"—and here she sneers as if smelling something most foul—"*your book?*"

"Yes, they're complaining *to you*. I'm trying to help *you* by reducing the number of . . . " I trail off and take a breath. Perhaps it's best to concede her right not to care. "OK, sorry, I'm almost done. I just want to confirm that you never, ever have last-minute tickets available the same day."

"No, it's impossible! Well, maybe one ticket, two tickets. But almost none! You must take this out of your book!"

"I will. And thank you again for your help. By the way, I know this is very unlikely, but do you maybe have any tickets available for today?"

"You have a reservation?"

"No, sorry."

"You want one ticket?"

"Yes."

She checks the computer. "OK, we have a reservation available at 2:25, and then one at 3:05, and we're pretty much wide-open after 3:30."

Visiting so many places and talking to so many people quickly eats up a day. From the moment I step out the door each morning, the imaginary stopwatch over my head ticks down the seconds until that last museum closes. The people I meet on my research rounds must think (and often say outright) that I seem terribly rushed. That's because I am.

Even when the workday's over . . . it's far from over. Just as the museums close, restaurants are opening for dinner, prime time to evaluate them at their peak. I have the unenviable task of stepping into one fantastic eatery after another—each one more tempting than the last—and then turning around and walking right back out. At some point in the evening, I might give in to the temptation to enjoy a sit-down dinner. More often, I just grab a sandwich, slice of pizza, or *döner kebab* to inhale as I walk back to my hotel.

Once back in the room, is it finally time to rest? Not hardly. Gathering the information is (often) the "fun" part. Writing it up is the real work. And the best time for that is when the day's findings are fresh in my mind, in that quiet window between dinnertime and bedtime. I'd love nothing more than to kick back and watch TV. Instead, I get very uncomfortable on the tiny, hard chair in the corner and balance my laptop on the chintzy desk as I squint at my marked-up book, brochures, and business cards. I write until I'm exhausted, and then try to finish up later, whenever I have a spare moment on the train or during a quiet afternoon.

A few fitful hours of sleep later, I'm up and at 'em—on to the next town to do it all over again. And when I'm done with that book, I submit the files to our editors and head to the next country.

Guidebook writers are perennial beta testers on material that will never be "finished." A guidebook is a living organism, unique in the publishing world. Most books, once in print, are immortalized forever. But with guidebooks, we know there's always another printing and another edition on the horizon. We do our best to ensure our books are up to date as of the moment we send them to the printer. But things can change, sometimes major things, and sometimes the day after the book ships. So we fix them as soon as we can.

Risa Laib was Rick's first guidebook editor. For 20-plus years, she oversaw the prolific expansion of the series, and she taught me most of what I know about editing and updating guidebooks. Risa often said she thought of each book as a palimpsest: an archaic vellum manuscript in which some ancient monk, at some distant outpost, wrote over existing text to make corrections or additions. These manuscripts, upon close examination, reveal many generations of amendments, layered on top of each other.

While the changes aren't as evident, any guidebook you flip through is just as much a palimpsest. It's difficult to say who even "wrote" each book. Rick Steves penned the first editions of many early guidebooks, and he still travels constantly to leave his marks. But so do other researchers and co-authors. And our editors make their own revisions.

Looking back on a guidebook chapter I worked on many years ago, sometimes I faintly recall which bits and pieces I wrote, and which ones Rick wrote, and which ones Risa or Jennifer or Tom or another one of our editors wrote. Most of the time, all I know for sure is that it's better than how I left it. Guidebooks are a team effort. If you've had a great trip thanks to a solid guidebook, take a moment to skim the list of credits—often squeezed in fine print at the back of the book—and imagine how many people worked hard to make your travels better.

Being a guidebook writer isn't quite what people expect, and it's certainly not for everyone. But for those of us who have a passion for travel, and who are wired to pack as much experience and learning as possible into each day on the road, and who are willing to forego slow dinners, lazy afternoon cocktails, and sleep . . . it's the job of our wildest dreams.

The Brazilian woman and I took a
couple trips together around Durban,
but not with the gaily decorated Zulu
rickshaw pullers; she said she didn't
believe in people being pulled by other
human beings.

—Mildred C. Scott,
  Jams Are Fun

PART TWO

Deconstructing Clichés

I had just sailed from Spain to Tangier, setting foot in Africa for the first time. My tour guide, Aziz, met me at the ferry dock and brought me to a restaurant where we sat down to a hearty lunch. I'm self-conscious about the very clumsy, very American way I use my knife and fork: Grip the knife in my right hand to cut, then drop it and pick up the fork to eat. I'm jealous of my suave European friends, who use their left-handed fork and right-handed knife, in concert, to eat with dexterity and grace.

But here in Morocco, Aziz watched me very closely as I ate. A wide smile slowly spread across his face. Finally, he blurted out, "I love the way you eat! So respectful."

In Aziz's culture, the left hand is considered dirty—traditionally used for cleaning yourself—while the right hand is used for eating. Many Moroccans use no utensils at all, only their right hand. By transferring my fork to my right hand, I was, unknowingly, being a very good Moroccan.

One of the great joys of travel is finding those little "ins" that help you understand the interplay between what people believe and how they live. Unfortunately, many travelers miss those details because they're mesmerized by clichés—captivated instead by belly dancers and camels and fezzes.

I can't blame people for getting sucked in by clichés. They make travel, an inherently destabilizing act, feel accessible and predictable. And, at times, they can be a useful shorthand. Take the first thing many travelers imagine when they think of Germany: the *Biergarten* with an oompah band. That's a cliché, yes. And, at the same time, many Germans truly enjoy a jaunty polka and a stein of *Weissbier* under chestnut boughs.

Clichés aren't necessarily the antithesis of authenticity. Sometimes a cliché is a distillation of culture. It's concentrated—usually too much so, as nuance and rationale get simmered out. But it contains aspects of truth.

For that reason, my approach is not necessarily to debunk clichés, but to deconstruct them. Often that means indulging in what travelers crave, just enough, while also challenging them to probe the depths beneath those clichés. I owe it to my readers to grapple with clichés thoughtfully—to understand where they come from and what they might actually tell us.

When writing about travel, there's an unspoken creative tension between accessibility and authenticity. An unexamined cliché is very accessible, but often less than completely authentic. Tourists who seek only clichés risk finding them and returning home feeling empty. When presented with Morocco, or Switzerland, or Iceland on a platter, many realize that's not what they want after all. They want something completely, unapologetically *real*.

Or do they?

One time I bumped into a former college professor of mine in a bookstore. He's still disappointed that I became a travel writer instead of a comparative literature professor (not recognizing that those are different shades of the same vocation). He acknowledged that our guidebooks aren't a total embarrassment. But he articulated one beef: "Rick Steves claims to be all about 'local' this and that. But in my opinion, he's driving people to places that are complete tourist traps!"

He went on to discuss a town in Europe he knows well, rattling off a few of Rick's recommendations and juxtaposing them, unflatteringly, against "real" local places that he personally prefers. But his favorites are in dreary neighborhoods far from anyplace a tourist would venture, and come with huge language and culture barriers that most of our readers wouldn't be willing to grapple with.

As his critique flared into a rant, I told him about the time that Rick and I challenged a local guide in Rovinj, Croatia, to take us to a truly local place. She walked us away from the touristy old town and into the back streets of the modern town. Finally we reached the crummiest, dankest, dreariest fishermen's pub you can imagine. Nude centerfolds were pinned to the peeling-plaster walls. The place smelled of spilled beer, vomit, urine splattered around the base of a urinal, and the sea. Several part-time fishermen, part-time alcoholics looked up from their chipped and smeared glasses just long enough to sneer at us. Our guide beamed proudly about her discovery; Rick and I glanced at each other awkwardly. This was "authentic" and "real," no question about it. It also had no place in our guidebook.

In reading travel writers I admire—and critiques of those travel writers—I can't escape the fact that travel writing is, perhaps unavoidably, rife with cliché.

Well, of course it is. Like the person who wants a "local" bar in Croatia, but would recoil at that fishermen's pub, deep down travelers crave some measure of cliché. And a good travel writer walks that razor's edge: seeking the balance of what people think they want, what they actually want, and what might make them run screaming.

Volcanoes, icebergs, and puffins in Iceland; Scottish kilts and bagpipes; *The Sound of Music* in Salzburg; French people being rude to Americans; the imposing language barrier that terrifies first-time travelers—all of these are clichés. But each one is also, to varying degrees, rooted in reality. And in the following pages, I explore each one. Sometimes I'll debunk; sometimes I'll reinforce; but always, I'll seek the truth behind the cliché.

Reykjavík, Iceland

Velkomin til Íslands!

*S*ettling into my rental apartment in downtown Reykjavík, I went to splash some water on my face. It came out scalding hot and smelled vaguely of farts.

You can prepare for a trip all you want. But there comes that moment when it becomes real. In my case, I had arrived on a volcanic island, where superheated water is piped into the city from boreholes in the countryside. Burning myself at the tap while smelling sulfur was a rite of passage. *Velkomin til Íslands.* Welcome to Iceland.

I was in Reykjavík to work on a new Iceland guidebook. And my constant companion—in spirit—was an Icelandic academic named Hildur. When we're writing a new book, we work our network any way possible to find local experts. Hildur was a friend-of-a-friend who was very excited to contribute. In fact, after I asked her for some pointers, she sent me copious notes to take into consideration as I scouted the book.

Wrapping up a research trip in Oslo, I printed out Hildur's notes for the next leg of my journey. As I boarded my plane, I realized I was about to fly east to west over the North Atlantic—a thousand miles across a frigid sea—just like those first Icelandic settlers, eleven centuries ago. Their journey was courageous, even foolhardy, and filled with peril as they followed a black raven to parts unknown. My journey was in Economy Plus, with free movies and drinks. But we both had a similar mission: to tame a new land. And I had one huge advantage: Hildur's notes in hand.

Devouring this material on the flight over, I heard Hildur's sensible, penetrating voice in every word. I also discovered that she's a stickler. She seeks comprehensive accuracy and abhors "tour guide stories"—simplified or exaggerated tall tales that guides love to spin for tourists who don't know, or care, that what they're hearing isn't strictly correct. Mixed in with Hildur's sharp advice about the best restaurants, museums, and so on, was a steady stream of disclaimers and debunking efforts—ripping these silly stories out by the root before they could sprout.

On the 45-minute minibus ride from the airport into downtown Reykjavík, the driver regaled us with a monologue of Icelandic factoids—so rife with half-truths and hyperbole, he might as well have scripted it just to torture Hildur. "While you're in Iceland, you have to try the fermented shark!" "Icelanders believe in 'hidden people.' They even get clairvoyants to negotiate with the elves when building a new road!" "If you buy one thing in Iceland, make it a stuffed puffin. If you buy two things, you have to get an Icelandic sweater. It's expensive—but warm!" I could feel a miniature Hildur perched on my right shoulder as she vigorously rolled her eyes, shook her head, and buried her face in her hands.

And yet, I found the driver's enthusiasm infectious. As one of those first-time visitors myself, I was entranced by the landscape we passed through: jagged black lava rock blanketed in a gentle, fuzzy, yellow-green moss. In that moment, I was just excited to finally be in Iceland, with its Vikings and volcanoes and puffins and "hidden people" and Björk.

Once I'd checked into my apartment and fried my face at the tap, I prepared to head out and explore. It was early summer, and through the windows, the rooftops of Reykjavík were bathed in bright sunlight. Parka-clad pedestrians, with fashionably fur-fringed faces, strolled by on the sidewalk.

I scampered down the stairs like a kid on Christmas morning and threw open the door, only to get whipped in the face by an arctic blast. After running back upstairs for a few more layers, I ventured out again. Bracing myself against the howling wind, I recalled Hildur's warning that wind trumps all. Icelanders define bad weather as "lots of wind," and good weather as "somewhat less wind." And despite the sunshine, this was a bad weather day.

Walking a few blocks to the center of town, I felt frigid gusts coming off the nearby harbor and heard the cry of seagulls. I passed a row of eye-pleasing old houses wrapped in corrugated metal and painted in bright colors—a practical, durable, and unaccountably beautiful cladding for this hostile climate.

Just past those Crayola homes, the street opened up into Ingólfstorg—an urban, concrete square busy with local fast-food stands and skateboarders. In the middle of the square stood two stony pillars, engulfed in steam billowing from hidden vents. These recall the legendary Reykjavík founder Ingólfur Árnason, a Viking who, upon exploring Icelandic waters around A.D. 874, tossed two beams overboard and sent his crew out to see where they washed up. The vapors rising from hot springs inspired him to call this place *reykja-vík*, "Steamy Bay."

Mini-Hildur, sitting on my shoulder, cleared her throat. *Actually, most of what you just said is wrong. Ingólfur was not a Viking, per se; at best he was a "Scandinavian settler during the Viking Age." Specifically, the beams he threw overboard were from his ceremonial throne, and if he did this, it's not really notable, as it was common practice for explorers to test prevailing currents and find a safe harbor. Regardless, there is no historical documentation to corroborate this story, which is as likely legend as fact, and the date is at best a guess. Oh, and the steam they saw was not actually here, but in Laugardalur east of today's down-town. And reyk doesn't quite mean "steam"—more like "smoke."*

The record corrected, I turned up Aðalstræti—famously "Reykjavík's first street"—to the square called Austurvöllur for a peek at Iceland's parliament. The Alþingi, pronounced "all-thingy," is boxy and just two stories tall, made of stacked volcanic rock; it could pass for a small-town post office or bank. Next door is the city's cathedral, which looks more like a Danish village church. Taken together, this "parliament square" was strikingly modest—a stark contrast to Iceland's bubbling, boiling, glacial, cinematic countryside.

Eavesdropping on a tour, I heard the guide say that the Alþingi was the "world's oldest parliament"—dating back to an annual gathering of clan chieftains in the summer fields of Þingvellir, beginning around A.D. 930.

As I jotted down this factoid, Mini-Hildur hissed into my ear: *Actually, this is an exaggeration, albeit it a common one. The Alþingi that met at Þingvellir in the centuries after settlement was very different from a modern democratic parliament. From about 1400 to 1800, it was an appeals court, not a legislature. Then there were forty-five years when the Alþingi didn't meet at all. It was reestablished in Reykjavík, in a totally new and different form, in 1845. And Iceland didn't become an independent nation until 1948 in any event, begging the question of whether it could truly be a "parliament" before then.*

Scratching out my notes as I shook my head with the weight of clarity, I circled back down to the main drag, Austurstræti. A forest of construction cranes rose high between me and the harbor. Reykjavík was taking advantage of its rebounding economy and tourist boom to undertake a "big dig" along its waterfront.

Venturing toward the mess to explore, I stumbled upon Reykjavík's indoor flea market, Kolaportið. Stepping inside to warm up, I found a warehouse filled with an endearing assortment of mainly local wares: used paperbacks, reclaimed furniture and housewares, posters, ironic Icelandic T-shirts, secondhand CDs by

Björk and Of Monsters and Men, and a few racks of those famous Icelandic sweaters.

At the far end of the hall was a small food section. The coolers displayed examples of another Icelandic cliché: "hardship" foods. Mixed in among the more familiar choices like lamb, cod, and haddock were sea bird eggs, horse meat, *harðfiskur* (air-dried stockfish), and whale.

With this last one, Mini-Hildur sucked in her breath: *Let's tread lightly here. Icelanders rarely ate whale. They were hunted mainly for blubber, and the meat was exported to Norway. These days, whale—which is exclusively non-endangered minke whale—is consumed mainly by tourists, plus some export business. I've heard most of it ends up in Japanese school lunches.*

Here we agree. Eating whale in Iceland is one of those clichés that requires care and context. It's understandable that a remote, near-Arctic island would hunt whales during its hardscrabble Settlement Age. But now that practice continues partly to feed curious tourists, eating whale as much on a dare as for the protein. In this case, blindly reinforcing a cliché can spur the continuation of an outdated practice.

I left the flea market and returned to the main drag. Following it to the west, I made my way across a busy street and soon found myself on Reykjavík's main walking, shopping, dining, and nightlife drag, Laugavegur. Low-key and slathered with street art, this strip is an inviting place to simply wander and browse. I did just that, making a slow lap past tacky "puffin shops," microbrew pubs, cozy cafés, indie bookstores, heavenly bakeries, boutiques selling top-end $200 Icelandic sweaters, thrift and vintage shops selling those same sweaters—gently used—for half-price, and lots of lively restaurants. I finally began to simply enjoy myself and let Mini-Hildur take a well-deserved break.

At the intersection with the steep, picturesque street called Skólavörðustígur, I looked up to see Reykjavík's hill-capping

landmark church, Hallgrímskirkja. The street was painted in a giant rainbow, which I followed up, past intriguing cafés and inviting shops, toward the church's lantern-like steeple. I felt like I was off to see the wonderful Wizard of Oz.

At the hill's summit, the plaza in front of the church was dominated by a dynamic statue of Leifur Eiríksson—or, as Icelanders call him, "Leif the Lucky" for how he found his way to North America half a millennium before Christopher Columbus. I could feel Mini-Hildur squirming on my shoulder, like the smartest kid in class desperate to be called on. But I ignored her and turned my attention to the church.

Icelandic architecture is utilitarian, but it possesses a simple, harmonious beauty. The Hallgrímskirkja—the most famous building in the country—is built of gray volcanic stone. The towering steeple is flanked with stairstep gables that evoke the basalt cliffs of Iceland's countryside.

From the church's narthex, I rode the elevator to the top of the tower. The cute Monopoly houses of Reykjavík splayed out from my feet, with cheery colors that popped in the bright sun—offering an ideal visual overview of the sprawling capital. *From the top of this tower,* Mini-Hildur said with an atypical awe, *you can see the homes of two out of every three citizens.*

Gazing out over most of the planet's Icelanders, I pondered the internal debate I was having with Hildur. On the one hand, I respect her approach. There's a lot of tourist-baiting nonsense in Europe—and perhaps nowhere more than in Iceland, which had, only a few years earlier, embarked on an ambitious and wildly successful bid to capture the imaginations of travelers. Clichés sell, and maybe their efforts worked too well, creating a monster. And now, seemingly to compensate for the excesses of her homeland, Hildur was handling the place with a puritanical reverence.

And yet, it's not all nonsense. And even if it were, it's fun. Even smart people need fun. My challenge was coming into focus: to balance Hildur's scruples with the joy of discovery (and, yes, appetite for clichés) of a first-time visitor. Hildur was the left brain; I was to be the right brain. (The tables were turned: Usually Rick is the right brain, and I'm the left brain.) Like Hildur, I wanted the book to be factually correct. But I also didn't want to piss all over the simple joy of being in Iceland.

The debate wasn't over; in fact, it would rage over the next three weeks. Throughout my time in Iceland, I would be both guided and, to some extent, haunted by Mini-Hildur's presence, whispering into my ear: *Actually, that's not quite right.* . . . On long car trips, we'd spend hours arguing the pros and cons of whether it's accurate to say, for example, that you could "walk through a chasm that separates Europe and North America," geologically speaking. Writing a new guidebook always involves this creative tension, and Hildur made the subtext explicit. And, no doubt, her concerns made the book stronger.

Did George Washington actually chop down a cherry tree as a child, then refuse to lie about it? Historians say no; the story seems to have been invented by a biographer. But the existence of this legend offers insight into American values (or, at least, how Americans like to view themselves). And so it persists. To the best of my knowledge, there are no outright falsehoods in our Iceland guidebook. But you will find phrases along the lines of, "According to legend . . ." or "Some Icelanders believe . . . ." That's because, in the end, travel writers aren't cliché exterminators. We're cliché curators.

Riding the elevator down the church tower to ground level, I was famished. I returned to a high-end grill restaurant I'd spotted earlier. Stepping inside, the whole space smelled like charcoal and mesquite. It felt hip, yet accessible. Periodically, a hazy cloche was lifted theatrically off a dish, releasing another puff of sweet smoke into the air.

I put on my best puppy-dog eyes and asked the host if they had any tables for one. "Do you have a reservation?" he asked in that stern way that typically means, "Ha!" But then he spotted a lone place setting at a counter made from a split tree trunk, facing into the kitchen. He seated me there, next to a Japanese hipster with a man bun poking out from under his furry hat. We exchanged the courteous nod of two singletons who find themselves dining together, and I turned my attention to the menu.

Despite Iceland's bum rap for its "hardship" foods, every single item here sounded delicious, melding international know-how and distinctly Icelandic ingredients: lamb, *humar* (langoustine), puffin, rhubarb, *skyr*, licorice, and yes, minke whale.

After placing my order, I pulled out my camera to photograph the sous chef blowtorch-searing a hunk of whale on a miniature hibachi. My neighbor snapped the same photo. To break the ice, we compared cameras. And soon, we were debriefing each other on our Iceland trips. Both of us were celebrating special occasions: I was on my first night in Iceland, and he was on his last, after three weeks of camping and skiing his way around the island. And we both had big journeys that began tomorrow: his to Tokyo by way of Helsinki, mine three weeks around the perimeter of Iceland with Mini-Hildur in tow.

My rack of lamb hit the table. It was incredibly tender and flavorful, with dipping sauces made of yogurt and rhubarb jam. As the lamb melted in my mouth, I asked my fellow traveler about his favorite place in Iceland.

"I don't remember what it's called, but it's a very long name," he began, quoting every traveler who's ever been to Iceland. He drew his hands apart as he said it, to emphasize just how staggeringly long the name was. "It was a wonderful little town on a fjord on the north coast. You drive north from a bigger town along a fjord. You go through a very long tunnel. Then more fjord. And then you drive through a shorter tunnel. And that's where this town is." He opened his laptop to show me photos: skiing down a steep mountain with a village in the distance and the midnight sun on the horizon. (Later I figured out which town he was talking about: Siglufjörður. And it was one of my favorites, too.)

We watched in silence as the chefs plated arctic creatures on wood shingles and glassy chunks of lava. Soon my dessert arrived: lemon meringue with salted licorice. I've learned that some people love licorice, and some people hate it. And those who love licorice, really love salted licorice. I knew I was going to feel right at home in Iceland.

Bidding bon voyage to my dinner companion, I headed back out into the chill of the evening. It was 10 p.m., yet it was lighter outside than when I'd gone in. It dawned on me that I wouldn't see true darkness until I flew home three weeks later.

I waddled my way back up the main drag to my apartment and fell into bed. All tucked in, catching the faint whiff of sulfur on my just-washed face, it was hard to fall asleep. I love the adventure of being at the start of a journey in a brand-new place.

Good first day, Mini-Hildur whispered. *But tomorrow, we must discuss that "Leif the Lucky" story. It's . . . more complicated than that.*

Scottish Highlands

The Soggy, Sunny Highland Games of Taynuilt

*P*ulling off the main street in the village of Taynuilt, I feel my tires shimmy on saturated turf. I follow muddy ruts to where a waterlogged attendant stands in front of a green shack.

"Is this the parking for the Highland games?" I ask.

"Aye, it is indeed," she says, peering out from the narrow slit formed by her rain hood. "Six pounds, please."

Taynuilt may have picked the wrong day for its annual celebration of Highland culture. Even though it's July, frigid gusts swirl misty waterspouts across the neon-green playing field. I park my car, bundle up, and feel my feet squish through the wet sponge of a lawn—with each step, wringing out peaty brown water that threatens to crest the tops of my shoes. (Why, oh why, didn't I pack the waterproof ones?) I'm considering bailing out and returning to the warmth of my B&B lounge.

But then a delightful scene unfolds before me: Rural Scotland is putting on its show, rain or shine. Everyone, unlike me, is wearing their Wellies (rain boots). A traditionally clad family piles out of their minivan, and dad helps his young sons adjust their kilts.

Bagpipes begin droning from every corner of the field as members of the pipe band tune up.

This is why I've sacrificed a precious day off to stand around in a wet field. Traveling in Scotland, you're awash in clichés: Kilts and tartans. Bagpipes. Whisky. Golf. Haggis. Lochs and castles. Midges and hairy coos. Few little countries carry so much cultural baggage, or leverage it so deftly for financial gain. Many tourists— on the predictable Edinburgh-Stirling-Fort William-Inverness-Edinburgh loop—are exposed only to tacky "tartan tat."

I'm driving around Scotland for a month working on a new guidebook. My mission is to deconstruct all those clichés and, if I can, uncover something deeper, something truer. And Taynuilt, a no-name burg a thirty-minute drive from nowhere in particular, might be my best chance to determine if there's any "there there."

A loudspeaker crackles to life, and a lovely, lilting Scottish voice cuts through the fog: "If you'd like to join the pipe band in their parade through the village, you can follow them on up to the Taynuilt Hotel in a few minutes." She proceeds to list off the day's events. And she explains the rain plan: There is none. Except for the Highland dancing, which has been moved inside the village hall.

I tag along with the pipe band—about eight bagpipers and a half-dozen drummers—as they start up the village's lone street. I ask the bass drummer where they're from. "Strathearn, in Perthshire. We came a long way for this. And according to the weather map, it's the only part of the country in rain."

Passing the village hall, I peel off from the pipers to peek inside. Fiercely focused lassies, done up in their best Highland finery, are dancing with precision and poise. They're hoping the weather will improve, so they can head outside.

I catch up with the pipers and drummers, who stand huddled in the alley next to the town's lone hotel. They're getting in one more round of practice before the big show. A crowd of about thirty people gathers across the street, waiting patiently. Finally the clan chieftain shows up with this family. Shivering in their kilts, they line up in front of the pipe band.

The band springs to life, and the ragtag parade marches through the village to the playfield. Ponchoed pipers and drummers fill the drizzly air with drone, whine, peal, and rat-a-tat-tat. They're trailed by villagers—and a handful of visitors like me—scurrying around them to snap photos.

By the time we arrive back at the field, it's a different scene. While still cloudy, the worst of the rain has passed, and—like ginger-haired earthworms—more villagers have emerged. The clan chieftain's family and pipe band take a lap around the racecourse before announcing the Taynuilt Highland Games officially open.

I survey the scene: The infield hosts the kilted, macho feats of strength. Ringing that is a running track for the footraces. Off to one side is a stage for the dancers. And sprawling alongside the venue are junk food stands, test-your-skill carnival games, and fundraising charities selling hamburgers, fried sausage sandwiches, baked goods, and bottles of beer and Irn-Bru. One greasy cart, with that indefatigable spirit of British whimsy, is called "Posh Nosh." Several sell deep-fried Mars bars—a proud Scottish invention.

In the center of the field, eight brawny athletes assemble for the feats of Highland strength. They're all wearing kilts, with track pants underneath and hoodies over top. The emcee, who has a marvelously dry wit and seems to revel in how folksy it all is, introduces the competitors. "Gary's wife tells me he's the most handsome man in Scotland. That's her over there watching Gary adoringly from the sideline."

She continues: "Stuart is our youngest participant, at just 16 years old. He just started a new job this week, and already he's getting high marks. They say he can lift anything." (We have a word for guys like Stuart back in the States: linebacker.)

The events are all variations on the same concept: hurling objects of awkward shape and size as far as possible. Things kick off with the weight throw, where the stocky strongmen spin like ballerinas before releasing a 28- or 56-pound ball on a chain into the sky. At a certain point, gravity has its way with the weight, abruptly altering its trajectory to plummet sharply groundward, where it embeds itself several inches in the wet earth. The hammer throw involves a similar technique with a 26-pound ball on a long stick.

In the "weight over the bar" event, the Highlanders swing a 56-pound weight over an incrementally higher horizontal bar—starting at 10 feet, eventually reaching 12 feet. As our emcee keeps reminding us, "That's like tossing a five-year-old child over a double-decker bus."

And then there's the caber toss: Pick up a 90-pound, 17-foot-long log, take a running start, and release it in an end-over-end motion with enough force to, ideally, make it flip all the way over and land at the twelve o'clock position. (On this day, most of the cabers wind up closer to six o'clock. I doubt I could lift the thing to begin with.)

Meanwhile, the track events are running circles around the musclemen: the 100-yard dash, the 1,500 meters, and so on. Trying to fabricate an exciting narrative out of the paltry turn-out for the women's 400-meter, our emcee intones, "Currently there are only two runners in this race. They are sisters. And they are competitors."

The most impressive event is the hill race, which combines a 1,000-foot mountain ascent with a six-mile footrace. The hill racers begin with a lap around the track before disappearing for about an hour. After several minutes, I begin to see their colorful jerseys bobbing up the side of a distant peak. By the time they finally start to trickle back into the stadium, even the emcee seems to have forgotten about them.

At long last, the sun emerges. People shed their water-proofs and bask in the hard-earned rays. The Highland dancers have escaped from the village hall to dance on a covered stage at the end of the field. While one set of little girls carefully toes routines for the judges, others practice on the sidelines. The youngest lassies, with less control over their swinging limbs, work hard but lack grace. The older dancers are nimble and dignified.

At one point, crossed swords are placed on the stage for the performers to delicately dance over, hopping benignly over the glinting blades. As an indication that the feats of strength may be more my cup of tea, I keep waiting for the dancers to pick up the swords and start fencing. (They never do.)

I tease. There are reasons—historical, cultural, superstitious—why Highlanders dance over weapons, and why they do all of the things I'm observing today.

Hopping over crossed blades originated as an intimidating war dance, illustrating dexterity and endurance—the Highland equivalent of army recruits running through rows of tires. And those feats of strength, of course, exude power and defiance—an essential stance when you're a hardscrabble small community, surrounded by rival communities, at the northern reaches of a realm that occasionally decides to flex its expansionist muscles. Even the hill race is excellent preparation for moving around this vast and hilly terrain.

Bagpipes occur in many cultures, but nowhere are they as closely associated with one place as in Scotland. The Highlanders used them to motivate troops on the battlefield. After Culloden—the pivotal 1746 battle that devastated the Scottish clan system—they were outlawed as an "instrument of warfare." To a Scot, bagpipes remain deeply patriotic.

Those tartans, too—that epitome of Scottish cliché—have authentic origins. Members of a clan lived in the same area, with access to the same natural dyes, and so they dressed in similar colors. It wasn't until the Victorian Age that these patterns were standardized, brightened, and neatly categorized clan-by-clan. Their continued embrace by modern Scots demonstrates a determination to preserve that connection to a distant past. And that speaks, as well, to why so many have turned out in this damp field, in the early 21st century, to remind themselves of those traditions. For the Scots all around me, these "touristy clichés" remain a point of genuine pride.

By the day's end, the passing bright spells have become steady sunshine. Cotton-candy clouds echo the candy floss that kids gobble as they watch the final few events, including the village-wide tug-of-war. A good time has been had by all . . . rain or no rain.

Heading back to my car, I realize this may have been the most satisfying, most culturally enlightening, most affordable, and least touristy experience I've had during an entire month in Scotland. There were tartans and bagpipes and deep-fried Mars bars, yes. But it was clear that they weren't there for outsiders like me.

I grew up in the town of Delaware, Ohio, about a 30-minute drive north of Columbus. We're not known for much. The birthplace of Rutherford B. Hayes—widely acclaimed as one of America's most forgettable presidents—was torn down long ago, replaced by a plaque in front of a gas station. We are, however, the home of the Little Brown Jug, one of the "triple crown" events of harness horse racing (and the namesake of a jaunty 1939 Glenn Miller single). Every September, everyone gets the day off school, and the fairgrounds at the north end of town are enlivened by carnival rides, junk food, and 4H competitions. And to kick things off, a horse parade winds through the city streets—followed, close behind, by a squad of pooper scoopers carrying snow shovels, who get bigger cheers than the equine grand marshals.

All of this is to say: I know authentic, genuine, small-town folksiness when I see it, and I love the hell out of it. And it's clear to me that the Taynuilt games are as real as they come. In the least likely place—the Scottish Highlands, inundated with "tartan tat"—I've found that elusive unicorn: a cliché that exists only for itself.

Salzburg, Austria

D'Oh! A Deer!

S alzburg's tour guides are understandably jaded. "Understandably" to me, anyway, because I'm not really a fan either. Don't get me wrong: Like many Americans, I grew up watching *The Sound of Music*—or bits and pieces of it—every Easter on TV. Some of the songs are catchy. Pretty scenery, and all that. But I never *loved* it. Growing up as the little brother of an *SoM* fan, and later being married to another, no doubt hardened my cynicism against the Von Trapp brats.

The thing is, I only have to deal with all this once a year—and at that rate, it's harmless and quaint. But if you're a tour guide in Salzburg, you have no choice: *The Sound of Music* is your life.

Sound of Music tours are a huge business, attracting some 100,000 Von Trapp pilgrims to Salzburg annually, at around $50 a pop. Our guidebook recommends two different *Sound of Music* tours: one with a big bus, and the other with a minibus. Both get an unusual number of reader complaints. To get to the bottom of things, I went on each one.

(You may be wondering why someone who isn't a fan of the movie would be given this assignment. I would counter that someone who isn't a fan of the movie may just be the *perfect* person for this assignment. My assessment isn't clouded by fond childhood memories of whiskers on kittens and schnitzel with noodles. And while we're on the topic, nobody actually eats schnitzel with noodles. That's a recipe for weeklong constipation.)

The *Sound of Music* phenomenon in Salzburg is emblematic of what some call "set-jetting" or "location vacation": organizing your travels around places you've seen on TV or in the movies. As someone who seeks authenticity in Europe, it would be easy for me to dismiss the *Game of Thrones* pilgrims on Croatia's Dalmatian Coast, or the *Harry Potter* fans flocking to random locations across the British countryside, as a silly nuisance. But I also happen to be a movie buff, so I get it. And, more important, I have observed people, sometimes in spite of themselves, coming to love those places in their own right.

But when the "set-jetting" becomes the end instead of a beginning, it stops being what I consider good travel. One of my guide friends in Dubrovnik has been asked to lead tours exclusively of *Game of Thrones* locations—"without any of that history or culture stuff." That's where she draws the line, and where I do, too. And I fear that these *Sound of Music* tours, while entertaining, cross that line.

And so here I am, in a minibus with six North American *SoM* devotees—the only one not singing along to "Doe, a deer . . . ." My companions for the day are two fifty-something Canadian women whose husbands skipped out on the tour to visit Hitler's Eagle's Nest in Berchtesgaden (smart guys) and four American college students. It's clear that the movie—50-plus years young and still going strong—exerts a powerful, cross-generational appeal.

Everybody on the minibus—young and old alike—knows every word to every song. They know when to sing "flibbertigibbet" and when to sing "will-o-the-wisp." They're full-on geeking out about each morsel of information. And everybody "oohs!" and "aahs!" on cue when our guide shows us, for example, the trees where the kids hang from the branches in their curtain clothes, or whatever . . . I wasn't really paying attention.

We pull up to a mansion on the shore of a beautiful alpine lake. This is not the actual Von Trapp family house. And it's only one-third of the movie Von Trapp family house. (The back of the house, and the interior, were each filmed elsewhere.) But even so, people gobble up the stories of the youngest Von Trapp falling out the wrong side of the canoe and being rescued by Liesl.

Our guide explains that The Gazebo (where Liesl hooks up with a teenaged Nazi) was built just for the movie, next to the mansion. But then, years later, cinephiles were still showing up in droves, making a racket, singing and waltzing and taking pictures. So they moved The Gazebo across the lake to a *Biergarten*. But the same thing happened: Tourists made a ruckus, disturbing the *Biergarten* patrons.

Just to be entirely clear on this point: The *Sound of Music* fans were so rowdy, they were bothering Austrian drunks chugging one-liter mugs of beer.

And so, The Gazebo is no longer anywhere near this lake. They moved it several miles away, to Hellbrunn Palace, where they placed it outside the wall near the parking lot, between the garbage cans and the toilets. And there, each day, a steady stream of tour buses pulls up to let 50 people take turns photographing

each other in front of The Gazebo, gazing wistfully into each other's eyes. Then they use the toilets and get back on the bus.

And what about The Meadow—the one where Julie Andrews spun herself silly? Like Hitler's Bunker in Berlin, its real location is shrouded in mystery: Everyone claims to know where it is, but each one of them will take you to a different place. (Apparently, the actual The Meadow is on private property, and strictly off-limits to the curious public.) But it doesn't really matter. Guides told me that any alpine meadow will do—so they just pull over wherever's handy. One of them said, "Local farmers can't figure out why all of these Americans are always spinning in their fields."

Our guide, an elderly Austrian, has a knack for doling out trivia at the appropriate pace. "Did you know that Audrey Hepburn also auditioned for the role of Maria?" he asks. "Yes, as a matter of fact, I *did* know that!" exclaim no fewer than three of my fellow *SoM* aficionados.

But there's a mirthlessness to our guide's delivery. I don't sense a deep-in-his-bones love affair with "The Lonely Goatherd." He seems to get a minor kick out of the story of the Trapp Family Singers . . . but would he lie down in traffic for Julie Andrews? As an *SoM* cynic myself, I can relate. When he asks if we have any questions, I can barely stop myself from asking, "So, Günther, how *do* you solve a problem like Maria?"

Day two. The big bus tour has a similar itinerary but more people. Lots and lots more people . . . 49 *SoM* fanatics on a 50-seat bus. Our lederhosen-clad guide recites his tightly crafted spiel with the poise of a stand-up comic. I imagine he's been regaling his audience with these same quips, puns, and factoids, twice a day, for many years. The bus offers a comfy ride and a higher vantage point. But loading and unloading at each stop is a chore. And, by the trip's end, rather than feeling the warm camaraderie of the minibus, I feel a need to escape.

All told, each tour has its pros and its cons, and both are just fine. So what's with the complaints? The disconnect, I think, is that the Austrian local guides cannot, and never will, match their customers' intensity of affection for the movie.

The Sound of Music is an American phenomenon. Yes, the exteriors were filmed in Salzburg. (And after these tours, I'm wondering if there's a square inch of the city that didn't wind up somewhere in that movie.) But fundamentally, it's an American movie, based on an American stage play, by American composers who wrote songs in English that have nothing to do with Austria's musical tradition. Most Austrians haven't even seen the movie; those who have, certainly weren't *reared* on it. Mozart is in their bones. But *The Sound of Music* is this weird thing that just happened to them.

And so, when our readers go on one of these tours, then complain that the guide was gruff, or the tour felt rushed . . . I'm not saying these people are wrong to be disappointed. But it's hard to blame the guide for maybe phoning it in just a tad.

Look at it this way: Imagine that some obscure-to-you movie was filmed in your hometown a very long time ago. Just for the sake of argument, let's say it was the 1990 Tom Hanks action-comedy *Joe Versus the Volcano*. So, *Joe Versus the Volcano* was filmed in your hometown. That's cool. But it's been decades now, and you've moved on. Everybody in town has gone on to bigger and better things. As it should be.

But here's the thing: People keep showing up, having traveled great distances at great expense to see everything in your town relating to *Joe Versus the Volcano*. They want to visit the shop where Joe bought his four waterproof steamer trunks that he later lashed into a raft. They want all of the tinseltown gossip about Meg Ryan's artistic journey in playing three different roles. They are desperate to stand on the very pier from which Joe set off on his sailboat trip to Waponi Woo.

Now, these people are willing to pay you a lot of money. Like, every day, a dozen of them will hand you fifty bucks apiece to show them this stuff. There are many other things in your town that you are legitimately passionate about. But these people don't want to see those things—and six hundred bucks ain't bad for a half-day's work, am I right? So you take them to see the vacant lot where Abe Vigoda and Lloyd Bridges had their trailers. But—and this is a big but—that doesn't mean that you enjoy it.

There's more to Salzburg than *The Sound of Music*. But you are really excited about *The Sound of Music*. And that's great! Just be prepared for an enthusiasm gap between you and your guide. They'll take you to the locations. They'll tell you the stories. They'll play the songs on the bus. And they'll do it all with a smile (as much as Austrians ever smile). But cut them some slack. And don't expect them to sing along.

France

Loving the French
(What's Not to Love?)

If I'm being honest, I'm always a little intimidated when first arriving in France. I suspect living in America has programmed me—contrary to the sum total of my lived experience—to think of French people as stuffy and snooty and unkind to outsiders. And then, with each visit, I have dozens of mini-epiphanies about how wrongheaded that is.

The fact is, the French aren't rude and abusive. They're reserved, and a bit formal. They believe in a certain orderliness to social interaction. They just want to be respected, and if you respect them, you'll get more than your share of respect in return.

The garrulous, "Howzit goin'?" American cowboy stampedes all over the French social order. We Yanks pride ourselves on our independence, on bucking conventions, on being on an instant first-name basis with every stranger we happen to ride the elevator with. And, in their place, those can be wonderful qualities. But it clashes with the French worldview.

One of my colleagues, who guides tours all over Europe, confessed that she finds France one of the hardest places to bring Americans. It's not because the French are unpleasant; it's because we Americans aren't very adaptable when on someone else's turf. And the French do expect us to respect their ways.

A Parisian shop clerk once explained this with a sublime simplicity: "In France, we don't want to be defined by our work. We want to be acknowledged as a human being first, and only then as a provider of services. So just say *bonjour* before telling us what you want from us. Treat our shops the way you would our living rooms. Would you walk into my house without saying hello?"

And that's really all there is to it. When you interact with any French person, first acknowledge their humanity. Just say, *Bonjour!* For extra credit, throw in a *Madame* or a *Monsieur*. And when you leave, say *Au revoir!* If you do this, and only this, the French will warm to you.

Another disconnect is Americans' tendency to be in a hurry. Time is money, and impatience is a virtue. But in France, they've mastered the art of fine living—and that means savoring the moment. Slow yourself to their pace (or, at least, meet them in the middle). They'll appreciate it, and you'll likely find that it's more enjoyable for you, too.

France is a country of introverts. As an introvert myself, I can appreciate how extroverts sometimes come on too strong—getting in my face with an aggressive chumminess that can feel fake and exhausting. As a nation that values extroverts, we'd do well to empathize with the French. Don't bowl them over with enthusiasm; just give them a gentle smile and a kind greeting.

Putting this approach into practice, I've had vanishingly few terrible interactions with French people. In fact, I find the French much warmer than many of their neighbors.

And what about that language barrier? Wait, what language barrier? I speak no French beyond a few pleasantries, but it's *pas de problème*. I find more and better English spoken in France than in Spain or Italy. People here can be a bit shy. When you ask locals if they speak English, many say, "A little bit. I will try." What a nice way to put it. And many of those who are "trying" express a mastery of English that eludes some native speakers.

Even when they don't speak English, they listen patiently, with a sweet smile, while I mangle their delicate language, as if stomping on a fine carpet with muddy boots. (Since I don't actually speak French, I accomplish this by speaking Spanish with a French accent. Yeah, I'm *that guy* . . . and they still seem to like me.)

If there's one caveat to this, it has to do with Paris. Look, it's a big, busy city. And, like New York, London, or Tokyo, it's a mix of kindhearted people and troubled cranks. Some Americans go only to Paris, maybe have one or two awkward interactions, and extrapolate those to the entire country. I've met my share of surly Parisians, too. But overall, I've had many more positive experiences there than negative ones. When standing on a street corner puzzling over a map, I've been approached by helpful locals offering directions more in Paris than anywhere else in Europe.

On a recent visit to Normandy, at my B&B's breakfast table, I met a stubborn American who embodies this cultural disconnect. It was immediately apparent that he'd come to France with a massive chip on his shoulder. Over breakfast, I was enthusing about how friendly the French are, and how welcome I feel as an English-speaker, when he cut me off. "Oh, yeah?" he snapped. "If their English is soooo great, why do I have to tell everyone bone-joor all the time?"

While his wife—a Francophile who clearly had been coaching him on this—died a silent death next to him, I replied, "To be polite. Is it really that hard to say *bonjour?*"

What I was thinking, though, was this: To not get along with the French, you pretty much have to be an asshole. (Pardon my French.)

That Wonderful Language Barrier

efore my first visit to Russia, I decided to learn the Cyrillic alphabet. I made flashcards for each letter and quizzed myself daily. Deep down I suspected that this was pointless: Would it matter if I could sound out Russian words when I don't speak Russian?

After landing in Moscow, I went for a long walk and dissected every word I saw, phonetically, letter by letter. And I was shocked at how many I understood. Loanwords from English looked exotic but sounded familiar: йóга—yoga, or Старбакс Кофе—Starbucks coffee, or Русские Сувениры—"Russkiye suveniry" (Russian souvenirs), or even the supermarket chain Дикси—Dixie. And I recognized proper nouns, too: Сталин—Stalin, or Италия—Italy, or Парк Горького—"Park Gorkogo" (Gorky Park). Simply noticing which words had migrated into Russian offered insights about how Russia relates to the rest of the world.

The fearsome cliché of the language barrier intimidates travelers. They view a foreign language as exactly that: a barrier to be overcome. I disagree. Grappling with language is one of the joys of being on the road. Not only is it a fun puzzle to solve; trying to understand it—even psychoanalyze it—can unlock cultural secrets.

To be clear: I'm not talking about *learning a language* before you visit a place. I'm talking about approaching language openly and constructively, rather than assuming it's a lost cause. You're smart. You've already mastered at least one language. Give yourself some credit to play around with another. Many of my favorite cultural eurekas have been earned through a willingness to get my hands dirty with Europe's languages.

In 2009, the time had come to create new editions of our best-selling Rick Steves phrase books. To ensure that our redesign was driven by the needs of a traveler, Rick sent me on an unconventional research mission: I went to Spain, France, Germany, and Italy for a few days each to gather new words, phrases, and cultural insights. For a word nerd like me, this was a dream assignment.

Hold up—*phrase* books? How quaint!

It's fair to question whether a printed phrase book has any place in 21st-century travel. With translation apps and the ubiquity of English, the monoglot traveler has a much easier path than Rick did during his backpacking days. On day one of my scouting trip—in Madrid—it was already clear that phrases like, "I would like to buy two tickets for the matinee, please," were included more out of a sense of propriety than practicality.

I quickly hatched a subversive counter-agenda for the project: Rather than stack the books with even more borderline-useless phrases, I'd turn each phrase book into a "cultural decoder" for stealing a glimpse inside the heads of Europeans. I'd use language to reverse-engineer a deeper cultural understanding.

And so I wandered through those four countries, scribbling down everything I saw and seeking cultural insights. For example, in Italy, when does a *bambino* become a *ragazzo*? Around age ten, I was told, which seems arbitrary but offers some insight about when society demands greater maturity from a wild child.

Grasping the subtleties of language can help avoid confusion. English tends to use "excuse me" and "pardon me" interchangeably. But Europeans distinguish between trying to get someone's attention *(Excusez-moi)* and quasi-apologizing for trying to pass or get out of someone's way *(Pardon)*. A Parisian told me they've observed Americans in a crowded Métro train—when approaching their stop—repeat, with increasing urgency, *Excusez-moi! Excusez-moi!* To Parisians, this is like shouting, "Hey, please, everybody! Can I have your attention? Everyone, *look at me!*"

These were phrase books, not grammar books. And yet, grappling with grammar, just a teensy bit, also pulls back the curtain on culture. English has long since done away with our "Thees" and "Thous," but most Europeans still differentiate between informal and formal "you": *du* and *Sie* in German, *tu* and *Usted* in Spanish, *tu* and *vous* in French, and so on. But how do you decide who's a *tu* and who's an *Usted*? When making a new acquaintance, you assess relative ages and social ranks and make a judgment call. Personally, around the time I reached age 35—which is also when my temples began to gray—I started hearing more formal "yous," in every language. And I heard more *tus* when wearing shorts and more *Usteds* when wearing long pants.

I fulfilled my obligation to add conventional "phrases" to the books. But I also submitted blocks of culturally enlightening text. What are the different ticket lines in the Madrid train station— and which one should I get in? What are the names of all those delicious-looking pastries in a French *pâtisserie*—and what's the flavor profile of each one? How do you navigate the food and drink stalls at a Bavarian beer garden—and where do you sit once you've assembled your meal?

Upon my return, my guerrilla crusade to de-phrase the phrase books met with resistance. Throughout the editorial process, more and more of my prose was excised. In retrospect, this was reasonable on the part of editors who believed themselves to be editing *phrase* books. While much of my material made the cut, in the end the phrase books are still phrase books, and they still sell like hotcakes. As a consolation, a fair bit of what I wrote was woven into our various guidebooks instead. And I've rescued some of my favorite observations for this chapter.

Universal words are a godsend to travelers. Once you learn that "cashier" is *Kasse* in German, you'll recognize it everywhere: *caisse* in French, *cassa* in Italian, *kasa* in Polish, *kassa* in Swedish, and касса in Russian.

Sometimes these pan-European words reflect history. Throughout Europe, furniture is "movables"—*muebles* in Spanish, *meubles* in French, *Möbel* in German, and so on. This recalls a time when the nobility would take cupboards and chairs with them when moving between their summer, winter, and country estates. The only thing you couldn't take along was the building itself, which is why real estate is "unmovables" (*inmuebles*, *immeubles*, *Immobilien*, and so on).

Idiosyncrasies between languages are also revealing. The people we call "Germans" are *Allemands* to the French, *Saksalaiset* to the Finns, *Tedeschi* to the Italians, *Duitsers* to the Dutch, and *Deutschen* to themselves. This, too, reflects history: Until the mid-19th century, there was no unified "Germany," but a loose collection of German-speaking kingdoms, fiefdoms, and city-states. Essentially, whichever Germanic group a culture came into contact with—the Allemands, the Germanni, the Saxons—became the term used for all Germans. The Slavs of Central and Eastern Europe dismissed this whole mess and, with a striking consistency, called them all "mute" (in other words, "people we can't speak with"): *Niemcy* in Polish, *Nijemci* in Croatian, Немецкий in Russian, and so on.

Similarly, the nickname each country uses for syphilis speaks volumes about international relations. To the Russians, it's "the Polish disease"; to the Poles, it's "the German disease"; to the Germans, it's "the French disease"; to the French, it's "the Neapolitan disease"; and to the Turks, it's simply "the Christian disease."

Let's talk for a moment about diacritics: those wee doohickeys that are appended above or below letters, mystifying foreigners and infuriating typesetters. Most Americans can handle simple accents, like á, and umlauts, like ä. (And by "handle," I mean "ignore.") But the Slavic lands provide a crash course in advanced diacritics. The "little roof" is easy—it's just like adding an "h" after the letter in English: č sounds like "ch" and š like "sh." But each language has its one-offs, like the Croatian đ or the Czech ď. Poland ramps up the difficulty, with ą and ł and ń and ż.

The (understandable) temptation is simply to blow right past these. But that's like skipping minus signs and exponents in mathematics. Each of these carats, curls, or hooks changes the pronunciation and the meaning, sometimes dramatically. Taking the time to learn each symbol gives you a rewarding sense of mastering something that most travelers simply pretend isn't there. And locals will ooh and aah when you're the rare tourist who's bothered to pronounce their hometown right.

There's one thing that is, for me, simply hopeless . . . undecodable: the words for "push" and "pull" in any European language. Maybe it's a mental block, but I can never memorize these. If you ever spot me in Europe, I'll be the guy pushing on a door marked *tiri* or *ziehen* or *ciągnąć*.

In college, I double-majored in German Studies, more or less by accident. I took enough classes to become fluent, and it was enough for a major. The phrase book project gave me a chance to dig deeper, not just into classroom German, but German the way Germans speak it.

One (non-textbook) word you hear constantly is *ja-ein* . . . yes (*ja*) and no (*nein*). Germans can be painstakingly precise, which makes a straightforward "yes" or "no" elusive. If the answer is 90 to 95 percent "yes," that's what you'll hear in most countries. But in Germany, it's *ja-ein*, which basically means "Yes. However . . . " And it's always followed by a lengthy digression coloring in the shades of ambiguity, which almost certainly don't apply to your circumstances.

Germany sits along Europe's religious fault line: Northern Germany—the home turf of Martin Luther—is Protestant, while southern Germany is Catholic. The Counter-Reformation still rages in the South, with its Rococo churches and bombastic frescoes. Driving through ardently Catholic Bavaria, you'll see at the entrance to each village a list of *Messezeiten*, noting the times for weekly Mass in the onion-domed church.

English is unruly. It's so widespread, sprawling across the far corners of the globe, with staggeringly many variations. And there's no unified body to tell us exactly how to speak or write. The closest we've got for American English are Merriam-Webster, the AP, and the Chicago Manual of Style—which, unhelpfully, are frequently at odds. But many languages do have a formal academy that provides definitive answers to vexing questions of spelling and usage.

An institution with the parodically Germanic name "Council for German Orthography" convenes to determine, for example, whether and how to keep using that pesky ß character, which looks like a capital B but can be replaced in print with a simple double-S and, mysteriously, is named "S-Z" (*Eszett*). Around the time I graduated college, having spent four years struggling to create the elusive ß on keyboards foreign and domestic—and memorizing exactly when I was supposed to use it—the Council decided, what the heck, from now on let's always just make it a double-S.

Sometimes the Council puts the kibosh on creeping shortcuts that have infected the language. At some point, an informal, efficient, and entirely reasonable movement emerged to leave out the extra "f" when combining words like *Schiff* and *Fahrt* ("boat trip"). Thank *Gott in Himmel* for the Council for German Orthography, which clarified that these shortcuts must never be tolerated, and decreed that the proper spelling is, and I am not making this up, *Schifffahrt*.

Imagine for a moment if the US Cabinet had a Secretary of Spelling, Grammar, and Usage, who could tell us whether to capitalize "internet," whether we need a hyphen in "e-mail," and whether any sane person can justify not using the Oxford comma. (Spoiler alert: no.)

And why do Germans capitalize all nouns? Nobody's ever given me a satisfactory answer on that one.

Of Europe's dominant languages, the one I'm least comfortable with is French. I can't, for the life of me, figure out how to pronounce written French, or how to transliterate spoken French. At least a few syllables' worth of letters always gets left out. How can it be that the pileup of words *Qu'est-ce que c'est?* is pronounced, simply, "kess kuh say"?

A breakthrough came when a Parisian colleague helped me assemble a handful of exceedingly succinct, all-purpose "Caveman French" phrases. For example: *Ça* (pronounced "sah"). Meaning "this" or "that," this tiny syllable is the puzzled tourist's best friend; when combined with pointing, it conveys worlds of meaning.

Also, there's *Ça va* (sah vah). While textbooks teach this as the casual way to say both "How are you?" and "I'm fine," it's so much more. As a question, *Ça va?* ("Does it go?") can mean "Is this OK?" In concert with a gesture, you can use *Ça va?* to ask, "Can I sit here?" or "Can I touch this?" or "Can I take a picture?" or "Will this ticket get me into this museum?" As a statement, *Ça va* ("It goes") is just as versatile. When the waiter asks if you want anything more, say *Ça va* ("Nope, I'm good").

Another handy one is *Puis-je?* (pwee-zhuh). Meaning "Can I?", *Puis-je?* is a more refined alternative for many of the *Ça va?* situations. Instead of saying, "May I please sit here?", just gesture toward the seat and say, *Puis-je?* Instead of, "Do you accept credit cards?", show them your MasterCard and ask, *Puis-je?*

While English speakers reserve *Voilà* (vwah-lah) for grand unveilings, the French say it many times each day. It means "Exactly" or "That's it" or "There you go." You'll hear it in response to the questions above: Unsure of how much your plums cost, you hold a euro coin out to the vendor and say, *Ça va?* He responds with a cheery *Voilà* . . . and you're on your way, biting into a plum.

So there—with seven syllables—you've got all you need to politely make your way through the majority of simple interactions tourists are likely to encounter in France. *Voilà!*

These "caveman" phrases carry a greater wisdom: Europeans are adept communicators, and so much of communication is driven by tone and gesture. Yes, the words are important, and it's fun and insightful to play around with them. But in the end, the specific words don't matter as much as you might think.

In any language, a monosyllabic grunt can suffice for effective communicators. And it takes just a few moments to identify and master those grunts. Europeans even crack jokes when they have almost no language in common; international words and a preschool vocabulary go a long way.

During my years as a tour guide, my favorite bus driver was a Slovenian named Bojan. On his first tour, Bojan spoke minimal English, but that didn't prevent him from expressing his sharp sense of humor. Driving down a highway, we got stuck behind a tiny, communist-era Polski Fiat—Poland's answer to the Yugo, whose miniscule size is matched only by its utter lack of pep. At the helm was a huge man, taking up the entire two-person front seat, crouched over the steering wheel, left elbow sticking out of the window. Bojan nudged me and said, simply, "Rucksack."

On another tour, Bojan was testing his new GPS against our standard way of navigating with paper maps. On one particularly complicated route, connecting a string of obscure Slovak villages in the foothills of the Carpathians, the female voice of the GPS correctly called several tricky turns in a row. Bojan quipped: "Smart lady!"

Don't fear language in your travels. View language like a menu in a restaurant: You don't have to order everything. But it can be fun, and instructive, to peruse.

Jams Are Fun

How to Drive in Sicily: Just Go Numb

We had some hot words. I don't usually fight unless
I think my cause is just, then I hang on until I win.
—Mildred C. Scott, *Jams Are Fun*

One summer, I spent three weeks driving 800 miles around Sicily as I worked on a new guidebook. That was no easy task. Not the guidebook work—the driving. While touring Sicily by car can be smart and efficient, the timid and the uninitiated find it challenging. Wait, is "challenging" the right word? No, I've got it: "terrifying."

The trick to driving in Sicily is never forgetting that you are *driving in Sicily*. It took me a few days to dispense with preconceptions about things like obeying traffic signs, or why it's a bad idea to triple-park in the middle of a busy street, or the importance of cars staying in their lanes (or, really, the very concept of "lanes").

Assuming you want to get where you're going, occasionally you need to drive like a Sicilian. Drivers who refuse to accept Sicily on Sicily's terms end each journey by popping a Xanax and prying their death-grip claws from the steering wheel. But, as with other things here, you'll do fine if you just go numb.

Entering a big city, forget everything you think you know about driving—just go with the flow. In the heart of Palermo, I pulled to a stop at a red light, instantly generating a chorus of furious honks from the column of cars behind me. I shrugged, checked both ways three times, and ran the red light . . . followed, without a moment's hesitation, by everyone else.

One great challenge is the motor scooters, or *motorini*, that swarm and buzz and hector like the midges of the Scottish Highlands. Knock-off Vespas weave between cars stalled in traffic, brushing past side-view mirrors as they bushwhack their own path through the urban jungle. Pausing at a red light in Catania, my car was enveloped by *motorini* squeezing around me on both sides. They gathered in front of me, cramming into the tiny no-man's-land between my hood and the cross traffic, forming an eager swarm at my front bumper. When the light turned green, a half-dozen tiny engines buzzed to life, like bees taking flight, and off they zipped . . . leaving me in a cloud of exhaust.

Compared to urban driving, joyriding in the Sicilian country-side is, for the most part, a delight. The roads are empty, and it's easy to make great time. But be prepared for the wild variability in Sicilian cruising speeds. On a road with a limit of, say, 100 kilometers per hour, virtually nobody actually goes 100 kilometers per hour (except me).

Approximately half of all Sicilian drivers go far, far below the speed limit. Roads are clogged with dinky, boxy Fiat Pandas from the early 1980s, which appear to have a maximum cruising speed of about 70 kilometers per hour. I spent enough long journeys stuck behind these to become something of an aficionado. (The lines on the 1982 Panda 45 Super are nothing short of breathtaking.)

Meanwhile, the other half of Sicilian drivers go far, far above the speed limit. And if you're going even a smidge below their preferred speed—even for a fleeting moment, even if there's a stop sign a hundred yards in front of you—they'll ride your bumper so close, it feels like you're giving them a tow.

Passing on blind curves is a high-risk national pastime in Sicily, and drivers take insane chances. On a busy parkway into Siracusa, a motorcycle screamed past me on the shoulder, at what must have been double my speed. As he shrunk into the horizon, I caught a fleeting glimpse of the daredevil driver riding sidesaddle, his bike leaning at a precipitous angle.

Navigation is tricky. Sicily's roads are potholed and inconsistently signed. And where signs exist, they can be more confusing than no signs at all. Highways close unexpectedly, and some imaginary roadways appear on maps despite never having been completed. I spotted several on-ramps to nowhere.

A word about roundabouts: I believe they are among humankind's greatest inventions, somewhere between penicillin and smartphones. We should have roundabouts at every intersection in the United States. I've driven miles and miles through the British countryside, zipping around the outskirts of major cities and through the historic cores of quaint villages, without ever coming to a full stop. When used as intended, roundabouts make traffic flow like poetry.

But in Sicily, a roundabout is treated as a lawless intersection: Everybody just aggressively plows through, willfully defiant of silly concepts like "right of way." Yield to vehicles already in the roundabout, and those entering from the left? *Per favore!* You just *go* and let Santa Agata sort it out.

All of this sounds like madness . . . chaos. But if you approach Sicilian driving with the right attitude, you find that it's a controlled chaos. The thing is, it works. It works not because it's "every driver for herself," as it might seem at first, but because there's an unspoken understanding of exactly the opposite: We're all in this together.

Other drivers are watching you. They see how fast you're going, how big your car is, and where you're headed next. They probably know more about your driving skills than you do. And they adapt—constantly, intuitively, and effectively. If you get stubborn and use roundabouts the way they were intended to be used, dammit!—you'll get everyone angry (at best) or cause a fender-bender (at worst). Put another way: If you're the only one using the roundabout "the right way," then you're the one using it the wrong way.

Road engineers in northern Europe are pioneering a new way to manage complicated intersections: simply remove all of the signage. There are idyllic English and Dutch towns where, upon reaching the village green, suddenly you see no traffic lights, no roundabouts, no bike lanes, no crosswalks, no instruction of any sort. You just have to pay attention. And so, everyone does: Drivers, cyclists, and pedestrians all make eye contact with each other, ensuring that they're all on the same page about what happens next. It sounds counterintuitive, but these intersections have less congestion and fewer accidents.

On my second or third day in Sicily, as I was cursing drivers who refused to abide by the universally accepted rules of the road, it suddenly dawned on me: Sicilians long ago intuited what those scientists have spent their careers researching. The road is a shared venture. And as long as we all look out for each other, we'll get through it in one piece. If you can do that, and just dive in, you might just come to enjoy it.

Failing that, remember: Just go numb.

Like All Things, This Tour Shall Pass

Confessions of a Tour Guide

n the heartland of Croatia, I was guiding a tour group through the gushing waterfalls of Plitvice Lakes National Park. Reaching the boat dock at the midpoint of the hike, one of my tour members discreetly asked when the next bathroom break might be. I explained that there were no toilets at this dock, but there was one at the other end of the 20-minute boat trip we were about to take. In the meantime, if necessary, he could use the bushes. Glancing around, he said, "No, I'm OK. I think I can wait."

We boarded the boat. A few minutes later, the wide-eyed tour member approached me with a renewed desperation. "Nope, can't wait. What are my options here?" We scanned the deck of the open boat. There weren't many. I led him to the steering cabin in the back, where the captain and first mate stood stoically at the helm. I stuck my head in the door and asked about bathrooms. They shook their heads vigorously and pointed to the dock we were approaching . . . 15 long, agonizingly watery minutes away.

At this point, what was going to happen was going to happen *now*. My tour member stepped into the cabin, made a beeline for a garbage can in the corner, and unzipped his fly. Finally grasping the urgency of the situation, the captain directed him, instead, to stand at the back of the boat.

And so we glided silently across the pristine lake, my tour member peeing off the back, and me standing in the cabin doorway to block the other passengers' view. To this day, I don't think any of his fellow tour members were ever the wiser. As for the people on the boat that passed us going in the other direction . . . well, that's another story.

As a tour guide, I spent many years leading groups of about 26 people on Rick Steves bus tours around Europe. While I enjoyed guiding, about a decade ago I realized I was being pulled in too many directions and decided to focus exclusively on content. It was the right choice; since my "retirement" from guiding, I rarely look back. But when I do, it's with fondness. (Mostly.)

People sometimes ask me how to become a tour guide. The answer: Be a great traveler . . . then do it with two dozen people in tow. Guiding is hard work. It's fun and rewarding. But, like researching a guidebook, it rarely qualifies as "glamorous."

Most of this book's stories emphasize the merits of independent travel. But taking a tour can be a great alternative—especially for extroverts, for people who hate planning their own trips, and for those who appreciate having an expert close at hand at all times.

Of course, that expertise is just one small part of a tour guide's duties. Not only do we have to master the culture, history, cuisine, language, and current events of each place. We're also travel agents, coordinating menus, museum reservations, and hotel rooming lists; shepherds, keeping our flock together and safe; navigators, making sure our bus drivers know where to go, and getting us there right on time; cheerleaders, keeping spirits high and grumps at bay; and, very often, psychologists.

But the psychology of a group is entirely different from the psychologies of 26 individuals. As an independent traveler, I often find myself cursing groups that cluelessly block Europe's sidewalks. I assume that, individually, each of these people is nice enough. But when you put a bunch of people together, some degree of their individuality shuts off. It's human nature: They become a gangly blob of humanity with limited free will.

Experienced guides become adept at wrangling their blob of humanity. They train their tour members to think as one, to share the hive mind of a great traveler—what we call "group think." That means being on time, looking out for each other to avoid losing stragglers, crossing the street and using public transportation in unison, and, yes, not blocking the sidewalk when listening to a local guide. The masterstroke of a great guide is a properly executed "precision dump": efficiently unloading a busload of tourists in a semi-legal parking space—or, sometimes, even at a red light—before the driver gets a ticket.

Traveling with a group has big advantages. For one, it's efficient: Sharing the expenses of transportation and guiding, booking blocks of hotel rooms, and enjoying a family-style dinner all help keep costs down for everyone. But there's also an intangible joy that sprouts from the fellowship of traveling with a group. Strangers become friends and forge close bonds as we all experience the same magic together. Of the hundred or so people who work in my office, I still share a special connection with ones I've been on tour with.

* * *

Each January, we fly our guides in for a week of intense strategy and business meetings, plus a big reunion party for the previous year's tour members. Our small town just north of Seattle is transformed into the United Nations—the temporary home of around 150 huge personalities from every corner of Europe and beyond.

My beat as a tour guide was Central and Eastern Europe. And each year, my wife and I still invite every guide from that region into our home for dinner, offering them a casual break from a week of conference rooms, happy hours, and catered meals.

At our most recent gathering, we jammed 24 Czechs, Hungarians, Poles, Slovenes, Bosnians, and Bulgarians under our roof. Despite our attempts to herd our guests to the dining room table, they insisted on squeezing into the tiny nook in the corner of our kitchen—sitting cross-legged on the floor and cracking each other up.

I learned a lot that evening, including how Czech parents send their kids to Native American-themed summer camps to live in tepees; what my nickname would be in Czech ("Kamerka"); and how Bulgarians have a tradition of letting their kids "ride" on the back of a freshly slaughtered Christmas pig for good luck. (Hearing this last story, several guides glanced over and said, "You writing this down, Cameron?" They know me well.)

At one point, a pocket of conversation grew animated, with gasps and peals of laughter. One of the Polish guides ran over and said, "Cameron! Do you have chicken dance?"

"Beg pardon?"

"The song, chicken dance! Can you play it?"

Dutifully, I found a way to stream the wedding-reception classic "Chicken Dance" to my speakers. A dozen guides squealed with delight, moved the coffee table to one side, and started clucking, clapping, and flapping their wings around my living room. It turns out, each one assumed this was a bizarre and shameful national custom. They were all tickled to discover it's international.

Because of these annual gatherings, and because we share an odd and vexing vocation, there's a powerful camaraderie among guides. Wherever guides venture with our groups, a certain magnetism brings us together. A popular city (like Venice or Paris) might have several groups in town on the same day. Officially, we avoid having groups cross paths, to preserve the specialness of each tour. But after hours—once our tour members are properly oriented and our accounting spreadsheets are filed—guides can't resist slipping out for drinks together. I once hopped on a milk-run train to meet up with a couple of guides three towns away. Sometimes it feels like there's an unspoken contest to gather as many guides as possible in one place.

My very first tour, in the spring of 2001, was a baptism by fire. Because of my (atypical) interest in the Slavic lands, I was tapped to be the assistant guide on the first-ever departure of a brand-new, 19-day Eastern Europe itinerary. I was working with a seasoned lead guide, Rick Garman, who was known for being well-organized, conscientious, and a great teacher. He deserved a far more experienced assistant for a new itinerary. But he got stuck with me—training a complete novice, to boot.

That would have been challenging enough. But then Rick Steves decided that he would also join the tour—ostensibly "just for fun," as a tour member. In reality, he was a firehose of ideas, suggestions, and critiques. The boss spent the entire tour at our guide's side, like a twitching golden retriever with a tennis ball in his mouth.

"When are you gonna tell them all about Martin Luther? Don't you think it's about time for another bathroom break? How 'bout you hand out some of those local candies after the next stop? Don't you have any local music to play on the bus? No, not that singer—the other one. Is that orange juice 100 percent real juice, or that ersatz stuff they drank under communism? Did you notice it's been a few days since the last picnic? You know what might be fun? Let's just drop them off in some random village, and give them a little local money, and tell them they have to go find their own place to buy a coffee so they can use the bathroom."

I had been warned that tour members keep informal track of the pros and cons of each hotel room: whether they had a view, or had to climb lots of stairs, or had a bigger-than-average room. It was my duty to manage room assignments, ensuring everything evened out by tour's end. However, I did not realize just how seriously some people take this until our first night in Prague, when I asked a tour member, "How's your room?" He fixed me with a piercing gaze and said, "It's fine. But I just want you to know that I have to climb seventy-two stairs to get there."

In Budapest, we decided to hire a local guide for a city bus tour. Our hotel assured us that they worked with an agency employing only the very best guides. When our guide showed up, she seemed energetic and personable. But the moment she opened her mouth, it was clear she spoke virtually no English.

We loaded our group onto the bus and set off on our tour, while our guide provided commentary in German with a smattering of English. She got the words "left" and "right" mixed up (which, one would think, should disqualify anyone seeking to become a tour guide). Soon after leaving the hotel, we passed one of Budapest's most venerable thermal baths. "And on left," she said—meaning, of course, "right"—"you see example of our baaahs. We are *sehr* famous for our baaahs." It just so happened, at that very moment a bus drove by on our left side. Stifling giggles, I watched as every tour member's head swiveled left to see the bus, instead of right to see the baths.

This went on for several embarrassing minutes. Rick Garman and I were sitting in the front row of the bus. Rick Steves scurried up from his favorite seat—in the back row—and whispered insistently in our ears. "Guys, this is a *disaster*. We need to get out of this."

Rick Garman instructed the driver to pull over at Heroes' Square. The local guide announced, "Now we have *fünf* minute to see square, then back to bus." Rick Garman politely but firmly explained that she would, in fact, not be getting back on this bus.

Seeming to understand, she got on the mic one last time. Dejectedly, she said, "So, *jetzt* must I say goodbye. I am sorry you no understand. This *ist mein* first tour *auf Englisch!*" We cut the rest of the city tour short and gave our tour members some free time.

A few days later, we were heading to a Croatian island where tourism had only just restarted following the Yugoslav Wars. As recently as seven or eight years earlier, we were told, refugees from the war-torn Croatian interior had lived in our hotel. Finally that war was in the past, Croatia was safe, and the hotel had been refurbished for paying guests.

I called ahead to the hotel with our arrival time, hoping to get our room keys as quickly as possible. It had been a long day, and everyone was more than ready to settle in. But the call took on a mysterious tone. "We want to give you a welcome drink," they said. "We have plans for this."

Upon arrival, it became clear that it wasn't just a "welcome drink." They had organized a full-blown reception involving the entire community, with our group as the guests of honor. Our tour members were instructed to leave their wheelie bags by the front door and take their seats on the veranda. Martini glasses with a bright-pink mystery cocktail were distributed. And then a band struck up and a troupe of elaborately costumed performers processed up the veranda to present a show of the local folk dances.

Just when we thought it was finished, the town's mayor stepped up to the microphone and, through a translator, explained that we were the first American group that had stayed on the island since the war, and they were grateful. Weary as we were, we were touched.

*   *   *

Tour guides spend the many bus hours teaching our tour members the story of each place we're visiting, and getting them oriented to the nuts and bolts of what's coming next: explaining what we're doing today, taking orders for dinner tomorrow, and making sure everyone knows the exchange rate and the location of the nearest ATM.

Tour members have varying appetites for information and—understandably—tend to zone out on the bus. So if something is important, I'll repeat it. And if it's really important, I may repeat it several times. One time, after I passed out slips of paper for mid-tour suggestions, one of my tour members hand-delivered it back to me. "You know," he said, "I was just about to write that you repeat yourself too much. But just then, someone asked about something I have heard you say at least five or six times already. So my feedback is: Keep up the good work."

On another occasion, we were at the bitter end of a very long day on the bus. We'd had some weather-related delays, and now, at long last, we finally checked into our hotel. My tour members met in the lobby and dutifully trudged 10 minutes through the drizzle until we were all squeezed under a leaky awning on the town's main square.

They were tired. I was tired. Tempers were flaring. But they needed to eat. As efficiently as I could, I did a speedy spin-tour of the square, pointing out easy restaurant options, ending with, "Any questions?" The soaked and famished group clenched every muscle, hoping the answer was no. But one woman pointedly raised her hand. "Yeah, yeah," she said with a hand-on-hip impatience. "But when are you gonna tell us where we should go to eat?" The rest of the group groaned and hissed in unison. (She survived.)

I led the first-ever departure of our Best of the Adriatic itinerary, which I'd co-designed with a couple of other tour guides, stitching together our favorite experiences. I was particularly excited to take my group to a tavern in the hilly, vineyard-draped interior of Croatia's Istrian Peninsula. I'd enjoyed a delightful meal there the year before, sitting out on a breezy terrace, with distant views of the sun easing itself into the Adriatic. It was a perfect memory. And as our bus pulled up to the restaurant, I couldn't wait to re-create that experience with my sunburned tour members.

But my heart sank as the owner walked us through the already-full terrace to go inside. There she'd laid out a glorious table . . . directly in front of the enormous hearth, where glowing coals did all of the cooking.

Already sweating from a very hot day, but with no other seating options available, we settled into the sweltering stone dining room. And then the owners—seriously overestimating the appetites of their honored guests—fed us at least two courses more than anyone could eat. By the meal's end, we were stuffed, and we could have wrung out our shirts. Several tour members reported heat rashes.

One unique aspect of Rick Steves tours is how we consider the bus driver an integral part of the tour community. We encourage the driver to get to know our tour members on a personal level.

While our tour members—and our drivers—love this interaction, we are violating Europe's established social hierarchy. Bus drivers inhabit their own parallel world. Many hotels have a tiny, off-the-books single—often with a view of the parking lot—just for drivers. In big cities, there are bars patronized exclusively by a Babel of drivers from across the Continent. And in places with a mass tourism tradition, it's the bus drivers—who have the power to whisper to an overwhelmed guide, "I know just the place for this busload of tourists to buy lunch"—who are treated like royalty.

My favorite driver, Bojan, trained with me on his first-ever Rick Steves tour. When I explained that we wanted him to socialize with our tour members—which was expressly forbidden by many tour operators—he was at first aghast, and then excited. It turns out he'd been stifling his gregarious instincts for his entire career. He made up for lost time, becoming dear friends with everyone on the bus. He even joined us on town walking tours and participated in my bus lectures when we arrived in his home country, Slovenia. He went on to work exclusively for us for many years until retiring, a very happy man.

On a later tour, Bojan invited me for a glimpse into the more traditional workings of the bus driver world. Our group stopped for lunch at an only-game-in-town roadside restaurant. Tucked in a corner of the sprawling dining hall was a special drivers' dining area, elevated and roped off like a VIP lounge. We were given menus without prices and were waited on attentively. From our privileged dais, we looked out over the congested dining hall, trying to avoid eye contact with our tour members as they shuffled through the self-service cafeteria line.

We also invite drivers to attend our annual guide meetings near Seattle. One year, two of our other Slovenian drivers flew in for the festivities—their first visit to the United States. I took them to a big box store, where they filled their oversized suitcases with electronics, jeans, and toys for their kids that would've cost double back home.

Throughout that week, while the guides were tied up with meetings, the Slovenes had ample free time. They got into a routine of having meals at the local diner. On their last night in town, they insisted on taking me and a fellow American guide out to dinner. When the bill arrived, they paid with exact change. In explaining our customs to them, it dawned on us that they had not been tipping all week long. The next day, after taking our driver friends to the airport, we stopped by their favorite diner with a few 20-dollar bills: "You remember those two Eastern European guys who kept coming here last week and stiffing you on the tip? Well, here's the thing. . . ."

Of course, a bus driver's primary responsibility is *driving the bus*. And a good driver has an uncanny mastery of their vehicle. They enjoy showing off for Americans who can barely back down their own driveways without taking out the mailbox. One tour hotel in Kraków had a parking lot accessed through a narrow stone gateway that provided a few inches of clearance on each side of the bus. The driver would give me a wink before executing a text-book three-point turn—along the busy ring road at rush hour—to gracefully back up between those pillars, to the astonished gasps and cheers of our tour members.

For a perfectionist, tour guiding is high stress. (That's partly why I left it behind.) You alone are responsible for the travel happiness of two dozen people. And yet, so much remains outside of your control.

Goodwill is the currency of a tour. You earn it, and you spend it. Unfortunately, the two biggest factors in determining your supply of goodwill—the weather and the character of the group—are entirely out of your hands. You can be the worst tour guide in the world, with a great group and perfect weather, and everyone has a blast. And you can be the best tour guide in the world, and have more than your share of "problem children" and rainy days, and you'll be running in the red the entire tour.

For the most part, our tours attract great travelers. We even have an explicit "No Grumps" policy. And yet, I'd estimate that, on average, there's about one challenging customer per tour. These are not bad people—just high-maintenance, or mismatched with our travel philosophy, or someone with a chip on their shoulder. Keep in mind: That's in aggregate. You can have four or five great groups in a row, and then, out of nowhere, you're stuck with a bus full of turds.

My worst tour ever was one of those turdloads. It was the last departure of the season—late October. The weather and time had both shifted to winter, which meant chilly temperatures and overcast daylight that abruptly turned to black by mid-afternoon. Something sinister was in the air.

The group that showed up to greet me was the motliest assortment of individuals I'd ever seen in one place. In isolation, none of them was notable, and anyway, you get used to juggling an oddball or two. But taken together, the chemistry was combustible. Challenging as they were, they were actually on their good behavior around me. Various spies tipped me off about a complicated web of grievances and grudges just out of view. It's clichéd—especially in the tour guide world—to talk about "herding cats." But my God, was that one shitshow of a kitten rodeo.

And yet, perhaps because they were such an odd bunch, we had some wonderful moments on that tour. It's liberating to realize that your well-laid plans can't possibly go further awry. After all, jams are fun. I loosened up and became more adventurous.

In the Hungarian countryside, after a wine-tasting that had everyone feeling cheerful, our translator suggested that we take the group to a locals-only thermal bath. It was just two simple, steaming hot pools in the middle of a farm field, at the base of a cascade of white travertine terraces that looked like a melting mountain of marshmallow. We changed into our swimsuits in split-shingle cabanas and simmered alongside Hungarian villagers in the hundred-degree water. A very good time was had by all.

A few days later, we arrived at Plitvice Lakes National Park, that wonderland of waterfalls and boardwalks in the uplands of Croatia. We woke up bright and early the next morning, ready for our three-hour hike, and saw that several inches of snow had fallen overnight. Some tour members were not up for a hike in the snow, but I offered to take those who were.

I have been to Plitvice perhaps fifteen times. And I have never seen it so beautiful as that morning. The plank walks connecting the lakes, streams, and cascades were covered in fresh powder, and we were the first and only human beings to experience this pristine morning. The blue-green waters shimmered with a pure luminescence against the snowbanks and flocked-white branches. All of us who went out that morning agreed it was sublime.

About half of the group had chosen to stay behind at the hotel. And what I had failed to calculate was exactly what they'd be doing there: spending the entire morning at the lobby bar, getting absolutely hammered.

Those of us who had experienced a morning of awe, and those who had drunk their feelings, all got on the bus together for a very unpleasant three-hour drive. Worse, that day's journey took us through a part of Croatia that had been badly damaged in the Yugoslav Wars of the 1990s. We drove by roadside memorials to fallen soldiers, burned-out husks of buildings, and church facades still splattered with bullet holes. The mood on the bus was weird and queasy, but I couldn't pass by these places without explaining them. And as I spoke of ethnic cleansing and lives ripped asunder by sectarian strife—normally one of the most powerful moments of the tour—the drunk half of the bus cracked jokes and giggled.

From there, the bus twisted down a long, serpentine road to the coastline, until we arrived in a small port city for a break. By this point, our bus driver—whose patience with this group, like mine, had been fraying for two weeks—had reached his limit. As we approached the parking lot at the town pier, he gunned the engine, raced toward the water, then stopped short just before the front tires went over the embankment. The drunks screamed, the sober hikers laughed, and I found a new respect for our driver.

A couple of days later, the tour ended. And I am very pleased to report that I never saw any of those people again.

On tour, you've got a built-in family, like it or not, for two weeks. And like a real family, you don't get to choose who you're stuck with. If things are going well, you savor it. If not, you simply shrug and say: Like all things, this tour shall pass.

At the Rome airport, I got a salami sandwich and tea. One sandwich called for another. I went back and they told me in Italian some other sandwiches they had. But I didn't know what they were, and I knew what salami was, so I took another one.

—Mildred C. Scott,
  Jams Are Fun

PART THREE

Food Is Culture

*C*learly, Aunt Mildred was no foodie. That's understandable. "Foodie-ism" comes with a generation gap, like the Charleston or the Beatles or the Beastie Boys. Still, just this once, I'll defy the wisdom of Mildred C. Scott: Go beyond the salami sandwich.

I proudly consider myself a foodie. Yes, this sounds pretentious and self-consciously trendy. But I've yet to find a better word to convey someone who prioritizes food in their travels. ("Gourmand" is dreadfully old-fashioned and sounds like no fun at all.) So I'm determined to take "foodie" back for travelers who live to eat.

You eat-to-live-ers may not buy this. You're in Europe for the sightseeing, for the history, for the scenery, for the people—in a word, for the culture. You may see food simply as a way to fill the tank for another day of travel. But food is every bit as central to the culture as any of these.

Complete this phrase: Swiss ___.

Switzerland is synonymous with cheese. It's part of their international brand and their national identity. In fact, the government invests generous subsidies in keeping this part of Swiss culture alive. (I also would have accepted "chocolate.")

Just as I love to deconstruct clichés and grapple with language, I geek out on psychoanalyzing European food. As an example, consider the cuisines of Italy and France—equally beloved, yet fundamentally different.

In Italy—the garden patch of Europe—cuisine revolves around quality ingredients. The fewer ingredients, and the less they're manipulated, the better. A gourmet salad is a tumble of roughly torn greens, maybe some coarsely chopped tomatoes and other vegetables, drizzled with fresh olive oil and *balsamico*. In Tuscany, I learned how to make the most delicious sauce ever to cross my palate. It has just five ingredients: tomatoes, olive oil, garlic, red pepper flakes, and salt.

This emphasis on fresh ingredients also makes Italian cuisine highly localized. Why are there so many variations on pasta? Because each one is engineered to highlight a particular sauce or topping, usually specific to a place and/or season. (Those pasta places where you "pick your noodles, then pick your sauce" make Italians furious.) Italian law even forbids restaurants from using frozen ingredients unless they're noted on the menu.

The French also prize fresh ingredients. But their approach is more driven by what you do with them. French chefs are technicians who endlessly tinker and experiment to create something delicious—even, and especially, with ingredients no self-respecting Italian chef would touch. Who, but the French, would look at snails oozing across a rain-dampened path and think, "I'll bet if I sautéed those in garlic butter, they'd be delicious"?

Beyond *escargot*, consider other famous French dishes: *Coq au vin* takes the toughest, least palatable type of poultry—rooster—and

135

simmers it in red wine and spices to fall-off-the-bone perfection. *Bœuf bourguignon* does the same with tough cuts of beef. And *confit de canard* is a duck that's been rendered, preserved in a can of its own congealed fat, then cracked open months later and cooked in that same fat. That's not a recipe. That's a science experiment.

So much of French cooking feels like it originated as a dare. And yet, it's delicious. And it's beautiful. French chefs are scientists, yes, but also artists who create masterpieces as pleasing to the eye as to the palate. French salads aren't just thrown together, as in Italy—they're *composée* . . . composed.

Or you can become a "foodie" simply because it's delicious. In Naples, I met up with a local friend, Vincenzo, who couldn't wait to take me to the best pizzeria in the birthplace of pizza. Choice of toppings? Psssh. Here you have just two options: marinara or Margherita. Like In-N-Out Burger back home, this *pizzaiolo* understands that when you achieve perfection, you keep things simple.

When the pizza hit our table, Vincenzo took a bite and rocketed into performative ecstasy. "Aha! You taste that? The perfect crust. Thin, soft, a leetle sour. You don't even need to chew it. You just put it in your mouth and . . . " He pantomimed a delicious glob of pizza sliding down his esophagus, ending with a big smile.

Watching me gingerly nibble at my slice, Vincenzo said, "*This* is the *correct* way to eat pizza." He cut out a wedge, rolled it up into a bundle, sawed off a crosswise chunk, and jammed it into his mouth. I tried it. And in one perfect bite, I got the gooey middle, the singed crust, and a squirt of tomato sauce—all in just the right proportions.

In some ways, I'm jealous of non-foodies. It would be so liberating simply not to care about what I'm eating. I can't imagine all the time and money I'd save. Instead, I obsess over every meal as an opportunity for a cultural experience . . . and when I settle for something easy and generic, I feel regret and a little shame.

Part Three: Food Is Culture

The next several chapters psychoanalyze the place food occupies in five very different European cultures. In Palermo's markets, we see how Sicily's history, culture, and climate have created some unique street foods. In Poland, I savor a budget feast while pondering the challenge of selecting "local" restaurants for my guidebook. In Provence, we immerse ourselves in seven markets that are an explosion of flavors, colors, and *hyper*-local produce. In Spain, we consider how the famous tapas scene is an expression of both culture and climate. And multicultural London demonstrates how the best "European" food can originate from very far away.

Come On,
Have Some Guts

*O*n a gritty Palermo street, standing amidst the chaos of a churning marketplace, Marco is an anchor of calm. "Let's begin," he says, with a twinkle in his eye. "Do we have any volunteers?"

Marco has spotted an opportunity to get his students precipitously high on the culinary learning curve. Following his gaze, I see it, too: an antique wheeled cart with a giant wok of mystery meat. Being a "volunteer" on a street food tour is high-risk, high-reward. I raise my hand. After all, I'm in Sicily to *experience Sicily*.

The vendor grabs my hand, flips it over, and lays a square of tissue paper on my palm. He proceeds to pile it with hot, gelatinous . . . something. It's from an animal—presumably deep, deep inside the animal—but beyond that, I'd hate to guess. My stomach sends a few trembles down my arm, jiggling the pale protein as the vendor spritzes it with lemon.

I taste it. And the flavor is . . . well, not half bad: pleasingly salty, generously seasoned with pepper and bay leaf, with a bright acidic zip provided by that lemon juice. The texture, however, is *all* bad. Like chewing on sautéed gristle.

"This is *frittula*," Marco says. "It's the leftover parts of veal—cartilage, fat and meat from the jaw, leetle bits of bone—all chopped up and fried together. What do you think?" The members of our group bold enough to sample it nod in agreement. The others look a bit green.

The diversity of food across Europe is astonishing. Each country, each region, each city, each *block* has its own specialties. And this is nowhere more apparent than in Italy, the land of *campanilismo*—where people feel a sense of community and shared pride with neighbors who live within earshot of the same bell tower, or *campanile*. Combining this with a seasonal, ingredient-driven approach to food, "Italian cuisine" splinters into thousands of local variations.

Today, I'm exploring one tiny corner of Italy's culinary landscape, in the city that many Italians consider the capital of street food. For efficiency's sake, I signed up for a food tour led by Marco, a gregarious Palermitano. And now that he's lined our guts with a baby cow's, he's plunging us further into the street market.

"This is one of three big outdoor markets in central Palermo," Marco explains. "It's been here for one thousand two hundred years. And it has not really changed in all that time." This seems like hyperbole. But if you ignore the *motorini* nudging their way through the crowds, this scene does convey an insistent timelessness.

We walk past tables piled high with the sea's bounty: big fish, small fish, tiny fish, shellfish. Occasionally, beefy fishmongers circle around each table and fling sloppy handfuls of water onto the styrofoam containers. They crow about their catch with a droning cadence that's a holdover from the Arabs who turned Palermo from a village into a thriving metropolis:

"Tutta fresca! Tutta fresca! Tutta freeeeeeeessss-caaaaa!"
"Prego-prego-prego-prego-prego-prego-preeeeeeeGO!"

On a marble slab is a gigantic half-fish, lying on its side, exposing a tree-stump-sized cross-section of red flesh. "Aha! Tuna season has begun." Bunches of mint lie next to the fish. Marco explains that this young, tender spring herb indicates the tuna has just arrived. Later in the season, they'll put out chrysanthemums, a symbol of death—to signal shoppers that their time for fresh tuna is running out.

"Freshness is important, because we eat it almost raw. You know *bistecca alla fiorentina?*" Marco asks, referring to the super-rare Tuscan T-bone. "This is like *tonno alla fiorentina*—sear it just 30 seconds on one side, 30 seconds on the other, and *finito!*"

"But it's not just the flesh. We think of tuna as the 'pork of the sea,' because we use every part. Well, except the fins. The heads are used to make fish soup. And we dry out the roe, then sprinkle it on pasta—that's called *alla bottarga.*"

Next to the tuna is a swordfish—its jagged upper jaw suspended from the canopy like a trophy. Standing over the cadavers, the fishmongers sharpen their comically oversized knives with the ear-piercing clang of metal on metal, and a glimmer in their eye that dares me to take their picture.

"Of course, in the past, the people of Sicily were extremely poor," Marco clarifies. "Most could not afford fish or seafood. The one exception was sardines. And not fresh ones—the cheaper ones, already a few days old and nearly spoiled. That's why a very traditional Sicilian dish is *pasta con le sarde*—pasta topped with sardines, pine nuts, fennel, and raisins . . . to mask the taste and aid digestion."

"*Pasta con le sarde* is also sprinkled with breadcrumbs. Anything in Sicily that's prepared *alla palermitana*—Palermo-style—has breadcrumbs. This, too, comes from poverty: People could not afford to grate cheese on their pasta, so instead they sprinkled it with salty breadcrumbs from yesterday's stale bread."

It occurs to me that poverty also explains the Sicilian tendency to turn offal into beloved street food. One century's hardship food becomes the next century's defining culinary style.

Greengrocers have their own top-of-the-lungs sales pitches to trumpet how their produce is both incredibly fresh and, somehow, also remarkably cheap. Tectonically speaking, Sicily has one foot in Africa, allowing it to grow tropical fruits that thrive in few other corners of Europe. Sicilians love to brag about their domestic mangoes.

Produce stands burst with bright-purple eggplants, plump tomatoes, and distinctly Sicilian zucchinis, three feet long. A prospective zucchini buyer picks up the vegetable and waggles it around, demonstrating its floppiness. "Eh, terrible quality. I'll pay half!"

Someone asks Marco whether vendors are honest. "Sicilians have a . . . *special* way of interacting with each other. First of all, we don't just speak Italian—we speak Sicilian. We learn it not in school, but in the streets. So if you talk to someone in Sicilian, they'll give you the local price. If you talk to them in Italian, or in English, you get a special price. Maybe a euro more." This "tourist tax" approach to gouging visitors has always been a pet peeve of mine. But hearing Marco explain it so matter-of-factly, for the first time in my life, it almost seems reasonable.

"And there's a kind of . . . what I would call 'gamesmanship' at the market," Marco continues. "Not just with tourists, but among Palermitani. Sure, sometimes maybe a vendor will try to cheat you in some way. It's almost expected. But if you figure it out and come back to confront him, then he respects you. He gives you something free to make up for it. I have relatives who won't come to the market—this is exhausting for them. But for others, it's fun. Kind of a game, a challenge."

On the other hand, once Palermitani forge a relationship with a vendor, they become extremely loyal. If you get sick, your

fishmonger may even deliver. Marco says, "My mamma has told me she's going to leave me two things when she passes on: Her house. And her list of market vendors."

We reach our next snacking stop: giant deep-fried rice balls. "What do you call this?" Marco asks. I'm one of the know-it-alls who blurt out the answer: *arancino*, of course! Marco clucks his tongue and jerks his chin up sharply—a definitive Sicilian no. "In Catania," he says, practically spitting on the ground as he names Palermo's rival city on the east coast, "they call it *arancino*. Here in Palermo, we call it *arancina*—feminine."

The Catania-style *arancino*—common in most of Italy—is rice, tomato, veal *ragú* (meat sauce), mozzarella, and peas. But here in Palermo, an *arancina* is flavored with bright-yellow saffron, another Arabic artifact.

As Marco slices into a steaming *arancina*, the inside pops with a perfect Pantone yellow. This is one of those foods—like croissants—that's infinitely better when fresh: burn-your-fingertips crispy outer shell; soft, warm, and gooey rice inside.

Leaving the market and wandering through town, we come upon a square in front of a dazzling Baroque church. Here we stop at another food cart. Inside the glass case are stacked sickly-looking hunks of French bread with a pinkish topping.

"These are *sfincioni*—sometimes called 'Sicilian pizza,'" Marco says. "It comes from an Arabic word for 'sponge.' The traditional one does not have cheese or other toppings—just tomato, and one ring of onion. Then they sprinkle it with black pepper and oregano. That's all. Simple."

Noticing our skeptical looks, Marco says, "I know, I know. These do not look appetizing. But what you don't realize is that he has a little oven inside the cart, where he grills up the *sfincioni*. And that makes all the difference."

The bells of the church clang as we watch the vendor stick his *sfincioni* into the cart, wait a couple of minutes, then pull out a deliciously toasted snack. It's flavorful, with a nice oregano zip, a little char on the bottom, and just the right oiliness. Who knew? (Marco knew.)

Continuing down a tight lane, we pop out at a ramshackle piazza ringed with food carts. The district of La Vucciria, close to the port, was hammered by World War II bombs, and some buildings were never rebuilt. Until recently, the area hosted a thriving street market. But now, as more Sicilians do their shopping at modern supermarkets, some traditional markets are struggling. Although its market has closed, La Vucciria is enjoying a new life as a hotspot for food stalls and after-hours cocktail bars. Little "for sale" signs hang from apartment balconies—flags of surrender flown by homeowners eager to vacate their newly rowdy neighborhood.

One stand serves octopus. That's it—just octopus. A small octopus, not much larger than your hand, is boiled in salty water, tinted black from the ink. When fully cooked, the critter is fished out with a hook, roughly chopped into tentacled chunks, and spritzed with a wedge of lemon. And that's *polpo bollito*, boiled octopus.

Another vendor has a glass display case with all manner of meat strung out on skewers. Nearby, a hissing grill kicks up a rich smoke. The vendor is chopping up juicy wands of spring onion, then wrapping them in thick strips of bacon. When tossed on the grill, the smell is heavenly.

And then there's Palermo's ultimate "gross street food": *pani ca' meusa*—spleen sandwich. Marco introduces us to a vendor who has served this grease bomb to celebrity chefs and travel TV personalities from around the globe. He fires up his big wok, drops in a dollop of lard, and stirs in chunks of organ meat.

"They call it 'spleen,'" Marco says as we wait. "But actually, it's mostly lung." Marco, *you're not helping*.

"Not everybody likes the taste. If you don't like organ meat, you may not like it. But for many Palermitani—including me—this is the most delicious street food we will try today."

The vendor lays strips of sizzling meat onto the pillowy bun, spritzes the requisite lemon, and hands the sandwiches around. Now, I have a rule that I am willing to try any food . . . once. And so, swallowing hard, I take a bite. And . . .

It's just as Marco described: a milder version of liver. It's deliciously salty and greasy—which helps it slide down. Some bites feel like thin-sliced, gristly meat. Others are chewy and sinewy.

Looking around the Vucciria bustle, I notice how locals and adventurous tourists coexist in harmony. Here stands a little scrum of curious street foodies. And across the square, Palermitani are just hanging out at cheap plastic tables. A big guy pulls up on a little *motorino* and idles while he chats, oblivious to the exhaust he's spewing all over people nursing cocktails. He greets the grillmaster with a long handshake and a tender kiss on the cheek. They wave their arms in conversation, before he remounts his *motorino* and buzzes off down a grimy street, and his friend returns to his grill full of guts.

144

Of the many Sicilian dessert choices, Marco has selected the most famous: cannoli. He explains the two secrets of a good *cannolo*: First, you don't fill the deep-fried pastry tube until you're ready to serve it. Second, it must be filled with quality ricotta cheese—mildly sweet, yet tangy, and dusted with powdered sugar.

"Around Palermo," Marco explains, "you see cannoli filled with all sorts of tourist-pleasing nonsense: pistachio creme, vanilla custard, Nutella, whatever. But these . . . these are not true cannoli."

Crunching into a quality *cannolo* in the shadow of Palermo's Moorish-style cathedral is like eating one for the very first time. And it gets me thinking about how, throughout Europe, food is so deeply rooted to a place.

Like the island itself, Sicily's street food has been influenced by a mélange of surrounding cultures, past and present, and even comes with its own cross-island grudges. It reflects both the bounty of the sea and land, and the poverty of the people. It has powerful flavors, with palate-awakening splashes of spicy and salty and sweet, always spritzed with a wedge of lemon. And it carries a sensibility of that artisanal perfectionism that possesses even grubby food-cart vendors with grease-smeared smocks. Not bad for a lazy half-mile walk across one city.

Kraków, Poland

These Pierogi Are Perfect

I'm back in Kraków once again, meeting up with a local friend. Tomasz, who leads food tours here, seems to enjoy the challenge of trying to impress me with his latest finds. It's a game we play: He proudly names a chic new bar or restaurant, like a cat bringing a mouse to my doorstep. "Oh, sure, that place," I say. "Ate there six months ago. It was . . . fine." And then he tries again, and again, until my threshold is cluttered with birds and chipmunks to sift through.

But this time, I sense he's holding back. I nudge him and nudge him until he relents.

"Well, OK," he says, glancing around, then breaking into an uncontainable grin. "There is this one place. It's where all of us locals go for lunch. Homeless people, artists, businesspeople, politicians—everyone sits together at shared tables and eats well. It's a milk bar, a very local one."

The milk bar is a uniquely Polish phenomenon. In communist times, the government subsidized these no-frills cafeterias to provide workers with a cheap meal out. While many things have changed since then, milk bars remain a Polish fixture where you can get a filling meal of traditional dishes for next to nothing.

Being both thrifty and a lover of Polish cuisine, I am an aficionado of milk bars. And Tomasz's tip sounds spot-on. It bills itself as a *jadłodajnia*, roughly "place for eating." Old-fashioned. Unpretentious. A weekday-lunch-only place.

The next day, I follow Tomasz's directions to the milk bar, just a half-block off the Main Market Square. I can't believe I've never noticed it before; it shares a courtyard with my favorite Kraków pizzeria. And yet, there it sits: Two open doors—one the humble kitchen, the other the tiny dining room. With basic tile walls, basic coat racks, basic tables, and no "decor" to speak of, it feels entirely practical, almost clinical.

As I enter, the cashier—a tired-looking salt-and-pepper-haired man in a striped polo shirt and jean shorts—looks mildly surprised to see me. As Tomasz instructed, I say, *"Angielski, po proszę."* He ruffles through the stack of tattered photocopied menus, pulling one from the bottom and handing it to me. He makes a sweeping gesture across the tiny room. Sit anywhere.

I find a seat in the corner. Reaching for the ersatz tissue-paper napkins, I take a small stack of about six of seven—approximating the absorbency of one Yankee napkin. Within seconds, an aproned woman appears tableside, cocking her head with a wordless smile: Ready to order? I beg for a few more minutes to consider my options.

The short menu is in three languages: German, French, and English. The dishes sound much better in French. Who can resist the *viande de pot-au-feu*? So that's what I order: boiled beef, plus a plate of "Russian-style" pierogi. The server disappears behind a tattered red-and-white-checkered curtain into the antiseptically tiled kitchen. Big pots simmer on a workhorse stove, tended by blue-smocked cooks.

Maybe one minute later, the plate hits my table. I take a bite, and complex flavors flood my taste buds. It's "boiled beef," yes, but that undersells it. (So does *viande de pot-au-feu*, for that matter.) It's slow-simmered to fork-tender perfection, smothered in a perfectly balanced horseradish cream sauce, with a side of potatoes halfway between roasted and mashed. On the side is a plate of beetroot salad: grated strips of perfectly tender beets, with shards of horseradish. Fantastic.

A minute later, a plate of pierogi joins the tableau. The boiled-dough casing is flawlessly *al dente*. The filling—potato, cheese, and caramelized onion—is generously peppered. Flecks of pork cracklings add a punch of meaty flavor and texture. They sweat fat that makes the water draining to the bottom of the plate shimmer like gossamer. I've had a lot of pierogi, and many are flavorless. But these pierogi? These pierogi are perfect.

Glancing around the room, I observe the steady flow of customers in and out. Everyone shares tables: Young people. Old people. Rich people. Poor people. And everyone is singularly focused on the food in front of them—classic Polish dishes, executed just right. One thing's for sure: I am the only one taking photos of my food. Mindful that this is the kind of place that locals hesitate to tell tourists about—*for exactly this reason*—I stow my camera and eat discreetly.

Not many people get excited about Polish food. And that's a shame, because it's delicious. Polish cuisine is hearty comfort food—high cuisine for hardworking peasants. In this country where virtually every square mile is rippled with farm fields, you can taste the land in the food. Poles have mastered umami—that enigmatic "fifth taste," sometimes described as earthy or savory. Beetroot. Potatoes. Braised beef and pork. Cabbage. Smoke. Mushrooms. Dense rye bread. Rich, fatty proteins. Fermented vegetables. Field greens. Slow-simmering broths. All of these are Polish staples, and all are quintessentially umami.

At the same time, Polish chefs get playful with punchy herbs and spices: Cutting through that smothering blanket of earthiness are bright bursts of dill and peppercorn and marjoram and caraway. And, of course, plenty of garlic.

A well-dressed, professorial man asks to share my table. We sit together in silence—sharing only the common language of satisfied "yummmms"—as I savor my last few bites. I notice a few splashes of purple beet juice on my shirt. I choose to think of these as prized souvenirs from a meal richly enjoyed.

Wishing my lunch companion a hearty *"Smacznego!"* I bus my dishes to the stainless-steel window where, periodically, a hand reaches out to collect them. On my way out the door, I pay the bill: 20 Polish zlotys, or about five bucks. For a meal so filling, I won't need dinner.

Back out on the street, I chew over whether to recommend this place in my guidebook. On the one hand, steering American travelers to a decidedly local hole-in-the-wall could irrevocably change the place, creating frustration and potentially spoiling its specialness. On the other hand, I have a relationship with my readers. They trust me to put them in touch with authentic pockets of local culture. I trust them to treat those places with respect. Strange as it sounds, I'd almost feel guilty about withholding these perfect pierogi from them. And Tomasz trusts all of us: When I see him again later today, I'll make sure he's OK with adding it to book.

In the end, I decide to include it. But, crucially, the way I describe it will thread the needle to ensure it attracts the "right kind" of traveler—the ones who will appreciate its quirks. In the gray area between the rave and the pan is a third path: a thoughtful write-up that shades in those nuances.

I'm a matchmaker between Europe and the North American traveler, and I've developed a sixth sense for that chemistry. Usually it works beautifully. And if it doesn't, Tomasz will be sure to tell me.

Provence, France

Seven Markets
in Seven Days

e didn't have a year in Provence. But we had a week. And that was enough for seven entirely different Provençal markets.

Many French people do much of their shopping at market day (*jour du marché*): a sprawling, weekly celebration of local produce that takes over the entire town or neighborhood. From anyplace in Provence, any day of the week, there's a market—or several—within a 30-minute drive. Needing a break during a very busy period of work, my wife and I retreated to Provence with a goal: seven markets in seven days. This turned out to be the recipe for a perfect vacation.

On a Saturday morning in late September, we drove to Uzès. The cozy main square, under artfully gnarled plane trees, was filled with a classic *marché provençal*: Mountains of plump produce, luscious pyramids of olives, and fragrant mounds of tapenade. Neatly stacked piles of salamis and gigantic wheels of mountain cheese. Colorful fabrics—tea towels, tablecloths, bolts of flamboyant patterns—flapping like flags in the warm breeze. Cheesemongers carving delicate curls from giant wheels of cheese, offering them

for a taste. Butchers and fishmongers standing over refrigerated cases of perfectly butchered cuts.

Tables groaned under the weight of bowls, platters, and spoons carved from olive wood. Bulging burlap bags of spices were artfully identified in neat cursive script on miniature chalkboards. Dappled sunshine, breaking through the leafy canopy, illuminated jars of golden honey. Each one was a slightly different shade of yellow. The seller seemed to know the bees personally . . . perhaps by name.

At the many produce stands, locals filled plastic tubs with carefully selected items: Carrots so perfect they belonged in a Bugs Bunny cartoon. Artichokes painted in an artful ombré of green and purple. Heads of yellow and green lettuce, shaped like starbursts. Heirloom tomatoes, red, orange, purple, and green. Monster shallots, unblemished heads of garlic, muscat grapes with tangy sweetness encased in tough skins, and on and on.

When it comes to food, the French are perfectionists—both in the kitchen and on the farm. America, the birthplace of mass production, demands uniform products (and produce) at low prices. But the French believe in *terroir*: the primacy of the land (*terre*)—its unique soil composition, microclimate, and topography—in shaping the final product. Each plot of land is an artisan workshop, not a factory, and each piece of produce is unique.

Consequently, everything in Provence just tastes better. Strawberries really taste like strawberries. Apricots really taste like apricots. Raspberries and figs and kumquats are explosive. The sundried tomato tapenade we bought in Uzès redefined our sense of what tomato can taste like. For Americans, tasting Provençal produce can be an epiphany. A local person told me she once observed a visitor weeping upon biting into a strawberry, and truly tasting one for the very first time.

Our goal at this market was to sniff out the Uzès specialty, *fougasse d'Aigues-Mortes*—a puffy, cake-like flatbread infused with the essence of orange blossom and sprinkled with coarse sea salt from the Camargue. Finally we spotted a baker's table, two aisles over. By the time we got there, we watched in horror as the very last piece of *fougasse* was bagged up and sold before our eyes. We pointed hopefully to one giant chunk that was set aside, but the baker shook her head apologetically. This piece, she conveyed with a shrug, was being saved for a fellow vendor.

Dejected—but heartened by a shopping bag bulging with tapenade, cheese, and red peppers—we headed back to the car. On the way, we passed a bakery selling *fougasse d'Aigues-Mortes*. It was, indeed, heavenly. This turned out to be a teachable moment: When we thought we'd missed out on that *fougasse*, we reassured each other that we'd find it somewhere else. But we never saw a single piece after we left Uzès.

On Sunday, we doubled up on markets. First up, we stopped by the humble market in the crossroads village of Coustellet.

This was the choice for purists, not tourists. The Coustellet market filled a dusty parking lot, where each vendor backed up a van and dumped their harvest onto rickety tables: fat tomatoes, gigantic leeks, huge gnarled peppers as red as a fire engine, fragrant basil plants pulled from the pages of a botany textbook, mounds of skinny multicolored beans, and three different kinds of eggplants (purple, white, and Thai).

We taste-tested various salamis and other cured meats, settling on a delectable smoked pork loin—tender as prosciutto, flavorful as brisket—that would become the main feature of several picnics. We also picked up a couple of tiny wheels of soft, young, local goat cheese, one encrusted with chopped shallots and the other with peppercorns.

From Coustellet, we drove a few minutes up the road to the granddaddy of all Provençal markets, in l'Isle-sur-la-Sorgue, a workaday town laced with gurgling canals. L'Isle-sur-la-Sorgue's famous market is impressively comprehensive—basically the opposite of Coustellet's. It's also exhausting. Parking was a headache; the canalfront embankments were hopelessly clogged; and the stall-lined lanes twisting to the main square were a human traffic jam. While l'Isle-sur-la-Sorgue's market is one of those things "you have to do once," on this, our third visit, we finally recognized that once is enough.

We took a market break on Monday. Then, on Tuesday, we headed into Vaison-la-Romaine in the Côtes du Rhône wine region. Vaison is a straightforward, user-friendly town that's more practical than cute. But that's precisely its appeal: It feels like a place where real people live, and have lived, for a very long time. The market here has been going strong for 600 years, which might seem impressive, if not for the 2,000-year-old Roman ruins that occupy the heart of town.

In Vaison, we heard far more French spoken than English. It had a few touristy stands, yes, but more of the market's footprint was devoted to practical goods: clothing, kitchenware, textiles, plants, and so on. We stopped by a stand selling every kind of pocketknife imaginable. We chose one, and the vendor razored skinny curls off a piece of paper to demonstrate its sharpness. It was a perfect birthday present for my dad, a pocketknife connoisseur. It came with a certificate of authenticity and a leather pouch, and before we left, the vendor pulled us in close for some advice: Don't keep it in the sheath for more than a few days at a time, or it might discolor the handle. In Provence, even cutlery is handled with the delicacy of fresh produce.

Wednesday was a sleepy market day in our area. So instead, we side-tripped about an hour to the city of Aix-en-Provence. There we met up with a local guide, Mathilde, who leads market tours and teaches cooking classes. She helped us further decode the *jour du marché* phenomenon—delving deeper than the simple "oh wow!" joys of sampling delicious food.

We began with the daily produce market on Place Richelme. Surveying the fruit and veggie stands, under towering plane trees, Mathilde quizzed us: "How do you tell the difference between a farmer and a produce reseller?" She responded to our blank looks with a crash course: If they display a wide range of produce—especially bananas, mangoes, or other tropical fruit—they're a reseller. Stickers on produce are also a sure sign of a reseller.

Produce from a reseller can still be good quality, Mathilde stressed. But knowing the difference can help you choose more carefully. "A farmer picks their produce only when it's perfectly ripe, to sell today at the market," Mathilde said. "When picking for a reseller, they tend to pick it just before it's ripe, to give it more time to be transported." Connoisseurs shopping for today show up early and seek out farmers first; if they strike out, they turn to the resellers.

"For top quality, watch for a stand selling only one item," Matilde said. "Only plums. Just berries. Apricots *seulement*. This is a very good sign." The expression "jack of all trades, master of none" probably did not originate in Provence. But it might as well have.

Leaving the market, Mathilde took us a block away, where we entered a classic *fromagerie*. The air inside the shop slapped us across the face with the individual aromas of a hundred types of cheese, from tiny *mini-bouchon* ("mini-plugs") of *chèvre* to wheels of mountain cheese as big as car tires. Mathilde bought a sampling of three cheeses: sheep, goat, and cow.

Cutting into the wheel of ewe's cheese and watching the insides ooze out, Mathilde noted that French cheeses are not pasteurized. That decadent creaminess comes with a subtle tingle on the tongue. Mathilde explained: "Pasteurization kills bacteria, both good and bad. When cheese is pasteurized, it no longer ripens or matures. We choose flavor over safety."

Biting into a tiny wheel of local goat cheese with a sprig of rosemary mounted on top, Mathilde said, "What grows together, goes together. Both the *chèvre* and the rosemary are from La Garrigue, the arid, rugged countryside around Provence. So they taste perfect together."

Trappe d'Échourgnac is a luxurious, mild cheese with tiny bubbles, which soaks in walnut liqueur until it forms a flavorful brown rind. "This one is not local; it comes from the Dordogne," Mathilde confessed. "But I wanted you to try a cow's milk cheese. And you may have noticed that we don't have many cows in Provence." Within France, cow's milk cheese predominates in cooler, wetter areas, where grass grows green. Warmer climates— like Provence—produce more goat and sheep's cheese, often rubbed in olive oil. (We didn't have the heart to tell her that the Dordogne cheese was our favorite.)

As we nibbled, Mathilde explained that the role of a *fromagerie* is not simply to sell cheese, but to age it. They buy raw cheeses, then mature them to perfection. In fact, the mastery of aging is the craft of a great *fromager*.

Mathilde began speaking in French with the shop clerk, both of them gesturing toward their feet. Excitedly, she translated: "They have offered for us to visit their aging cellar. This is a great honor!" We followed the clerk behind the counter, then through a maze of narrow hallways to a steep staircase.

Arriving in the cellar, we were surrounded by priceless mold. Big wheels of cheese sat upon shelves, and small wheels of cheese were neatly stacked on wooden trays. Some of the cheeses were fuzzy, as if flocked with cotton. All of them awaited that perfect moment of ripeness. Our feet crunched on the gravel floor. Mathilde explained how that floor encourages the perfect humidity and temperature, a steady 54 degrees Fahrenheit.

And then, feeling like we were leaving a secret hideout, we twisted our way back up into the warm sun. Bidding Mathilde *adieu*, we were grateful for the urbane break from our week of French village life. But tomorrow, it was back to small-town Provence.

On Thursday, we awoke in our B&B near the pastel hamlet of Roussillon, perched on its orange hilltop overlooking the lush Luberon. We were nearly *marché*-d out, so Roussillon's pint-sized market was ideal. It resembled other markets we'd browsed, but in miniature: just a few stalls filling a parking lot and some nearby lanes, covering the essential bases. One new-to-us feature we appreciated was the gingerbread man, carving off wedges of tasty gingerbread flavored with lemon or with lavender.

We finished our browse in a matter of minutes. And then, after a parking-lot picnic assembled from the spoils of several days' worth of markets, we set off on an easy hike through the ochre cliffs just below town. The landscape was so vivid, it almost hurt our eyes: soaring orange and yellow cliffs, green trees, azure sky, and big, puffy, white clouds. It's no wonder that so many artists have found inspiration in Provence, where the landscape, too, feels handcrafted.

On Friday, we completed our market marathon with a bang: the classic *marché provençal* in lovely Lourmarin, in the foothills of the Luberon Mountains that separate inland Provence from *Le Med*.

The roads radiating out from Lourmarin were speckled with parked cars under plane trees. Closer in, each street was closed to traffic and lined with market stalls. We recognized several vendors who were by now familiar to us. Lourmarin's market felt like a "greatest hits" collection: technicolor produce, big bundles of lavender lashed like wheat stalks, fragrant soaps stacked in neat piles, olives overflowing wooden buckets, straw baskets in every shape and size, stacks of sausages and wheels of cheese, display racks draped in vivid fabrics, and on, and on, and on, and on.

Lourmarin gave us one last injection of the sensory delights of Provençal markets. At one stand, a lavender vendor poured a few fragrant seeds into our palms. At another, we felt a crispy macaron break into sheets of meringue on our tongue, then slowly dissolve like a sweet bath bomb.

We took advantage of this last-chance shopping to stock up on a few items still on our list: another bar of that incredible-smelling bath soap; a carton of tiny-but-mighty strawberries to snack on in the car; a few lavender sachets for a cheap souvenir that also freshened up our luggage; and a jar of raspberry jam that truly tasted like raspberries. (We hoped it would be as good as the homemade jam at our B&B. Amazingly, it was.)

Pulling out of Lourmarin and heading for Marseille's airport—and our flight home—it was striking how quickly we re-entered the world of traffic-clogged superhighways, smog, and *hypermarchés* (France's answer to big box stores, and the antithesis of a *marché provençal*). Already our idyllic memories of Provence were fading into a happy haze—as if it had all been a very pleasant dream. But it was real, and I have the lavender sachets to prove it.

Browsing the markets of Provence, I'm impressed by the remarkable care and precision with which Europeans handle their produce. Just as France has more than a dozen types of strawberries—big, small, tart, sweet—each producer fills their niche with a perfection that feels like a satisfied sigh. Where I come from, if you want top-quality produce, you pay a premium—usually at a twee farmer's market that feels like a hipster music festival. "Farm-to-table" is on trend in certain corners of the USA these days, but in France, it's simply a way of life. It's understandable why Provence exerts such a powerful allure on expats. Peter Mayle had the right idea.

Spain

The Trouble with Tapas

*T*he crock of *gambas al ajillo* is still sizzling when it hits the table. The tiny pink shrimp, hazy with garlic, spit flecks of oil. It smells like heaven. But on past visits to Madrid, I've learned a hard lesson: If you dig right in, you'll suffer tenderized taste buds for the rest of the trip. So I wait.

When they're cool enough, I begin to eat, mindful of the second hazard of *gambas al ajillo*. And yet, I still manage to drizzle a pinstripe of oil on my shirt. My wad of tissue-paper napkins are no match for the stain—swiftly disintegrating into garlicky tatters—so I toss them into the marble trough at the base of the bar. Oh, well. Sometimes you have to sacrifice a shirt for a good meal. Especially in Spain.

Spanish cooking is Spanish culture—bullfighting and flamenco and Picasso—on a plate. Uncompromising. Unrelenting. Aggressive. It's about choosing a flavor profile, then doubling and tripling down on it. If French cuisine is about technique and nuance and surprises, Spanish cuisine is the opposite: a firehose of flavor. Sea creatures, just scraped from the ocean floor, wiggle and ooze on the bar, soon to be skewered on a toothpick, sautéed, or broiled. As for greens? A Spanish chef never met a vegetable they didn't want to submerge in olive oil and garlic.

Spanish cooking could be accused of being one-note. But there's no question that its one note is flavor-forward. Personally, it can overwhelm my palate, much as the tapas culture can chew up the timid traveler and spit them back out. They run screaming and take solace in a Whopper at Burger King.

When I'm in Spain, I make a point to become a temporary Spaniard. And here in Madrid, that means finding a street where Madrileños outnumber visitors. In a residential neighborhood near the Prado (but not *too* near) runs Calle de Jesús, three blocks with a dozen different tapas bars. I reach Calle de Jesús at prime tapas time: Saturday night, 10 p.m. Each bar is overstuffed, with would-be patrons on the sidewalk peering into steamy windows, waiting for someone to leave.

I choose a bar and squeeze inside. A weekend vibrancy bounces off the colorfully tiled walls. Madrileños stand in clusters, precariously perching their plates and glasses on narrow counters, waving their arms in conversation. It's a miracle glassware isn't flying everywhere.

Behind the bar, five uniformed bartenders scurry to and fro. They're in the weeds, but they remain perfectly coordinated: perfectly coordinated, shouting instructions to each other as they toss plates like frisbees to diners. Observing one bartender expertly tong two ice cubes each into four glasses held in one hand, in seconds flat, is like watching a pitcher locate a split-finger fastball at the bottom crease of the strike zone.

As somebody leaves, I make my move and shimmy along the bar to the far end, hoping to find a few centimeters of countertop where I can stake my claim. This attempt allows me to survey the full lineup of *canapés* (little sandwiches) under glass. I wave my arm until the bartender takes note. He points me all the way back down to the other end of the bar, where he's spotted a space that just opened up.

Once I'm in place, he shoots me a "whaddaya want?" sneer, curling back his upper lip to reveal impatient teeth. I rattle off my order: open-face salmon sandwich and a *banderilla*. Named for the tasseled darts the bullfighter jabs into the fleshy neck of his victim, this is a tiny, raw shish kebab of pickled items pierced with a toothpick.

But I've upset the delicate order of things: There are two kinds of *banderillas* in that glass case, each with a subtly different preserved fish peeking out between chunks of pickle and pepper. Which one do I want, for God's sake? We don't have all night here! If you're an indecisive diner who appreciates when the server helps explain your choices . . . well then, *Jesús* help you on Saturday night in Madrid.

I point to one *banderilla* at random, and in seconds the food is before me. The salmon is incredibly tender. And the *banderilla* is an *explosiva* pop of vinegar and salt, with a slight anchovy finish. It's so good, I order a second.

Finally enjoying my food, I contemplate the peculiarity of Spain's tapas culture. Except it's only peculiar to me; tapas are ideally suited to Spain's sunbaked climate. Who wants to cram into a tight restaurant at 6 p.m., when temperatures are soaring? It's much more civilized to go out in the cool of evening. Dusk is the time to stroll and mingle, and to drop into bars for a bite. This also suits the Spaniards' extroverted nature: Bar-hopping creates plenty of opportunities to reconnect with an endlessly replenishing selection of friends and neighbors.

Standing at the counter, I consider how some of my friends back home would love the tapas scene . . . and even more would absolutely hate it. And that's the trouble with tapas.

A few years ago, my wife came with me to Spain for the very first time. Envisioning foodie "small plates" eateries back home, she couldn't wait to check out the fabled tapas scene. We arrived late

one rainy Friday evening in Bilbao. By the time we'd checked into our hotel, it was around 9 p.m.—the dinner rush. This was going to be fun.

But then . . . it really wasn't. The bars were jammed. We could barely get inside. And when we finally managed to muscle our way to the counter, we couldn't get served. Even as a tapas veteran, I was overwhelmed.

Tapas are a beautiful cultural experience. But you have to work for it. As long as you can accept the latter, you'll enjoy the former. Here are some pointers.

Every town in Spain has a street (or several) lined with tapas bars. Any time I arrive in a new town, my first question is where to find that street. And my second question is which bars do certain things well. Every place might do a serviceable *pulpo* (octopus). But discerning locals know who does it best—tender and delicious rather than rubbery.

Tapas are mix-and-match. Some bars are hip, foodie, and fusion; others are old-school, serving just the classics to traditionalists. Spaniards would never eat an entire meal in one location.

They stroll from bar to bar, at each place ordering a drink and a plate or two to share. And over the course of the evening, they assemble an impromptu, progressive dinner.

Upon entering, you'll run into a wall of people. Don't bother looking for the end of the line. There is no line. Instead, tuck up your elbows like chicken wings and plow through the melee until you reach the counter.

Once situated, survey the options lined up on the counter or under glass. While tempting and easy, these are designed to attract attention. At many tapas bars, the best options are ordered from a menu. In more traditional places, you'll squint at the handwritten menu, hanging in low light at the back of the bar. Even if it were in English, it'd be next-to-impossible to read. You can try asking for a printed English menu, but even those can be far from straightforward. (Trendy eateries relish unhelpfully clever names. Is "Flavors from the Briny Depths" some sort of seafood salad? Paella? Dredged sewage with a seaweed garnish?) Do your best to identify some of the key ingredients, then choose with a spirit of adventure.

Ready to order? If you smile demurely and expect to be waited on . . . waiting is exactly what you'll do. The onus is on you to get the bartender's attention. Wave your hand, make eye contact, and boldly say *¡Por favor!* or *¡Perdón!* (Observing the displays of dominance required to get fed helps me understand why the national pastime involves the ritual slaughter of an innocent animal.)

The bartender's job is not to chitchat, or to conduct a dialogue on the provenance of the ingredients. And forget about substitutions. Watch how hard the bartenders work—a perpetual-motion machine of order-taking, drink-pouring, and cashiering—and you'll appreciate why they seem rushed.

So, be prepared. Once you get the bartender's attention, cut to the chase—clearly and succinctly. "Glass of vermouth, beer, grilled beef loin, *tortilla española. Por favor.*"

Order sparingly and share everything. Then repeat. It's hard to resist overdoing it at your first stop. But pace yourself! Remember: The whole point is to assemble a moveable feast. Pro tip: To avoid getting drunk too quickly, Spaniards alternate between hard drinks and soft drinks (that's why most bars have *cerveza sin alcohol*—N/A beer—on draft; say "thervetha seen").

Because of the communal nature of tapas, everything is family-style by default—don't you dare order something just for yourself. While those attention-grabbers in the showcase are saucer-sized tapas, most of the menu are plate-sized *raciones*, better for sharing.

If this all seems overwhelming, go earlier in the evening for a less intense experience. Spaniards eat dinner late, starting around 9 p.m. But most bars are open all day long and start to lay out early-bird tapas at what approximates a Yankee dinnertime—say, 7 p.m.—to catch office workers for a bite on their way home. As you master the art of tapas, you can start nudging your dinnertime later and later. Eventually you might achieve the all-in, late-night, fully authentic Spanish tapas experience. If not . . . there's always Burger King.

London, England

Where the World's Food Comes to You

*I*t's an April Saturday morning in London, and I'm waiting at a bus stop in front of the Bermondsey Tube station. As usual, it's cold and drizzly. And, as usual, I have an empty coffee cup in my pocket.

The weather can't be helped—it's a spring day in a city synonymous with fog. As for the coffee cup, this is my London routine. Any time I finish a takeaway flat white, I'm stuck with a cup, because garbage cans have been removed from central London as an anti-terrorism measure. Londoners arrange neat rows of discarded cups and bottles on curbs and half-walls, as if improvising shrines to the garbage-collection gods. But it kills me to leave my trash just sitting there in the street. So instead, I stuff the cup into my jacket pocket until I reach a less target-rich corner of the city.

And Bermondsey is exactly that. It's a middlebrow neighborhood on the South Bank of the Thames. While posh apartments line its riverside, its innards are a knot of housing blocks and warehouses, bisected by an elevated railroad artery. It's the kind of place where startup microbreweries are tucked between self-storage facilities and auto-repair garages. There's no reason for tourists to visit Bermondsey unless, like me, they're heading for the Maltby Street Market—Rope Walk for short.

After 10 minutes of patient shivering in the bus shelter, a no-nonsense, single-decker bus pulls up. I climb on, ride it a few stops, and hop off at a yellow-brick railroad viaduct. I walk under the bridge—feeling the ground shake as an express train rockets overhead—and pass a graffiti mural over a tidy pile of garbage bags, to which I add my pocket coffee cup. Rounding the bend, I arrive at my destination.

Rope Walk is simple. Two dozen vendors fill a narrow corridor squeezed alongside the viaduct—about as long as a football field, maybe 30 feet wide—with a festival of artisan food carts: Scottish salmon mounted on slices of dark bread, Venezuelan *arepas*, Vietnamese banh mi, fresh-pressed juices, Spanish *jamón* carved right off the hock, intriguing modern spins on scotch eggs, Brazilian steak wraps, Middle Eastern flatbreads with savory toppings, German-style sausages, gyoza steamed in wicker baskets, slabs of grass-fed, dry-aged, rare-grilled hanger steak, and on and on.

The drizzle intensifies. I pop up my hood and do another lap—still deliberating on the perfect Rope Walk progressive brunch. I spy my appetizer on a rickety table in front of a tapas bar: *calçots*, oversized green onions charred on a grill. Just before this trip, a co-worker mentioned she'd finally had this springtime delicacy in Barcelona. I've been dying to try it, too. I have no trips to Catalunya planned, but no matter—in London, the world's food comes to you.

Through broken English (with lots of Spanish), the vendor hands me a newspaper-wrapped bundle of steaming, oozing spring onions and explains how to eat them: carefully peel back the charred outer layer of the onion, revealing the sweet, slimy, tender cooked stalk in the center. Dip it into Romesco sauce and munch. File this one under "Looks weird; tastes amazing."

On to the main course. I settle on a tried-and-true favorite: grilled cheese. One stand specializes in giving this French invention an English spin. I opt for a flavor bomb: Cropwell Bishop Stilton cheese (imagine a fearless mashup of gorgonzola and cheddar) with pear chutney and bacon. I stand patiently in the mist while they griddle up my sandwich to order. It's worth the wait, and every bit as decadent, melty, and delicious as you'd dare to dream. The cheese packs a wicked punch, balanced and mellowed by the chutney. The bacon may be gilding the lily, but who can argue with culinary genius? Best of all, just the right amount of cheese has oozed onto the grill, hardening into a crisp, salty, slightly charred petrified puddle.

To wash it down, I head next door to the Sicilian lemonade stall. In Britain, "lemonade" usually means "sicky-sweet lemon-lime pop." But this is a true Sicilian *limonata*, as authentic as the guy from Catania who pours it: fresh-squeezed lemon juice, sprightly and not too sweet.

The sun begins to break through the clouds. And, while I've had the place largely to myself, now Londoners are emerging like thirsty snails and filling the pavement.

Before leaving, I grab dessert: a salted caramel brownie. It's rich, decadent, and gooey—dripping with thick, salty-sweet caramel, and topped with crunchy crystals of solid caramel. A couple of bites is enough for now. Fortunately, my coffee-cup pocket is currently vacant. I wrap the brownie in a bag, jam it in my pocket, and begin walking toward Tower Bridge. As another train rumbles overhead, I start whistling a tune. I have a busy day of work ahead of me. But no matter. As usual, Rope Walk has provided one of my favorite meals of the trip.

It used to be clichéd to say that British food was bad. Now it's clichéd to say that it no longer is. If you still believe that soggy fish-and-chips and microwaved shepherd's pie are the peak of British culinary achievement, you're a lost cause.

The secret is simple: "British" food is no longer strictly British.

Traveling around Europe, you observe how cultural chauvinism finds expression from place to place. In some countries, outside influences are viewed with suspicion, even hostility. In Provence, where we explored seven entirely different markets, and in Tuscany, where people aspire to "zero-kilometer" meals, quality is defined as intensely local. And in one Croatian city I know well, an expat attempted to open a "global food" eatery for backpackers, serving burritos, hamburgers, and pad thai. It was a hit, until it closed abruptly. The owner told me that members of his waitstaff—acting on behalf of a word-of-mouth community movement to keep Croatian food Croatian—were actively sabotaging him.

But Britain's approach to food is starkly different. People here seem to recall with more regret than nostalgia the food they grew up with. They're determined to do better. And that means being open to the world. Fortunately, this is a British forté.

Britain no longer rules the waves. And, for the most part, it's OK with that. Today's Brits find a comfortable, sensible, and dignified existence in being what once was, but no longer is, the mightiest land on earth. It requires a rare combination of confidence and humility to let yourself be challenged and changed by outside influences. If anything, the Brits take this to extremes with a penchant for cultural appropriation. But British foodie culture is increasingly mindful of this problem, too. (And it's still preferable to shutting down a place for having the temerity to serve tacos.)

London is Europe's greatest melting pot city. With each visit, I'm struck by the remarkable variation in languages, accents, skin tones, and clothing all around me. And I see this new face of London most vividly in its many street markets.

On a sunny Saturday, the park called London Fields is jammed with hundreds of people enjoying the tree-filled lawn after gorging themselves at food trucks. It's a Millennial Woodstock without the mud or music. Strolling a world of tattooed new dads, with coiffed beards and chunky vintage eyeglasses, pushing prams, you realize that Hackney is where London's hipsters go to breed.

At the southern edge of London Fields is Broadway Market— the name both of this area's Victorian main drag, and of its open-air festival of foods and crafts. It's a magnet for all that's chic and global, with an edge of pretense: seasonal organic produce, designer creams and lotions, farm-fresh meat and eggs, handmade fashions, twee craft projects, "bespoke" anything and everything. Nearby, a leafy primary school playground hosts wildly creative food trucks and other pop-up culinary offerings.

And if it's Sunday morning, you'll find me on Brick Lane, in London's achingly hip East End. This commercial artery has, for centuries, been the point of arrival for persecuted refugees. In the late 16th century, Huguenots escaping Catholic violence in France founded a thriving weaving industry at nearby Spitalfields. By the 19th century, the Brick Lane area became a magnet for both Irish people fleeing the Great Potato Famine and Ashkenazi Jews displaced by the pogroms of Eastern Europe. And in the 1970s, Bangladeshi refugees arrived here in such numbers that Bengali street signs were added and the neighborhood was dubbed "Banglatown."

At the intersection with Fournier Street stands a structure that embodies the story of Brick Lane. The Huguenots built it in 1742 as a Protestant chapel; it became a synagogue in 1898; and, since 1976, it has been a neighborhood mosque with a skinny, modern minaret—a glittering stiletto with a metallic sheen that catches and disperses any light penetrating the cloudy London skies.

It's fitting that today's hipsters have taken root in one of London's most historically diverse corners. Walking the length of Brick Lane on a Sunday, you can dip into the UK's largest assortment of vintage vendors; a cavernous food hall devoted entirely to vegan and vegetarian street food; and the courtyard of the old Truman Brewery, brimming with yet more market stalls and food stands.

Brick Lane and its side streets are slathered in wildly colorful street art and lined with fascinating businesses. A Black-owned chocolate shop displays overflowing baskets of intensely dark pralines, powdery with high-octane cocoa dust imported from Ghana. Two short blocks away, a hole-in-the wall with faded tile from pre-Thatcher times sells traditional Jewish bagels, topped with salt beef, herring, or salmon.

If the way to a culture's heart is through its stomach, there's no doubt London revels in its status as a multicultural hub. Contrast this, once again, to the dreamy bounty of Provence. In France, the birthplace of *terroir*, food is *hyper*-local. Here in London, it's precisely the opposite: a gathering place of flavors from around the globe. Both philosophies have their place, and both are delicious.

Paradoxes like this—the way that things from so near, and so far, can be equally enticing—are part of what keep me coming back to Europe. Just when you think you've sorted out a definitive rule of thumb to guide your travels, Europe subverts it.

Jams Are Fun

There's a (Gastrointestinal) Bomb on the Bus!

Jams are not all mine!
—Mildred C. Scott, *Jams Are Fun*

As Aunt Mildred acknowledges, some of the best jams are those experienced vicariously. Especially the really nasty ones. In my years of tour guiding, I encountered several bumps in the road. But I never endured the unenviable moment of knowing that my entire group was about to fall desperately ill.

During busy season, our tours run back-to-back, two days apart. Guides try to keep each other in the loop about problems that pop up en route. That is, when it's not already too late. As it happens, two days is also very close to the gestation period of the Norovirus—a brief, but extremely unpleasant, gastrointestinal illness sometimes called the "cruise ship virus."

Many years ago, one of our guides—let's call him Brett—was leading an itinerary with a stop at a storybook village in Germany. Each tour group had lunch at the hotel, spent the afternoon sightseeing, then loaded up the next morning to head south to castle country in the Bavarian Alps.

Leaving town and en route to the Alps, Brett got word that something unusual had happened on the previous tour: at dinner on that first night in Bavaria, several guests had to excuse themselves; by the next day, most of the group was violently ill. By this time, the office had triangulated that Patient X must have worked in the kitchen that prepared the group lunch. Upcoming tours had already been re-routed. But it was too late for poor Brett.

Arriving at the hotel, Brett compared notes with the shell-shocked innkeeper. Having just cleaned up the rooms of the previous group, the innkeeper was all too aware of what awaited Brett's group that night. All they could do was to wait, and to hope that the virus would somehow miss them.

That night at dinner, Brett kept a close eye on his group. Mid-meal, one tour member got up in a hurry and never came back. Brett wondered if this was an omen of things to come. After dinner, everyone went to their rooms. And a few hours later, the virus hit Brett full force.

I'll spare the gory details. I will say that, in clarifying the story with Brett, I asked him, "So, with all these people who got sick. Which . . . I guess, which *end* was the source of the problem?"

Brett turned white as a sheet and answered a little too fast: "Both. It was . . . it was both ends at once."

Always looking on the bright side, Brett notes that this was the first place he'd stayed that had radiant heat in the bathroom floor, which proved both convenient and cozy.

Dutifully, Brett showed up to meet his group the next morning for an excursion to Neuschwanstein, "Mad" King Ludwig's fairy-tale castle. Of his two dozen or so tour members, only about five showed up, and three of those looked pretty green. Brett boarded the bus with what was left of his group and explained the day's plan—pausing at one point to run back to the hotel bathroom for a few minutes, then getting back on the bus, and the mic, without skipping a beat.

The few hardy souls who made it to Neuschwanstein joined the castle tour. Upon reaching the King's Bedroom, however, one tour member realized that she was in dire need of a toilet. The castle guide sternly informed her that there were no WC options nearby. When she made it clear that this was about to happen regardless ("Just tell me which corner" was the approximate sentiment), the guide suddenly remembered that there was, in fact, an option: the King's Private Toilet Chamber, tucked behind the canopy bed, with antique plumbing that still worked just fine in emergencies.

The innkeeper took good care of the many tour members who'd stayed at the hotel, and the others when they got back. And by morning, the worst had passed. The group piled onto the bus for the long, twisty drive over the Brenner Pass to Venice—miraculously, without major incident.

Arriving in Venice, they enjoyed a gondola cruise on the Grand Canal, followed—as always—by a champagne toast. But this time, the toast was more festive than ever.

At one African airport where I seemed to be the only white person there, two girls were at an information desk in the waiting room. When my plane was called, one of them got up and walked with me to the plane. I never got that kind of service in the United States, and I wonder if we would give it to African tourists traveling here.

—Mildred C. Scott,
  Jams Are Fun

PART FOUR

All Alone;
Never Alone

*T*here are people who have never eaten a meal in a restaurant by themselves. Those people really should try it sometime. I do it dozens of times each year, all over Europe. "Table for one?" has, by default, become one of my travel mantras.

If you can live with the social stigma, dining solo carries many advantages. After all the two-tops are long since booked, there's often a single place setting hiding out somewhere. Once seated, the entire restaurant is a production of top-flight people-watching, staged for your entertainment. And when the food arrives, being alone lets you fully focus on what's on the plate. How many times have you gone out with friends to a hot new restaurant, only to get caught up in the conversation? Looking back on the meal, you realize you were so focused on what was coming out of your mouth that you barely registered what was going into your mouth.

"Solo travel" is its own genre. And while some people marvel at what it must be like for me to spend a quarter of my life on my own in Europe, that thought rarely even occurs to me. Traveling solo is my natural state.

Don't get me wrong: I also enjoy traveling with other people. My favorite travel partner is my wife, Shawna. One of the questions I'm most often asked is, "How does your wife feel about you being gone so often?" I am fortunate to be married to an outrageously generous person who sees how happy my work makes me, and supports it. When I'm away, we talk every single day. And we also look for any opportunity for her to join me in Europe. Each spring, as I plan my year's travels, I try to talk her into tagging along with me in Iceland, or Croatia, or Italy, or Portugal. I can usually twist her arm.

Still, my work requires me to be alone most of the time. And I've learned to make the best of it. After some experiences, I call Shawna and say, "I sure wish you'd been there." But other experiences have that much more impact (or, at least, a different impact) when I savor them entirely by myself. Hiking a Swiss mountain meadow or an English moor all alone, you're not distracted by chitchat about things back home; it's easier to be fully present.

Alone, you break out of the group think of a travel pod and become more of an individual, seeking contact with other individuals. The people you meet make a bigger impression—they're richly sketched characters who loom large in later memories. If you gobble sugar nonstop, you can barely taste sweetness anymore. But if you have just one square of chocolate each day, it feels like someone injected it straight into your taste buds.

All of that said, there's one big catch about "solo" travel: The traveler is never truly alone.

Every trip is spent appealing to the kindness of strangers and being pleasantly surprised when they exceed our expectations. In *Jams Are Fun*, Aunt Mildred describes the many "life savers" who made sure she got where she needed to go. I've learned that you don't have to be a sweet old lady to enjoy that treatment. For weeks at a time, I swing like Tarzan, from stranger to stranger, through the jungle of Europe. And so far, they've never let me fall.

I find Europeans easy to connect with. They're comfortable in their own skin; they have a clear sense of identity, both personal and cultural. And when I'm in Europe, I find myself becoming a different person. Back home, I get caught up inside my own head, critiquing each conversation after the fact. But Europe makes me fearless, candid, inquisitive. I ask questions guilelessly, and I gobble up the answers. And the Europeans I meet—who seem flattered by my interest—open up and generously share their worlds with me.

But the locals are just some of the characters who populate our "solo" travels. Our trips are also enriched by the fellow travelers we meet on the road.

I was born in Denver, Colorado. When I was a baby, on Sunday mornings my parents could hear the crowds cheering at Mile High Stadium across town—a joyous sound wave that rippled through the thin air. I must've caught that particular altitude sickness, because even after we moved to Ohio, I remained a die-hard Denver Broncos fan. And to this day, I can walk into any bar on earth where people are wearing orange and blue and start high-fiving strangers.

Travel is similar. The more you travel, the more you become aware that you're part of a community. When you encounter a fellow traveler-at-heart, you sense a bond that transcends your differences. You speak the same language; to borrow a trendy phrase, you feel *seen*. I think this partly explains the borderline-cultish allure of the "Rick Steves" phenomenon. Rick has been described as a "travel guru," and I can attest that his fans and followers feel tapped into something big, beautiful, even mystic. It's not about him; it's about all of us.

The following stories explore that strange mix of aloneness and community that we experience on the road. In Italy, I consider what it's like being an introvert in perhaps the most extroverted place on earth. You'll meet a Slovenian family that challenges my notion of how families work. On the moors of South England, I connect with larger-than-life personalities and commune with empty nature. In Tuscany, we become a temporary member of yet another family, who have perfected the delicate art of introducing American guests to traditional farm life. And finally, I flash back to the formative semester abroad I spent in Salamanca, Spain, and consider how my host family helped shape me into the traveler I am today.

Italy

An Introvert in the Land of Extroverts

ecently I flew home from London. Normally those nine-hour flights are a sedate affair, but this time was different. The plane was jammed with a big group of Italians, heading to Seattle for an Alaska cruise. They rolled onto the plane with fanfare, jamming bags every which way into the overhead compartments, gesticulating wildly, really making a meal out of finding their seats. A couple of hours into the flight, I couldn't get to the bathrooms because a half-dozen people were crowding the aisles. At first, I thought they were all waiting for the lavatory. Nope. They were just socializing after dinner.

Italy mystifies travelers. Especially introverts like me.

I'm sure Italy has plenty of introverts. I've met some shy, retiring Italians. But not many. I suspect that Italian introverts have to adapt to their outgoing society, so they learn to do a good impression of extroverts. (I live in Seattle—a.k.a. Introvert City, USA—where it's very easy to surrender to your loner instincts. Italians don't have that option, unless they want to become hermit shepherds.)

For evidence that Italy is an extrovert's paradise, you need only walk down the street—any street, anywhere in Italy—at about 6 or 7 p.m. What you'll find is entire neighborhoods out and about, strolling, greeting each other warmly, sharing an ice cream cone or a cocktail. In Italy, every night is a party. It's no wonder those Italians on my flight got so fidgety somewhere over Iceland. They needed their *passeggiata*, even if it had to happen in the aisle between rows 40 and 55.

Italian culture is organized around social interaction. The centerpiece of any Italian town is the piazza—the community living room and meeting place. Germans, meanwhile, have a *Marktplatz*—the market square, a place of business. At dusk, the *Marktplatz* is locked up tight. But the piazza is just waking up. Italian squares are not designed strictly for commerce; they're made for socializing.

Italians' social intelligence is off the charts. I have Italian friends who can size me up and intuit exactly what I'm thinking with one glance. They have a sixth sense for people. They *get it.* I enjoy doing guidebook research in Italy, because what is often the hardest part of my job in other places—explaining that I'm updating a book and just need to ask a few questions—is effortlessly understood, accepted, and accommodated. Even if they don't have the answers I need, they're right there with me.

Have you ever been in Italy, and someone starts talking to you in fast-paced Italian, and you protest that you don't speak their language—and they keep going? The more you object that you don't understand, the more you realize that . . . no, wait . . . you do, in fact, somehow understand. Not everything, but a little. Just enough.

It's not that they don't realize you don't speak Italian. It's that they don't care. Because they know that communication is about more than words.

All of that said, there are downsides to Italy's extroversion. I spend a great deal of time—probably *weeks* out of my life—walking behind slow-moving people on the sidewalks of Europe. And no nationality is more adept at occupying the maximum amount of space with the minimum number of bodies than Italians. As extroverts, they expand to fill their container.

It can be tough to be an introvert in Italy. "Fun" quickly turns to "wearying" as your social capacity is exceeded. And it's hard to feel like you're ever *alone* here. From time to time, I retreat to my hotel room—the introvert's final refuge. But in Italy, you can usually hear everything going on in adjacent rooms, thanks to minimal soundproofing, paper-thin doors, and echoey hallways.

For years I chalked this up to cheap construction. But on a recent trip, trying to get to sleep around midnight and hearing an animated conversation echoing through the stone staircase just outside my room, it dawned on me: Perhaps, out of a deep-seated desire to be among others, Italians don't mind hearing other people. Maybe they even find it . . . comforting?

In the end, I've come to appreciate the way Italy forces me to stretch my boundaries. Italians have a gift for getting you out of your shell. Rick Steves (a textbook extrovert) has a mantra: "Extroverts have more fun. If your trip is low on magic moments, kick yourself and make things happen." I have taken those words to heart since my first big European backpacking trip. And I find that in Italy, becoming a temporary extrovert comes very naturally. And, sure enough, it's more fun.

High in the Mountains
with Tina's Dad

igh in the Slovenian Alps, through a driving rain, Gorazd grips the steering wheel. He follows an unpaved road up, up, up above the tree line. As we disappear into clouds, Gorazd's tires grind against the gravel. But I'm not worried. I know I'm in good hands. After all, this is Tina's Dad we're talking about.

Tina Hiti, whom you met near the beginning of this book, has a knack for turning any friend into a member of the family. Whenever I'm in Slovenia—which is often—she takes me in and makes me feel very welcome.

Tina lives in an alpine village about a 10-minute drive from Lake Bled. Over two decades of visits, I've gotten to know Tina's entire clan very well. Her partner, Sašo, was my assistant guide on two departures of our Adriatic tour, and he's now an ace lead guide in his own right. Tina and Sašo have two sons, Anže and Tomaž, whom I've enjoyed getting to know as they've grown up. One quiet, cloudy October afternoon, my wife Shawna and I hung out at the Lake Bled ice rink with Sašo, watching their tots—at an age when most kids are still mastering walking—zipping around the ice like future all-pros.

Because of the difficulties in getting a mortgage, Slovenes make full use of any family property. So when they moved in together, Tina and Sašo converted her parents' attic into a functional, comfortable, multi-room apartment. At well over six feet tall, Sašo has to crouch under low beams. But nobody seems to mind; it's a cozy and well-equipped family home.

Visiting Tina and Sašo's home always shakes up my worldview. Why is it that in many parts of the United States, kids can't wait to move out? Why do my wife and I, and each of our parents, and each of our siblings, all have houses with multiple spare rooms? Isn't the European approach more cost-effective, more sustainable, and better for "family values"? Tina and Sašo have their privacy and their own space—but Grandma and Grandpa are just steps away, ready to babysit.

Of course, knowing Tina means knowing her parents. Her mother, Breda, is silent, smiling, and strong. And her father, Gorazd, is also soft-spoken and reserved, with a quiet kindness.

One misty fall day, I had dinner plans with Tina's family. But she called me in a panic: Her dad was out foraging for mushrooms when he slipped on wet leaves and tumbled into a ravine. Slovenian mushroom hunters have an ethic of never, under any circumstances, revealing their favorite places to forage. Gorazd knew that nobody had a clue where he was. He was on his own to crawl out of the ravine, regain his footing, and make his way back to civilization.

I always thought of Gorazd as you do the parents of your childhood friends: simply "Tina's Dad," full stop, without any real identity of his own. But then, one year, I was in Slovenia researching some new material for my guidebook. Tina, who had planned to take me to a remote mountain valley called Logarska Dolina, came down with a terrible cold. So the night before our trip, she called to tell me she was out.

"But you will go with my dad," she said. "It will be great. He speaks great English, more than he lets on, and he knows the mountains better than I ever will."

I'll admit, I was disappointed. But I showed up the next morning to meet Gorazd. He was a stocky but fit guy with gray hair, wearing a track suit . . . in short, someone's dad. But his warm smile reassured me that we'd have a fun and productive day. And we did.

Gorazd drove us through Slovenia's breathtaking landscape, alternating between cold rain and sunny spells, to Logarska Dolina. He wanted to experiment by taking a near-vertical detour through Austria, using a middle-of-nowhere border crossing that might be closed. (This was back when there were actually borders.) When we pulled up to the ragtag checkpoint and saw a couple of bored guards, we were pleasantly surprised that we'd be able to cross, and they were pleasantly surprised that we'd given them something to do that day.

Two hours of burly granite mountains later, we arrived at Logarska Dolina—roughly meaning "Woodsmen's Valley." As the sun finally emerged for good, Gorazd took me around to the scenic

viewpoints, rural rest stops, and picturesque tourist farms that I needed to check out for my book. And, as Tina had promised, Gorazd knew the area like nobody else.

Observing the steeply angled green pastures that huddle just below the tree line, Gorazd joked, "They say cows here have shorter front legs than back legs. That way, they can stay upright while they graze." Another Slovenian dad joke: "Dogs have to hold onto the grass with their teeth and bark through their butts."

Corkscrewing up yet another gravel byway—poetically dubbed "The Panoramic Road"—Gorazd brought me to a tourist farm on a rocky shelf with stunning views. He grew visibly excited when he saw a sign that said *kislo mleko*. "Ah, yes, this is the specialty here," he said. "It's like yogurt. You must try it."

He ordered two crocks filled with the stuff—"like yogurt," yes, but with a yellowish-brown film on top. My spoon broke through the firm outer layer and carried a cross-section of the contents to my mouth. Two flavors dominated: sour and what I can only describe as "barnyard."

Choking down the pungent mouthful with a swig of water, I pressed Gorazd for more details. "*Kislo mleko* means 'soured milk,'" he explained. "They make a light yogurt. No pasteurization. Then they put it in the barn for a few days to sour, naturally."

Scraping the final globs out of his crock, Gorazd declared, "Delicious! Tastes like the cow." (He intended this as a compliment.) I went back for more, hoping to acquire a taste for this mountain specialty, and failing. Tina tells me that finishing my bowl earned me Gorazd's undying respect. Apparently, he still talks about it.

Tina had mentioned that her dad was a good hockey player. But that undersells it. On the way back to Lake Bled, Gorazd explained that he and his brother were both Olympians in the 1970s and 1980s, when the core of the Yugoslav hockey team came from their mountain hamlet. While his playing days are behind him, her dad has coached for decades. His brother operates a bar inside Lake Bled's hockey arena; on the wall hangs a giant photograph of the Hiti boys in their prime.

It's always rewarding to see someone embark on an unexpected "second act" later in life. And in the dozen or so years since he took me to Logarska Dolina, Gorazd has blossomed into a fine mountain tour guide. With my encouragement, Tina added her dad to her guiding business. So now, travelers from across North America hire Gorazd for a drive into the mountains.

Gorazd and Tina always get me thinking about the way generations pass along family identity, one to the next. Young Gorazd was a hockey star who skated for socialist Yugoslavia; now his daughter is a proud citizen of Slovenia, of the EU, and of the world. They're fundamentally different people, products of different times, even different countries. But they share a carbon-copy adoration of their mountains and a respect for tradition. Now I see Tina—and Gorazd—passing those same traditions on to Anže and Tomaž, ensuring that the Slovenian cultural chain remains unbroken.

Here's another example—macabre, perhaps, but touching: On November 1, Slovenia celebrates the Day of the Dead. Across the country, Slovenes spend days decorating the graves of lost loved ones. Then, on All Hallows Day, they travel from cemetery to cemetery, paying their respects. Tina tells me that each November 1, she takes Anže and Tomaž to ten different graves, in six different cemeteries.

I was fortunate enough to be in Slovenia one year for this beautiful celebration. In the main cemetery of Ljubljana, everyone was wearing their Sunday best. I squeezed along the gravel lanes between elegant tombs decorated like parade floats—each one trying to outdo the next. Later that night—as the sky turned from overcast white to somber black—I returned to the cemetery, which was again full of people. Underfoot, half-sheathed chestnuts skittered through crunchy leaves. Thousands upon thousands of flickering candles filled the somber space with soft, dancing, red light. Old friends and distant cousins bumped into each other— for the first time in ages—at the grave of a shared loved one. Even when it began to rain, nobody left. Families huddled together under umbrellas, their tear-streaked faces shimmering in the candlelight, laughing together at treasured memories.

Travel is rife with epiphanies. And some of them are inconvenient, even uncomfortable. As I observe the deepness of connection that many Europeans feel to their heritage, I'm struck by the contrast to my own life, and my own country.

Many of the Europeans I meet seem to understand and accept who they are on a primal level. Meanwhile, many Americans struggle with finding a sense of meaning. Existential crisis is our national pastime. Some eschew family traditions as corny or pointless, then scramble to find other things to fill that void. We turn to meditation, or materialism, or religion, or political movements left and right, or travel. Many of us still haven't found what we're looking for. I wonder sometimes how much this owes to our itinerant nature.

My all time-favorite joke is this: What's Ohio's biggest export? Ohioans.

It's true. Everywhere I go—across the USA and around the world—I bump into fellow members of the Ohio diaspora. Middle America doesn't just grow America's corn and potatoes; it grows Americans, who are pulled out at the root to be sorted, distributed, and transplanted across our land. Of course, a great many people spend their lives in the place where they grew up. But when I look at, say, my circle of friends from high school or college, or even members of my own family, I'm struck by how far-flung we've become. We think nothing of moving hundreds of miles away from someone we were once inseparable from. I know Anže and Tomaž better than I know the kids of guys I grew up with, guys I consider brothers.

Tina lives within steps of her parents, well into her forties. In the States, some might consider that deeply uncool. And yet, I know few people cooler than Tina. She has a strong individual identity, a progressive political outlook, and a passion for getting out and experiencing our world—which she's now passing on to her kids. Living close to home doesn't make her any less adventurous or worldly; in fact, those traits are reinforced by having a strong foundation to return home to.

I'm not saying Tina's approach is for everyone. Many people have very good reasons to leave, to sever their past lives. Others of us have the privilege of choice. And speaking as someone who has lived for the last 20-plus years 2,500 miles from "home," Tina and Gorazd make me wonder whether I made the right one. When we relocate to a new place, we gain something. But we also lose something.

Under Tina's roof live three generations. And I'm certain that traditions are passed more easily within that family than within mine. (When I want to read Aunt Mildred's book, my in-laws have to ship it to me from half a continent away.) The boys already love hockey just as much as their grandpa does. I'm sure, if he hasn't already, Gorazd will soon introduce them to the joys of *kislo mleko*. And Tina tells me he's already whispered to Anže and Tomaž where they can find those elusive mushrooms.

Dartmoor, England

What Lies Beneath

On my first trip to England, I stayed in the village of Bovey Tracey on the outskirts of Dartmoor National Park. I was a houseguest of the parents of my sister's then-boyfriend, Sven—one of those tenuous connections that backpackers leverage to score a few free nights in a beautiful place. Sven's mom was a no-nonsense lady, belied by her name, Lovey. But Sven had prepared me well: The sure way to her heart was by making my bed every morning and offering to help clean up after dinner. (One of his friends had come by this intel at a terrible cost.) My hospital corners and dishwashing duty earned me Lovey's loyalty, and I was made to feel very welcome.

Eager to show off the beautiful landscape at their doorstep, Lovey drove me around the moody moors. The sky was misty and gray, cloaking Dartmoor in clouds and mystery. We pulled over at the foot of a grassy hill and hiked up a rutted path through soggy turf. At the top of the mound was a massive pile of rock called Hound Tor. It looked like some giant had dumped out a bag of boulders on a green hill. Lovey explained the opposite was true: The elements had slowly eroded away the grass and dirt, revealing the rock that was always there, just below the surface.

Years later I was excited to return to Dartmoor on a guide-book-research trip. I'd seen only a tiny corner of the place on my previous visit, but it left a huge impression. It seemed so vast and lonesome and enigmatic. There was much to be found in Dartmoor, and I wanted to find it.

I had booked a room at a remote countryside B&B just outside the hamlet of Murchington. I spent a busy day running down leads in Cornwall, made the long drive east to Dartmoor, and arrived at the B&B late in the evening.

I was greeted by the animated proprietress, whom we called "Maureen" in the book—but she instructed me to call her Mo. Mo was a short, plump woman, dressed in overlapping layers of patterns as loud as her husky alto, all wrapped up in a heavy gray shawl. Her face was painted as if for the stage, and she spoke with a theatrical affectation. I had to make a split-second decision whether I found her irritating or charming.

I opted for charming. And she rewarded me by lavishing me with hospitality. Feeling sheepish about my late arrival and too tired to venture back out for dinner, I had plans to retire to my room and finish off a half-bag of cashews in my backpack, hopefully supplemented by some individually wrapped digestive biscuits I imagined sitting in a little basket by the tea service.

"My first question for you, dear Cameron of Seattle," Mo said expansively, "is whether you will allow me to make you dinner."

"Oh. Well. Thank you, but no. That's not necessary."

Mo eyed me with suspicion. "So you've eaten already then, have you?"

"Um. Not really, but I have something."

"Nonsense!" Mo said. (It was probably "Nonsense," but given Mo's propensity to chew the scenery, it may have been "Poppycock!" or "Balderdash!" or "Pish Posh!") "You are a guest in my home. I will whip you up something straightaway."

Mo invited me to have a seat at her kitchen counter and proceeded to cook up a storm. All the while, she chattered nonstop about life in her small backwater of Devon with as much drama and intrigue as the rise and fall of Rome. She spoke of wayward young horses escaping paddocks, the ever-fluctuating quality of the various eateries in and around Chagford, and the vicar who'd just taken a new post three villages over. She noticed that the belt loop on my jeans had ripped out, and offered to mend it for me.

At one point her husband John doddered into the kitchen. He was tall, slender, and gray-haired, with an easy and gentle smile. When he spoke, it was softly and kindly, and always interrupted by his wife, to which he responded with more easy smiles. Mo was the flamboyant star of the show; John was the straight man.

As I sat and ate Mo's delicious dinner—pan-fried pork chops with potatoes and vegetables—she said to me, with a twinkle in her eye, "You know, John and I used to work on the *Queen Elizabeth 2*!"

"You don't say," I said, superfluously. "Tell me more."

"We performed in the shipboard lounge. I was a singer—you know, torch songs and classics, and all that. And John was my piano player." John reinforced this story with a smile and a cocked head. In that instant, a crystal-clear vision popped into my mind: John, in a tux instead of a cozy sweater, seated at the piano. And Mo squeezed into a sequined, slinky red dress, wearing even more makeup than she was now, curled up on the piano like Michelle Pfeiffer.

This place snapped into focus. For these two—and especially for Mo—running a B&B in the middle of nowhere was simply another gig. It gave her an entirely new, captive audience for whom to perform.

Over the next couple of days, I tooled around Dartmoor, exploring. I climbed Hound Tor again—this time on a sunny day—and summitted a few other tors. My tires rumbled over cattle grates, which kept free-range livestock vaguely contained within vast, rolling terrain. I pulled over at roadside pullouts and tiptoed around steaming piles of sheep droppings to reach long, perfectly spaced, arrow-straight lines of rocks embedded in the spongy turf. It's a landscape that feels somehow mystical and otherworldly.

But what made the biggest impression about Dartmoor was its people. With each stop I met a new and memorable character—perhaps not quite as dynamic, but certainly as intriguing, as Mo. The accommodations and restaurants we listed, and any new ones I checked out, were utterly quirky. English B&Bs sometimes veer into the cookie-cutter. Especially after a busy morning of dropping into ten or twelve, it's hard to tell them apart. But in Dartmoor, each business and each person I encountered was unique as a snowflake.

Dartmoor is one of those places where people don't live accidentally. If you live in Dartmoor, you live in Dartmoor *on purpose*. There's always more to the story. Perhaps, like Mo and John, you're seeking a second act. Perhaps you're escaping something, or looking for something. Or, for reasons that only you can understand, you simply want to live far from the predictable rhythms of mainstream society. Remote and mysterious places attract fascinating people, and that's just one reason why I like them very much.

* * *

"When you get to the sign that says 'Way Down,' go up."

This was just one of the bewildering steps that Mo outlined the next afternoon when I asked for directions to Scorhill Stone Circle. It came in the middle of a perplexingly detailed route that involved multiple turns, unmarked and unpaved roads, and crossing what should be a dry riverbed unless it rained more yesterday than she realized. And once there, Mo warned, I wouldn't see a sign for the circle, nor could I see the circle itself from the road. I'd have to trust that I'd parked in the right place, step through a fence, walk across a field, and the circle should—*should*—appear before me. (If I hadn't parked in the right place after all, it was possible I'd be wandering into a military firing range.)

Scorhill Stone Circle is a sentimental favorite of Rick Steves'. He stumbled upon it decades ago, while exploring Dartmoor as a teenaged backpacker. It had recently been added to our guidebook, but the previous researcher's instructions for finding it essentially said, "It's a few miles that-a-way; try to get a local person to tell you where it is." I was hoping to clarify things. But I was discovering the reason for the vagueness.

After reviewing the turn-by-turn instructions with Mo three times—including once while scrutinizing my Ordnance Survey map—I was ready to head out. Getting in my car, I looked over the notes yet again. They sounded like the written equivalent of a treasure map to pirate booty, right down to the obfuscating riddles. As I turned off onto progressively smaller roads, smooth paving gave way to cracked tarmac gave way to gravel and dust. Much of the drive was through a dense forest. The sky above me was opaque with tree branches that enclosed the road in a tunnel. In some places, a stone wall on either side was thickly covered in ivy, with an unforgiving few inches of clearance for my side-view mirrors.

The road eventually dead-ended at a fence. There I left my car and let myself through a gate. The fence demarcated where the thick forest ended, and where began the moors—that uniquely English, and uniquely evocative, landscape of low-lying scrubby vegetation.

The terrain rose with a gentle incline. As I walked up through the heather and broom, I passed anxious sheep, who bleated and backed away. Then I crested the hill. And before me, in the hazy late-afternoon sunlight, was the ultimate Dartmoor tableau.

Far ahead, at the low point of a broad basin in the moor, I saw the rocks of Scorhill Stone Circle. They rose from the green-brown turf like dragon's teeth, worn by the centuries to irregular nubs. The setting sun cast a spotlight on the circle, sending long, narrow shadows across the scruffy landscape. And nearby stood a pair of Dartmoor's famed wild ponies.

My step quickened as I carried on downhill toward the stones. The fence, my car, and the modern world disappeared beneath the rise behind me. To herald my arrival, the wild ponies pranced—they actually pranced!

Approaching the stones, I found myself holding my breath, like I was entering a grand cathedral or a cemetery. Nobody quite knows who erected these circles, or why. But there was no doubt that this was a special place.

I wandered quietly from stone to stone, touching each one to feel its rough texture, hearing only my own footsteps, a subtle wind, and the occasional snort of pony's breath. I thought back to a few days earlier, when a guide had driven me around the Penwith Peninsula, at the very tip of Cornwall—also known for its many stone circles and lines.

My guide had explained the concept of ley lines: invisible axes of perhaps magnetic, possibly metaphysical power that criss-cross Britain. Going back to prehistoric times, he said, people would follow these lines. Improvised footpaths became primitive, rocky roads, which eventually became the modern motorways of today. Without realizing it, people follow ley lines across Britain all the time.

The intersections of ley lines, he claimed, were particularly important. And often those intersections were considered sacred sites. A stone circle—like this one—might later become the site of a village church. And if that village grew, perhaps that church would become a cathedral. Again, modern Brits worship—and tourists snap photos—in places of prehistoric power.

He told me all of this as we stood in the nave of a tiny village church built of heavy, dark stone with narrow slits for windows. I was skeptical. But then he handed me two L-shaped metal rods, showed me how to hold them loosely in my fists, and told me to walk down the church's aisle toward the altar. And just as I reached the transept, an invisible force grabbed both rods and swiveled them in my hands until they crossed. The more I fought them, the harder they pulled.

Clearly, these were "tour guide stories"—pseudoscientific tales that would cause a real scientist to pull their hair out. My rational mind knew the movement of the rods was essentially a parlor trick. (Perhaps I was simply dowsing for water, and the rods found it under that church.) And yet, I couldn't shake the feeling that the rods sensed something I didn't.

I'm not saying I'm a believer in ley lines and the like. But I must admit that, in moments like this one, I enjoy suspending my skepticism and rolling with it. It's like going on a roller coaster or watching a scary movie: Even if you know you're not in mortal danger, the illusion is exciting. And there's just something about certain places—especially Britain, and Dartmoor and Cornwall in particular—that fires my imagination, temporarily unmooring it from rational thought.

Why would someone build a stone circle? You might as well ask: Why would someone build a cathedral, or a skyscraper? The mysteries of Dartmoor, and of prehistoric Britain, underlie everything that's modern and apparent. And if you're lucky, you may experience moments that hint at what's been just beneath the surface all along—like those rocks that nature revealed at Hound Tor.

I'd lost track of time. The sun was approaching the horizon, and I had a long and confusing drive back to Mo and John's place. I turned my back on the stones, nodded appreciatively to the ponies—who stood calmly, inquisitively, not fearfully, as they watched me leave—and headed up the hill back to my car.

As I hiked up and out of the moor, I thought about how one of the joys of travel is trying on different ideas, seeing how they fit, and deciding how to file them away in your constellation of beliefs. I am a logical person. But travel counterbalances that logic, in a way that feels healthy. In a world that craves decisiveness and clarity, travel fills me with the opposite.

Val d'Orcia, Italy

Waiting for Luciano's Knock

*I*n the heart of Tuscany, the stone farmhouse called Cretaiole floats like a mirage in an olive grove, overlooking the cypress-fringed hills just outside of Pienza.

Two decades ago, Isabella was an upwardly mobile city slicker from Milan, early in her career but already feeling burned out. On a winter getaway, she escaped for a week to this rustic farmhouse B&B. That's when she met the farmer's son, Carlo.

After a long-distance romance, they got married, and Isabella moved down to the farm. Isabella and the Moricciani clan initially clashed as she found her place in their traditional world. But eventually it became clear that this city mouse/country mouse union was ideal for the Italian concept of *agriturismo*: government-subsidized working farms that also provide accommodations, restaurants, or educational activities.

Cretaiole is the perfect expression of an *agriturismo*. Carlo and his father, Luciano, produce olive oil, wine, cured meats, eggs, and vegetables. Meanwhile, Isabella handles the *turismo* end of things, applying business savvy, a remarkable attention to detail, and a rare intuition for what travelers really want.

Each Saturday, about 20 visitors—mostly Americans—gather to begin a week-long stay in the cozy apartments that Isabella has

carved out of the antique farmhouse. Throughout the week, she orchestrates activities that balance cultural insight and comfort: pasta-rolling parties, truffle hunts, farm tours, olive oil appreciation classes, wine tastings, meaningful nature hikes, and so on.

Carlo is a farm boy. But, as evidenced by his marriage to a brilliant businesswoman, he's also smart and cultured. He's a certified olive oil taster—with a palate so refined, he has the papers to prove it. Still, Carlo is more at home on a tractor or trekking through the fields than in front of a group of Americans. One morning, during the weekly orientation session, Carlo fidgeted and glanced nervously at the encroaching clouds. Finally he asked Isabella's permission to be excused so he could go for his constitutional.

Cretaiole's resident cats are just how I like them: curious, playful, and starved for attention—they show up on your doorstep each morning to beg for burned toast. And the rest of the day, they camp outside your door, looking for any chance to slip inside. Once I asked Carlo what their names were. "They don't have names," he said flatly. "They're farm animals." Watching

Carlo affectionately play with the feline companions he refuses to christen, I came a little closer to understanding what it means to be a farmer.

Every night at around ten o'clock, there's a knock on the guest room doors. It's Old Man Luciano—Carlo's dad—inviting people down to the veranda for a nightcap. There's no point fighting it. Yes, you're tired from your busy vacation. But Luciano has been working the fields all day, and he's ready to party.

Trading pajama bottoms for jeans, you make your way to the glass-enclosed veranda. Luciano has laid out small plastic cups and bottles of his three homemade spirits: grappa (grape brandy), *limoncello* (Luciano's version is just grappa soaked in lemon rinds), and Vin Santo—the prized "holy wine" made with concentrated grapes, fortified with grappa, then aged in casks.

Luciano pours everyone their slug of choice and puts on his Sinatra records. As the sprits flow and Frank croons, Luciano nudges his guests to the dance floor. Emboldened by the Vin Santo—and by the Tuscan romance of it all—couples who haven't slow-danced in eons clutch each other and sway to the music. Occasionally Luciano cuts in for a dance of his own.

The old man, who speaks no English, loves to talk. Despite his guests' protests that they don't speak Italian, Luciano just keeps chattering away—making himself understood through meaningful eye contact, essentially willing his meaning into your mind.

Recently Luciano discovered the Google Translate app. So now, when he wants to convey a more complex point, he borrows someone's smartphone. He speaks into it with a measured, gentle ease—his voice submerging the phone in Italian charisma—as he gestures with his hands. After a pause, the phone spits out a rough translation in Siri-speak. It's a jarring juxtaposition. But, like the traditional-meets-modern mix of the *agriturismo*, it works.

Luciano is stubbornly old-fashioned. One of his relatives joked, "His idea of progress is getting two new sheep for the farm." Luciano may be the paterfamilias, but his daughter-in-law, Isabella, is the brains of the operation. By converting his farm into an *agriturismo*, she created a bridge between Luciano's old ways and a steady influx of visitors from the modern world. This has given Luciano a newfound purpose in life: getting to know people from faraway lands and sharing his traditions with them. This old dog is learning some new tricks, and loving it. Most of the time.

One November day, Luciano invited his *agriturismo* guests to participate in the olive harvest. A few hardy and curious souls showed up to put in a couple of hours' work: spreading out tarps under each tree, gently raking plump olives off spindly branches, then stooping over to gather them up.

At the day's end, as the sky became a deep purple, Luciano built a campfire in the grove. He pulled out a straw-wrapped bottle of homemade wine and cut slices of bread to toast on the open fire. He rubbed each crispy slice with garlic, drenched it in a generous dollop of his bright-green, fresh-pressed olive oil, and handed it around. "*Bruschetta,*" he said, holding up a piece. "This is the *real* peasant cuisine."

Luciano's exhausted work crew huddled around the fire and crunched into our reward for a hard day's work. But Luciano wasn't quite as impressed with us as we were with ourselves. He sat close to me and whispered, "Here's the thing about this *agriturismo* stuff: It's an awful lot of *turismo* and not nearly enough *agri.*"

Much as I love the curmudgeon, I disagree. I find Cretaiole perfectly in balance. Europe has a knack for preserving and sharing these pockets of traditional culture—connecting its agrarian roots with the modern, outside world. Luciano can grumble all he wants, but he can't hide how much he adores having a new set of visitors to befriend and ply with firewater each week. And he doesn't even have to learn English to do it.

* * *

At Cretaiole, Thursday night is pasta-making night. Guests return from a busy day of tooling around hill towns and wineries to make the local hand-rolled noodles, called *pici*.

Everyone packs into the veranda, squeezing behind tables with a hubbub of anticipation. In front of each small group is an oversized, rough-wood board with just the right texture for rolling noodles.

In one corner of the room, Isabella stands at a small table and addresses the group. Before her rises a 10-pound mountain of flour. She explains the procedure with the seasoned confidence of someone who's taught hundreds, maybe thousands, of travelers how to make perfect pasta.

First, she dredges out a crater in the top of her flour mountain, turning it into a volcano. Into the caldera she cracks eight eggs. With precision, she beats the eggs with a fork, gradually sprinkling in water—a few trickles at a time—as she pulls in more and more flour from the lip. With each stir, the sea of eggy goo threatens to breach its container. But gradually, imperceptibly, liquid becomes solid. And with one last vigorous stir, it's a mound of sticky dough.

It's time to knead. Isabella explains the importance of keeping the "cut"—or, in more pleasant terms, the "smile"—facing you at all times. After each knead, you rotate the dough a quarter-turn, then repeat. It's a steady, rhythmic, almost meditative motion—like waves crashing on a beach: Pull, push, push, rotate. Pull, push, push, rotate.

Each family huddles around their communal wad of dough, taking turns kneading. Isabella circulates through the room, gently correcting our technique. "Done?" someone asks. She sticks an accusing finger deep into the dough and withdraws a sticky fingertip. "Not done yet," she says. "Keep going."

Finally, it's time to make the pasta. *Pici* (pronounced "peechee") are peasant noodles—hand-rolled rather than extruded.

The technique is deceptively tricky: Cut off a hunk of dough, hold it in your left hand, and roll it with your right. Continually massage the dough with the heel of your hand against the cutting board, while gently tugging on the dough clump to tease out a strand. Too little pressure, and you create thick, inedible ropes. Too much pressure, and it breaks into bits. But if you do it right, you get a noodle shaped like a four-foot-long earthworm.

Families take turns rolling their *pici*, offering each other tips and encouragement. Some people go fast. Others go slow. Some pick up the technique immediately, cranking out long strands of uniform noodle. Others spend most of their time pinching together broken strands while nervously eyeing Isabella across the room.

In the garden shed outside, Isabella has brought a 20-gallon pot of water to a rolling boil. To season the noodles, Isabella pours three generous handfuls of coarse salt into the water. It tastes as salty as soup. Then she drops in the *pici*; they squirm around the bubbles like tiny, furious eels. In just five minutes—when the

water starts to foam up—it's al dente. Isabella tosses the *pici* with some meat *ragù* she's been simmering all day long, then takes the giant, overflowing, stainless-steel bowl back to the veranda.

We eat. The noodles we made are firm but tender, and each one clings to just the right amount of flavorful *ragù*, exactly as it was designed to do. Orgiastic *yummmmmm*s fill the veranda.

We're seated near Carlo, who's watching my wife Shawna dig into one of her favorite foods. He's appreciating how much she's appreciating the meal. He says something to Isabella, who translates: "Carlo says that many American women try to pretend they don't enjoy food. They talk about dieting all the time, don't want to eat too much. He likes how Shawna just doesn't care about this. She just lets herself enjoy it. We love this in Italy—we call it *buon gusto*." Carlo nods and smiles a charismatic smile. Shawna decides to take it as the compliment it was intended as, and unapologetically twirls another spindle of *pici* onto her fork.

Around the many small tables, lined up for one long serpentine Last Supper feast, the guests of Cretaiole chatter and drink and eat and laugh. Old Man Luciano walks through, carrying bottles of Vin Santo that he'll be sharing later in the evening. Once-strangers, now-friends discuss all they've experienced this week. Those glorious frescoes at Monte Oliveto Maggiore. The wonderful truffle hunt through the woods near San Giovanni d'Asso. That stunning scenery on the drive to Monticchiello. Those relaxing thermal baths in Bagno Vignoni. That coppersmith in Montepulciano. People swap the Italian words they've learned and the Italian gestures they've mastered.

Digging into our *pici*, we screw our index fingers into our cheeks, then wave our hand alongside our head: *Delizioso!* Time stands still around this convivial dinner table—so far from home, yet familiar—as we all celebrate whatever mysterious force brought Isabella and Carlo together . . . and took the rest of us along.

Acorns and Corncobs:
A Semester Abroad

*T*he first time I set foot in Europe was at Madrid-Barajas Airport in August of 1996, arriving for a semester abroad in the historic university town of Salamanca.

Our planeload of Ohio college students boarded a bus and drove three hours across the featureless Castilian plain to where Salamanca rose up like a mirage. The town center, draped over a gentle hill, bristles with steeples and is dominated by the husky buttresses and domes of its giant cathedral. The city exudes a desperation to assert how important it is, sorely overestimating how hard it is to be important when you're in the middle of nowhere.

Our bus was met by a contingent of host families, and I was introduced to the working-class couple in whose home I'd be living for the next few months. My host mother was animated and wildly expressive, lavishing me with welcomes. My host father, with a subversive yet good-natured smirk, seemed to have taken on, as his life's mission, counterbalancing his wife's exuberance. I introduced myself as Moisés—Moses, my middle name—which is what I go by in Spanish, because "Cameron" is perilously close to *camarón* ("shrimp").

We piled my bags into their tiny car and drove to their seventh-floor apartment, where I met three host brothers. The oldest one, Fran, was my age, and each of the others was two years younger than the last. My host grandmother (who would never say a word the entire time I was in Spain) smiled sweetly from her rigid-backed chair in the corner. It was lunchtime, so we all gathered around the big table that took up one-third of the living room.

After eating and unpacking, I headed out to explore. It was just a few minutes' walk to the ring road that surrounds the old city center. Inside this outer belt, Salamanca has a majestic air. Returning there recently, for the first time since college, confirmed my impression that Salamanca is the finest small city in Spain. Its handsome townhomes are built with a lemony sandstone, giving it a cohesive gentility. Its golden lanes and stunning main square are slathered with stone carvings so delicate and detailed they call them "silverwork-like" (*plateresco*).

I strolled those wide pedestrian streets, pulled along by the current of Salamantinos doing their *paseo*: aimless laps that are just an excuse to socialize and stretch your legs. We flowed past an enchanting array of storefronts, from glitzy chains to quirky curiosity shops. To this kid from Ohio, it all felt so . . . European.

Our classes, all in Spanish, covered local history, culture, language, art, and film. Our grammar professor was the favorite. He looked like a skinny, Spanish Mr. Bean, with glasses and a pencil moustache. And he had a sharp, wry, wicked wit. Many of his tongue-in-cheek examples involved his exaggeratedly strained relationship with his wife. To illustrate the subjunctive, he'd say, *"No te compré ese reloj para que lo pongas en una caja"* ("I did not buy you that watch so that you would put it in a box.") How can you tell that a teacher is effective? When you can still recall their lessons, word for word, decades later.

Sometimes our professor would call out a grammatically incorrect flourish that was common among less educated Spaniards. Invariably it was something I heard every single afternoon at the dining table.

I came to understand that, while some of my classmates lived in posh penthouses, my host family struggled financially. All three of my host brothers were in school; my host mother kept house and cooked; and my host father sat in the living room, day in and day out, wearing his rumpled cardigan and zoning out in front of the TV. Eventually they told me he'd lost his job quite some time before. While I may have been less comfortable than my classmates, this arrangement succeeded at pulling me out of my bubble to experience a life that was truly different.

As far as I could tell, the family's only sources of income were my host father's unemployment checks and the stipend they received for hosting me. I was their meal ticket. Therefore, my host mother treated me like a prince. I was the guest of honor, and her three sons were freeloaders she was burdened with.

Lunch—eaten as soon as I got home from class, around 1:30—was the big meal of the day, and on Sundays we shared a cauldron of *paella*. Being finicky about seafood, I ate the saffron rice but picked out the mussels and other sea critters. Looking back, I regret how long it took me to become a more adventurous eater.

Dinner was simpler, often eggs or a bowl of cereal. Once or twice each week, dinner consisted of a fried egg, a fried hot dog, and French fries. We'd go through a couple of bottles of cheap, weirdly sweet ersatz ketchup every week. Health food this was not.

I'd been warned that Spaniards curse a blue streak, but nothing could have prepared me for the torrent of obscenities that hung in a profane cloud above the table at each meal. Two favorite interjections, often used in conjunction, were ¡*Joder!* (our F-word) and ¡*Coño!* (a particularly unkind term for the female anatomy). These were sprinkled liberally into our every conversation, as if they had their own shaker next to the salt and pepper. "¡*Joder!* ¡*Coño!*" my host brother would exclaim. "Pass me the effing ketchup! ¡*Coño!*" In front of Mom. In front of Grandma!

Many Spaniards enjoy being out very, very late. At 11 p.m. or midnight, entire families strolled the streets with toddlers in tow. My family had hosted several students like me over the years, and most of them were aficionados of the late-night culture. Each Friday, my host mother would ask hopefully, "¿*Vas a marchar?*"—Are you going out partying? On my first weekend in town, I returned to the apartment around 1 a.m.—which, to me, seemed late. The next morning my host mother asked with great concern if I was feeling well. I told her I was fine. "Oh, such a relief! I was so worried when I heard you come home so very early last night."

The TV was never turned off. During lunch, we watched dubbed reruns of American sitcoms—mostly *Full House* and *The Fresh Prince of Bel-Air*. One time, just making conversation, I wondered aloud at the commercial break: What's going to happen next? My host brother cleared his throat, looked at me with grave seriousness, and said, "Carlton is going to cheat on the test, both he and Will get grounded, and Geoffrey quits but then comes back when Uncle Phil gives him a raise." It became clear they had seen each episode many, many times.

As an American, this embarrassed me. If we're exporting our culture to the world, I'm not sure I'd lead with these shows. Seeing long lines of Spaniards waiting in front of Burger King, however, I concluded that there's no accounting for taste, on either side of the Atlantic.

At dinnertime, it was variety and game shows. That fall, one out of every three Spaniards watched *La Parodia Nacional*, a weekly extravaganza in which a troupe of singers and dancers (with names like Tony las Vegas and Renata Tiramisú) performed original songs that parodied the latest headlines, with lyrics submitted by everyday Spaniards. The costumes were high camp, the performers hammed it up, and the jokes were recycled shamelessly.

The main purpose of this show appeared to be injecting new insults and stereotypes into the culture, and reinforcing old ones. I learned that, for Spanish men, being cheated on by your wife is the ultimate humiliation—and that, upon being cuckolded, a Spaniard sprouts literal horns from his temples. (I recently discovered a few episodes online, and *La Parodia Nacional* instantly shot to the top of my list of "Things That Have Not Aged Well.")

Nearing the end of my time in Salamanca, on a drizzly Saturday morning in November, my host family announced at breakfast: "Moisés, today we're going to *la granja*!"

It turns out, *la granja* was the family farm. The idea that my host family owned land was hard to fathom. Shoehorned into their tight apartment, they seemed pure urbanites. Piling into the family car—and jamming three of us in the tiny back-seat—they explained that *la granja* was a family property, going back generations.

When you leave Salamanca, there's no sprawl. It's just ten-story concrete apartment blocks, and then, abruptly, the lone-some expanse of Castile. After about an hour driving through sun-parched husks of crops, now rotting in the autumn damp, we drove up a gravel driveway.

My host brother, Fran, took me on a walk around the farm-stead. Leaves crunching beneath our feet, we passed through an oak grove. Fran rustled around in the undergrowth and pulled out an acorn.

"Ah, *bellota!*" he said with pride. "The *bellota* is so import-ant here. We feed them to pigs to make *jamón iberico de bellota.*" The ultimate Spanish staple is air-cured ham—*jamón*. And *jamón iberico de bellota* is the connoisseur's choice: made from black-footed pigs, freely roaming the forests of western Spain and feasting on a diet of top-quality acorns.

"The *bellota* is perfect nutrition," Fran said. "Even people eat it!" Noticing my failure to hide my disgust, Fran took a big, toothy bite of the acorn, finally managing to sever, chew, and swallow a tough chunk. "*Delicioso*," he said through a wince. He offered me a bite. Gamely, I bit into the nut, which flooded my mouth with an astringent cocktail of bitter and sour. All I could muster, through clenched teeth, was, "*¡Sí, fuerte!*"

Heading back toward the farmhouse, we passed a bin full of corn cobs. "Do you ever eat this?" I asked.

Fran grimaced and laughed. "Corn? Of course we don't eat corn. That's animal feed!" He shook his head and muttered to himself again, "Corn . . . ." In Ohio—where sultry summers push up towering stalks of corn—sweet corn on the cob, slathered in salty butter, is considered one of God's most precious gifts. I'll admit, I was a bit hurt . . . probably not unlike the way Fran felt when I balked at his acorn.

Then I thought about the *castañas* that vendors had just started roasting in rusted metal bins on the sidewalks of Salamanca. Back home we call them "buckeyes" and slap them on football helmets. But here, *castañas* are the roasted chestnuts of Christmas carol fame . . . filling the air with a seasonal aroma. And, unlike that acorn, they're delicious.

Returning to the farmhouse, my host father—who had changed into purple-stained denim overalls and a cockeyed trucker hat—announced he was ready for our help. He opened the door to a far-from-sanitary barn with a poured-concrete tub in the corner.

Wine in unlabeled bottles always flowed freely at the family dining table. They had told me it was *casero* ("homemade")—but until now, it never occurred to me that *they* were the ones who made it.

Fran pulled on a pair of rubber galoshes and climbed into the tub. His father began pouring in buckets of grapes, and Fran squashed them underfoot. Watching my host father make wine—using a method handed down across the generations, relying more on instinct than science—I suddenly recognized in him the soul of a farmer.

"Moisés, now it's your turn!" I pulled on the boots and started stomping. It was gratifying to watch the liquid trickle from the mash of skins and stems out the concrete spout and into a plastic bucket.

When the bucket was full of *mosto*, Fran's father poured it with precision into an opening in the top of an eons-old wooden cask. When all the grapes were stomped, he corked the cask, and we headed back to the car. "Now the grape juice ferments," my host father explained. "We'll come back next week to check on it."

As we returned home at the end of a long day on *la granja*, the mood was festive. After dinner, Fran turned to me and said, "Do you want to do shots?" The question surprised me—it was the first time they'd suggested this (and I'm not much of a drinker).

Noticing my puzzled expression, Fran said, "It's something special. It's like a sweet liqueur—but it has no alcohol." This only made me more confused.

"It was a gift from Melanie," Fran finished. This drew excitement and fond nods from the family around the table. "¡Sí! ¡Sí! Melanie! ¡Qué buena chica! Melanie was one of our host students, from *el estado de* Vermont."

Still not quite sure what I was agreeing to, I watched Fran go to the liquor cabinet and return with a leaf-shaped bottle. "*Delicioso,*" he promised with a wink, as he opened the bottle and poured the viscous, amber liquid into shot glasses. We all picked up our glasses, raised them in a toast, and slugged them down. A familiar sensation filled my mouth: maple syrup.

"*¡Uf! Me repite*," Fran said, wheezing and burping—like he'd just slammed a slug of *aguardiente*. I stifled a laugh and was about to explain that people don't usually drink maple syrup straight. But quickly, I realized that it doesn't matter what Vermonters do with maple syrup. My Spanish family's improvised custom brought them joy. Who was I to tell them they were wrong?

A semester abroad is intensely formative for those of us privileged enough to experience one. Living in a place where people eat acorns, only animals eat corn on the cob, and a family celebrates with shots of maple syrup helped set me on the road to becoming a temporary European.

Jams Are Fun

It's Gonna Be a Noisy Night

Of the 11 million people living in Tokyo, it seemed like
5 million of them must have been in the airport that night.
—Mildred C. Scott, *Jams Are Fun*

I am an inveterate insomniac. It's hard to imagine a worse malady for a travel writer. (Xenophobia, maybe?) While I sleep well enough in my own bed, I struggle with getting a solid night's sleep on the road. And, it seems precisely because I am such a light sleeper, I am a magnet for nighttime noise.

Late at night or early in the morning, the bar next door disgorges its rowdy customers onto what had been a serene street. Or my neighbors come back from a late dinner and crank up the volume on their TV. Or a prewar elevator grinds its way up the shaft immediately on the other side of the wall from my bed . . . and, even with my head burrowed under a pillow, I can feel the gears trundle over each rusty bolt.

The solution might seem elegantly simple: Request a quiet room. Which I do, repeatedly—when I reserve; when I call to confirm the day before; and when I arrive at the hotel. And yet, by fluke or by fate, I often wind up with a very noisy night.

(Side note: When you ask for a quiet room, and they smile sweetly and say, "All of our rooms are quiet," what they really mean is, "None of our rooms are quiet." And when they say, "We are in the very center, so you have to expect a little noise," they're actually saying, "We totally cheaped out on the windows.")

Some parts of Europe—ahem, Iberia—have a different (or nonexistent) understanding of "quiet." People live their lives against a steady soundtrack of buzzing motor scooters and rumbling buses and late-night revelers, to the point where they just don't hear it anymore.

Once I checked into a downtown Lisbon hotel where the clerk offered me two room choices, while prodding me toward his idea of the better option: the one with the view. I inspected both rooms. Sure enough, one looked out over a picturesque street— but every time a bus went by, the windows rattled. The other one faced an interior courtyard, with a view of ugly HVAC venting, but blessedly silent. When I told the receptionist my choice, he was stunned. I explained that the buses would keep me awake, and he said, "Wow. It must be very quiet where you live!"

On another trip, upon arriving in Spain, I toughed out three noisy, sleepless nights in a crummy small-town hotel. From there I headed to Madrid, determined to change my luck. My room was spartan but acceptable, and it overlooked a quiet courtyard. My dream of finally getting over jet lag, it seemed, was nearing reality.

That night, I returned to my guesthouse around midnight and heard the loudest snoring of my life. The banshee's howl echoed throughout the linoleum-lined hallways, all the way to the front door. As I curled around the corridor to my room, the noise got louder and—unbelievably—louder still, until I realized it was coming from the room next to mine. Lying in bed, I could hear the snoring through the wall; I could hear the snoring echoing out into the halls and back through my flimsy door; and I could even hear the snoring bouncing around the courtyard and through my window. Earplugs stood no chance.

Waking up the next morning (can it truly be called "waking up" when you've barely slept?), I found a dead-silent Hilton down the street and splurged on their last available room. When I explained the situation to the guesthouse owner, he said, "Yeah, I don't blame you one bit. *En mi vida*, I have never heard anything like that. Those people need a doctor."

On a recent trip to Hungary, I had yet another frustrating "noisy room" experience. While this actually happened exactly as described, it also serves as a sort of Platonic ideal of that moment when, upon checking in, you realize it's gonna be a noisy night.

Stepping up to the reception desk on a sunny Saturday afternoon, I give them my name and say, "I mentioned this in my reservation—can I please be assigned a quiet room?"

"Oh. Hm," the receptionist says, scrunching up her face, pondering an unsolvable riddle, tap-tap-tapping on her keyboard. "Well, you see, today we have a wedding."

"Ah," I say. Having read online reviews, I know all too well about this hotel's epic wedding parties. Which is why I asked for a quiet room. Months ago.

Working very hard to reassure me—and failing—she continues: "So, the wedding is on the first floor."

"O . . . K . . . " Waiting for the other shoe to drop.

"Buuuut," she continues, looking up from her keyboard with a triumphant smile, "your room is on the *second* floor."

Wondering whether numbers work the same here in Hungary, I glance at the mailbox-like key caddy behind her. I can see that the hotel has five floors and, sure enough, the second one is directly above the first one. "Hm. Well, do you not have anything on a higher floor?"

"No, unfortunately, we are full house tonight. We have the wedding. Plus we have two groups."

"Hm."

"However," she begins helpfully, "your room is at the opposite end of the hall from the wedding. So I hope you will not have problems. And if you do, you can just . . . call." She gestures toward the phone at the reception desk.

"So," I say, "If it's midnight, and I'm trying to sleep, and someone's wedding music has a thumping bassline, all I have to do is call the reception desk, and you will immediately bring the proceedings to a halt and circulate among the guests, individually shushing them until they are all speaking in barely audible whispers?"

"Yes, of course!" she replies cheerfully. "That is always our policy here at Good Sleep Despite Wedding Hotel."

"Marvelous!" I exclaim.

"And then, in the wee hours of the morning," she continues graciously, "I will personally scale the bell towers of nearby churches to remove clappers from any early-morning bells, lest they disturb your rest. Once stationed in the belfry, I will employ my silenced sniper rifle to dispatch any chirping birds near your window. With these tried-and-true methods, we can guarantee you the highest quality of sleep."

Except she doesn't say that. And I don't either. We both know what she really means: If you need to scream at somebody—without results—at 2 in the morning, she'll take the abuse. And then I'll just toss and turn furiously for another hour or two, until the party subsides just before dawn . . . with its pesky church bells and birdsong.

Knowing I've been beat, I take my keys, hang my head, and sulk up to my room. On the way, I pass a DJ hand-trucking his amplifier toward the ballroom, and another guy hauling up crates of jostling beer bottles.

To their credit, they have located me as far as they could from the wedding party—while still being just one floor above. (Seriously, guys?) However, looking out the window, I realize that in order to get me away from the wedding, they've situated me overlooking the town's main walking street. Opening the window, I hear the mellow hubbub of pedestrians, plus a street violinist who seems to be slowly executing an elderly cat. It's mostly pleasant now (cat killer aside)—at seven o'clock. But this is a college town. On a Saturday night. On the final weekend of nice summer weather. By midnight, I assume, a rave will break out 20 feet below my bed.

At that very moment, I begin to hear a thumping bass beat vibrating through the walls. The wedding DJ must be warming up. But no—it's coming from the other direction. It's coming from *outside the hotel.* Sticking my head out the window and craning my neck, I can just barely see the main square, just a block away. Something's going on there.

Heading out to investigate, I find the square filled with a commotion that seems excessive even for a Saturday night. They're throwing some sort of wine harvest festival. Food stalls are grilling up meat and potatoes and onions. Just then, a DJ mounts the big stage, grabs the microphone, and introduces an old Britney Spears song. It's loud. No, I mean *REALLY LOUD.* The bass vibrates through my back molars, and my eardrums start to tingle.

"This is just the beginning!" the DJ shouts to the crowd. "We're gonna keep this party rockin' ALL! NIGHT! LONG!"

My ultimate "noisy night" experience has already gone down in the city lore of Dubrovnik, Croatia. A particularly conscientious local resident, whom I'll call Karlo, rents some of the nicest rooms in town. Karlo is a perfectionist who does everything with care and professionalism. The moment I saw his rooms, I knew that my readers would love the place.

They did. So much, in fact, that Karlo's rooms started to book up months ahead. Over the next few years, I would email Karlo before each visit, hoping to have a firsthand experience staying at his place. Each time, he apologized profusely for being fully booked.

Finally, Karlo's best room happened to be available for my five-night stay. I looked forward to it for weeks, and Karlo was even more excited than I was. When I checked in, he fussed around earnestly, making sure I had everything I needed, eager to ensure my stay was a pleasant one.

The room was, in a word, great. It was neatly appointed with style and comfort in mind. It had a beautiful view, through green-shuttered windows, of Dubrovnik's orange rooftops. It even had its own private garden to relax in—almost unheard-of in this tight and congested town.

That first night, I fell into bed and immediately drifted off into a very deep sleep.

About four o'clock in the morning, I awoke with a start. I perked up my ears—hermetically sealed with earplugs—and couldn't hear a thing. But I *felt* something. A rumble, inside the wall or floor, sending sound waves up the leg of my bed, through the mattress, through the pillow, and through my earplugs. I did my best to ignore it. But after two or three hours of tossing and turning, I got up and began my day.

Later that morning, I bumped into Karlo, who was staking out my room to check up on me. He asked how I'd slept. I didn't want to upset him, but I thought maybe, just maybe, there was something he could do to address the noise. So I told him.

His excitement turned to self-flagellation. He was, of course, aghast. He apologized profusely (his go-to move), said he had no idea what was making the noise, and pledged to look into it.

Night Two: I slept like a rock. Until four in the morning, when I was again reverberated awake.

Karlo—obsessed with the situation—tracked me down the next morning, and I admitted that it had happened again. Still aghast, still apologizing profusely, Karlo spent much of the day visiting each of his neighbors, and the nearby buildings, to track down the source of the noise.

Night Three: At this point, I was becoming something of a connoisseur of the noise—the sensation, really—that had become my nightly four-o'clock companion. Having given up on sleep, I grew Zen about exploring the contours of The Noiseless Noise. It felt like having a tooth drilled while numbed by Novocain—but, critically, without actually *hearing* the drill. Just feeling that steely bit whirring deeper and deeper into an unfeeling tooth. Sensing its persistent vibration throughout your body, concentrating in the center of your brain where, finding nowhere else to go, it can only *be*.

Karlo, now fully apoplectic, continued his quest even after I told him, in no uncertain terms, not to worry about it anymore.

"Karlo," I said, "it's really OK. It's not your fault. I can deal with it. These things happen."

"No!" Karlo said defiantly. "It's not OK! It! Is! Not! O! K! Being in your book has changed my life. Changed! My! Life! Everyone who stays here loves it. And I am mortified that you finally stay at my place and you cannot sleep! It is unacceptable! I will find the answer, I swear to you!"

Night Four: It happened again. I'll spare the details because it was identical to the first three nights, only worse because I was now working on a cumulative 20 hours of sleep over four days.

At this point Karlo had interrogated everyone who lived in earshot of his building. And I think he was starting to suspect that I was making it up. Maybe he feared that I had some neurological condition whose symptoms include phantom vibrations. And to be honest, I was beginning to wonder the same thing.

Night Five: Miraculously, my four o'clock friend never showed up. However, I had to get up early regardless to pick up my rental car for a long road trip through Bosnia-Herzegovina, so the unexpected silence bought me only a couple extra hours of sleep.

Karlo, who'd offered to drive me to the rental car office, met me outside my front door.

"Cameron!" he practically shouted when he saw me. "There was no noise last night, was there?"

"No! It was wonderful."

"Aha! I finally solved the mystery." Karlo's downstairs neighbors, three floors below me at the base of the building, had hired plumbers for some remodel work. The plumbers decided that—because the apartment was uninhabited anyway—they could make some extra income by doing the work in the dead of night. And so, each morning at four o'clock, a couple of overly earnest tradesmen showed up and began drilling and drilling and drilling into the wall 30 feet below my head.

"This is, of course, completely against city regulations!" Karlo swore. "Don't worry! They will never do something like this again. The next people who stay in that room will have total silence!"

Privately failing to take solace in the good fortune of others, I reassured him again that I completely understood and did not hold him responsible. Even so, Karlo apologized ten more times during the five-minute drive to the rental car office, then sent me three more emails that week with more apologies. "Dear Cameron, I continue to ache with regret about the inconvenience caused . . . "

Over the course of that trip, the tale of the early-morning plumbers spread like wildfire through the Balkans. In each town I visited in Bosnia, Croatia, and Slovenia, local friends told me, "Hey, I heard about your room in Dubrovnik. Karlo feels *terrible*."

In Romania, Everything
Is (Not) Possible

Making Travel Television

*I*n a threadbare hotel room, Rick Steves sprawls on the
bed, propped up against the headboard, laptop on his
belly. Simon, Karel, and I sit in a semicircle around the
bed, squirming in our hard wooden chairs, watching Rick roll
words around in his mouth. Were the Hungarians "rulers" or
"overlords" of Transylvania? Was Vlad Țepeș a prince or a duke?
And, to describe Nicolae Ceaușescu, what's another word for
"megalomaniac"?

We're in the middle of nowhere. More specifically, we're in
Maramureș—Romania's remote northwest corner, where horse
carts outnumber cars and Ukraine looms just across the river. We've
come all this way, ten hours on potholed roads from Bucharest, to
film a TV show. But it's been pouring rain for two days straight.
And so, even though we fly home in just 24 hours, we're killing
time. First we shot everything we could indoors. Then we shot
everything we could under umbrellas, tiptoeing through six inches
of mud and goat dung. And now we're "scrubbing the script" while
praying for sun.

The clacking of keys ceases. And in the silence, the same
awareness dawns on all of us: No more raindrops. We look to the

window, where a sunbeam tries to punch through clouds as dense and as dark as a Maramureş peasant's felt vest. Buoyed by adrenaline (and an immovable deadline), we scramble to load up our gear and chase down some sunshine.

I've worked on several episodes of the public television series *Rick Steves' Europe*—scouting, scripting, and field-producing. Like guidebook research, making travel television is unglamorous, difficult work. Especially in Romania, where we filmed in 2016.

Romania is a special place. And I use that word in its most loaded sense. After exploring Eastern Europe for two-plus decades, I've yet to find anywhere that can match Romania—in complexity, in fascination, in its capacity to frustrate. I blame Nicolae Ceauşescu, that, yes, megalomaniacal dictator who completed his regime in front of a firing squad. Traveling in Romania, it's clear that Ceauşescu really did a number on this place. And, more than 30 years after his death, people are still scarred from that trauma.

If it seems cruel to "punch down" at a troubled place like Romania, I assure you that I am merely an agent of karma. This country confused, abused, and discarded us, all for the crime of promoting them on American broadcast television. Besides, Romania derives masochistic pleasure from punching down at itself. Being a "temporary Romanian" means being exasperated with Romania. The unofficial national motto is "Such a beautiful place. Such a pity it's inhabited."

Rick Steves personally writes most episodes of his TV series. But in cases where he's unfamiliar with the destination, he turns to me for help. Since I'd recently spent time in Romania, Rick asked me to return and sort out which sights, experiences, and nuggets of history and culture should make the cut, and then shape all of that into 30 minutes of television.

My first step was contacting the Romanian Ministry of Tourism. Within minutes of emailing them, I received an enthusiastic phone call from someone I'll call Silvia. She was a fan, and pledged to help make the show a success. Little did I know that Silvia—and every other Romanian we would meet—are pawns in a game that nobody really controls.

Silvia offered to set up a scouting trip, so I sent her our ambitious agenda, ranging hundreds of miles across the country: Bucharest, Transylvania, Bucovina, Maramureş. But as the date of my arrival crept closer, details were conspicuously sparse. The day before my trip, I finally received a partial list of hotels, and not much else.

I landed at the airport of Cluj-Napoca, a regional capital in Transylvania. I was met by a pair of young and eager helpers: Cristofor, a tour guide, was upbeat as a puppy dog. Later he would tell me that he feels most at home in nature—taking his wife and kids on multi-day hiking expeditions through the Carpathians. Andrei, our driver, seemed quick to toggle between jovial and serious. Both were disproportionately excited to meet me; the moment Cristofor and I shook hands, Andrei snapped our photo like I was a visiting dignitary. They pledged to help me in whatever way they could. "Everysing is possible!" Cristofor said gamely, with a broad smile.

There remained, however, an air of mystery. I asked Cristofor for a printout of our day-to-day plan, to ensure it matched my wish list. "Everysing is possible!" he reassured me. "But the one I have is rough. Please, let us wait until it is finalized, and I will give you a copy." But he never did, nor would he let me peek at the thick packet of papers he referred to all day long. It seemed I was in hands other than my own. And those hands had an agenda, unforgivingly rigid and known to everyone but me.

We planned to film some of the many fortified churches scattered across Transylvania, each one originally belonging to a community of Germanic settlers who left after World War II. Stepping into one of these fortresses of God, you feel you've traveled back in time to a medieval German world. Silvia had arranged visits to two or three churches, but I had a different church in mind.

"Everysing is possible," Cristofor said. Then he began conversing in Romanian with Andrei. This quickly escalated into a heated argument. Finally Cristofor said, "OK! It's not in the plan but I think we can make it fit, if you don't mind getting to the hotel a little later tonight." "Thanks," I said. "Everysing is possible!" he replied.

This happened frequently: Cristofor would announce our next stop in real-time. I'd request a change. And Cristofor and Andrei would go nine rounds in furious Romanian. Then Cristofor would smile and say, "Everysing is possible!"

The resolution was never a replacement; my request was simply tacked on to an already overstuffed agenda. The days were exhaustingly long. We'd pull up to the hotel at 8 or 9 each night and eat a huge Romanian peasant dinner of fatty meat and heavy starch, leaving me no time or energy to write up the day's scouting before I collapsed into bed. I kept careful notes and vowed to type them up as soon as I got home.

Something else strange kept happening. When we'd pull up to a sight, Cristofor would ask me to pause out front so that Andrei, our very own paparazzo, could snap our photo.

On a particularly overprogrammed afternoon, Cristofor began telling me about our next stop: a salt mine that had been converted into a health spa. We were already running a couple of hours late. And our schedule mandated a lengthy tour of the complex.

This was the breaking point. I know what makes for good TV. And an underground health spa—aging bodies lying still in the dark—isn't it. Besides, they'd already shown me enough of Romania to fill five or six mind-numbing hours of television.

"No," I said. "No, no, no. No way. I do not need to see that. Please. I'm exhausted. I have all of the information I need and more. Can we please, please just go to the hotel?"

"Everysing is possible!" Cristofor proceeded to have one of his knock-down-drag-outs with Andrei. This one was epic, as they spat angry rejoinders at each other as if I weren't there, for maybe ten minutes. Finally Cristofor dusted himself off and said, "OK! Here is a compromise. We will take you to the spa. It's not far—maybe ten, fifteen minutes out of the way. You get out of the car so we can take a photograph. And then we move on. OK?"

And that's what we did: Drove to the spa entrance. Bought a ticket. Took a very staged-looking photo of Cristofor and me shaking hands, like Nixon and Elvis. And then, mercifully, we were on our way.

As we drove on, I leveled with them: "Guys, I know you want to help me. But this just isn't working. You're running me ragged around this huge country with no regard for what will actually improve the show. You fight constantly, and I have no idea why."

They softened. And I finally got some answers. It turns out, Romania's new government was waging a war on corruption. The Ministry of Tourism was a public institution, and my scouting trip was funded by taxpayers. Silvia had the unenviable task of weaving together an itinerary that satisfied a wide range of stakeholders across the country—taking my wish list into account, but also assuaging many other interests.

Once that itinerary had been set, every element of the trip was opened up to auction. Each hotel stay, each museum admission, each meal that I experienced had been awarded to the lowest bidder. Cristofor and Andrei were legally obligated to ensure that I went to every single prescribed stop. If I wanted to "skip" something, it raised the possibility that someone was pocketing the money spent on getting me through that door. And so everything had to be meticulously documented with photographic evidence.

In an instant, my exasperation with Cristofor and Andrei—with all of Romania, really—melted into sympathy. Cristofor was Mommy, trying to give me what I wanted. Andrei was Daddy, the enforcer tasked with fulfilling the trip's legal requirements. It's no wonder they spent the trip bickering. They—and I—were all trapped in a Kafkaesque quagmire much bigger than any of us. They were doing their best amid a maddening situation. Which, come to think of it, could be another national motto for Romania.

I have a mental image of some hulking, concrete, peeling-plaster government ministry on a gloomy back street in Bucharest. Deep in its labyrinth of dusty halls is a filing cabinet. In that filing cabinet is a folder with my name on it. And in that folder, paper-clipped to a sheaf of documents, is a stack of photographs. The subject of each photo is the same: Cristofor, smiling his shit-eating "Everysing is possible" grin. And me, looking like an exhausted deer in headlights.

Back at the home office for the winter, I finally had time to write the script. First, I transcribed my reams of notes, then I put all of those options into a centrifuge and distilled it to the best 3,200 words. Except it wasn't 3,200 words—it was more like 5,000.

Rick and I briefly considered two episodes on Romania instead of one. But our viewers want us to be selective. We agreed: One tight, "best of" show was the smart strategy. That meant we had to cut some strong material. Bucovina and its glorious painted monasteries, which I'd spent two days scouting, were jettisoned.

We emerged with a "shooting script." This is a blueprint, but only a rough one. Until the final voice track is recorded—weeks after the episode is shot—the script is a living, evolving organism. As we film, we continually reconsider, refine, and rewrite.

We spent that spring in preproduction, arranging the details for the shoot. We got in touch with our favorite local guides and booked our preferred hotels. And we entrusted Silvia with the critical task of obtaining permissions. You can't just show up at a museum or a church and start filming. And in Romania, so shackled by a bloated and illogical bureaucracy, this would be especially important.

By early summer, we were ready to begin filming. On a layover at the Frankfurt airport—me coming from Salzburg, them coming from Seattle—I met up with our producer, Simon Griffith, and our cameraman, Karel Bauer. They were weary from their redeye, but unflappably eager to start exploring a country that was new to them.

Simon is the silent, bearded man viewers often see at the dinner table with Rick. As the series producer, he's both the brains and the brawn behind well over one hundred episodes of *Rick Steves' Europe*. He knows just what makes for good TV and helps Rick (and me) whittle down all those "great ideas." Simon hails from New Zealand and is the best possible version of a Kiwi—which is to say, an easygoing perfectionist. Simon is also generous with a laugh, a superb conversationalist, and a great traveler. If Rick's scriptwriting, on-screen performance, travel savvy, and enthusiasm are a churning sea of creativity, Simon is the steady hand on the rudder that keeps each episode pointed at the horizon.

Karel Bauer, one of our camera operators (or "shooters"), is—like Simon—equal parts artist, technician, and athlete. I've watched Karel scale rusty rungs welded to a granite cliff, then

hang on with one hand while capturing a "high-wide" with the other. For one challenging-to-film sequence—which opened our Romania show—Karel hung out the window of our van to film Rick riding a horse cart, while Simon held onto Karel's belt with one arm and steered with the other. And yet, Karel also has the soul of a painter, with an eye for composing shots that capture exactly the right details and mood.

We touched down in Bucharest, zipped to our hotel, unpacked the gear, and—all too aware that our sunny afternoon could turn into a rainy tomorrow—immediately headed out to film, jet lag be damned. It takes six days to make a 30-minute TV show. That may sound like a lot of time, but it feels rushed.

Filming a travel TV show is all about "covering the script"— every landmark, every idea, every word that's mentioned must be supported by visuals. We do that by shooting "b-roll": establishing shots, scenery, details, works of art, slice-of-life scenes, and so on.

Each shot has to "read": It must effectively illustrate what's being described. For example, scouting in Bucharest, I noticed that passersby, when walking in front of an Orthodox church, would pause in the street just long enough to make the sign of the cross. But this intimate gesture was too subtle for our camera; it didn't read.

And so we bailed on that detail. We call this "killing our babies"—giving up on ideas that don't work, or don't fit. It's a gruesome metaphor in the arts, but apt. If we're sweeping through the script to tighten things up, we start calling each other "King Herod."

The counterpoint of killing babies is positive serendipity: capturing a magic moment on the fly. Keeping the script flexible allows the best show to present itself. On a previous shoot in Croatia, we were walking through the floodlit main square of a hill town after dinner when we heard a chorus of heavenly voices through an open window. Tracing the music to its source, we discovered a practice of the town's choir performing traditional a capella folk songs. It became a highlight of that episode.

The majority of any episode is b-roll. The rest is establishing the host on location: Rick talking to the camera, exploring a museum, interacting with locals, and so on. Most of the audio is "voiceover" (or "VO")—when Rick's disembodied voice narrates what's on screen. This is recorded in a studio long after the footage is shot.

But when Rick speaks directly to the viewer, it's called an "on-camera" (or "OC"). We typically use on-cameras to cover a topic that's difficult to convey visually. (When describing a larger-than-life historical figure, like Nicolae Ceaușescu or Vlad Țepeș, you can only lean so heavily on archival photos or paintings.) Once filmed, an on-camera can't be changed. Rick is a master of putting each one into exactly the right words, then memorizing it on the spot. He sits cross-legged in a quiet corner, murmuring the lines to himself, while Simon and Karel set up the shot. By the time they're ready, usually he is, too.

This also means he has to nail all those foreign words. One afternoon, Rick and I stood together in a Bucharest park as I coached him. "Repeat after me: chow-SHESS-koo . . . chow-SHESS-koo . . . chow-SHESS-koo . . ."

When filming an on-camera, we do as many takes as necessary to ensure that Rick's performance, the audio, the background, the light, and everything else is perfect. If there are shadows on Rick's face, Simon pulls out a lightweight LED unit or a collapsible reflector disc and aims it just so, often standing on tiptoes, holding his arms in the air ("like a mighty tree trunk," he jokes).

Background noise is a constant concern. One evening, with the sun low in the sky, we found the perfect wheat field where Rick could stand to describe this land's ancient inhabitants. The catch: It was next to a highway where semi trucks intermittently rumbled past. The challenge: Could Rick deliver his lines in a gap between trucks? (Yes, he did . . . eventually.) On another occasion, I had to ask a jackhammer crew to take their break early, and bought them a round of beers for their trouble.

The outtakes at the end of each episode are rife with examples of flubbed lines, badly timed background noise, or passersby looking awkwardly at the camera. With so many potential screwups, on-cameras are the most time-consuming bits to film. One 15-second on-camera can be shot in just a few minutes, if all goes well . . . or closer to an hour, if it doesn't.

When filming, two overriding concerns are time and weather. Two expressions are used liberally: If a spell of sunny weather helps us get ahead of the game, we are "in a commanding position." Killing time waiting for rain to clear up is, in the parlance of a frustrated film crew, "getting boned by the weather." Used in a sentence: "If we hustle and work ahead in covering the script, we'll be in a commanding position. That way, if we get boned by the weather tomorrow . . . it's no big deal."

TV insiders are stunned to learn that we film a 30-minute show in six days with a crew of just three people—including the host. This is possible only because Simon and Karel both wear multiple hats. Even when they have an extra pair of hands (mine), there's not much I can do to make things easier . . . just get out of the way and try to keep up.

Simon personally lugs heavy gear all over Europe (a task usually relegated to an entry-level "grip"). When done shooting, Karel lifts up his camera. Simon quickly collapses the tripod and perches it on his shoulder, then puts on a backpack filled with another 20 or 30 pounds of sound and lighting equipment and carries it all to the next shot—all while talking through the script with Rick.

Meanwhile, along with shooting, Karel also handles sound. In addition to the camera-mounted mic, Rick always wears a hidden microphone (taped under his shirt). If the scene involves dialogue with someone else—such as a local guide or a market vendor—we mic up that person, too. And then, while he's filming, Karel is listening to the audio track through headphones to ensure it's clean and usable.

Watching this team in action is inspiring. While Rick sits in the car, tinkering with the script, Simon and Karel haul their gear out into a field. There Simon stands—like an artist at his easel—next to Karel, offering gentle direction. If anyone has earned the right to be jaded, it's these two. But they love what they do, are fully present in Europe, and it shows. Their relaxed smiles open more doors than any

amount of paperwork. When they're done shooting, they pause for a moment just to take in the beauty around them (and often pull out their iPhones to snap a photo for their personal reel). And when Rick finishes interviewing a local guide for the camera, Simon and Karel quiz the guide with follow-up questions.

As filming got underway, it became clear that my scouting trip had been just an appetizer of the perpetual torment that Romania had in store for us.

We all have that co-worker or acquaintance who's an irredeemable asshole. And then we learn that they are having serious troubles at home. It makes their toxicity, if not acceptable, understandable. Frustrations soften. Annoyances become endearing. But then they do something—again—that infuriates you. Empathy only forgives so much. An asshole is still an asshole.

But here's the thing: The Romanians themselves weren't assholes; it was Romania, collectively. The individuals we met and worked with were, almost to a person, gracious, helpful, and capable. They tried to assist us—they really did. But ultimately, all of them answered to a higher power, and that power relished saying "no."

On our first evening in Bucharest, tourism bigwigs threw us a blowout welcome dinner. Over the bacchanalia of traditional Romanian food and drink, our contacts broke the news that the Palace of Parliament, which we were planning to film the next morning, was a no-go.

Romania's Palace of Parliament, the biggest building in Europe, was the pet project of communist dictator Nicolae Ceauşescu. To tell the story of this darkest stain on Romania's history, we felt it essential to film the palace's vast and opulent interior—which Ceauşescu spared no expense to slather with lavish decor, even as his own people starved to death.

Lacking formal permission, our contacts suggested that we try showing up anyway. We could buy a tourist ticket, they spitballed, and send in Karel with the regular tour to film it on the fly.

The next morning, we were greeted at the Parliament's visitor entrance by a half-dozen tourism officials—effectively powerless, but there to cheer us on as we flouted their own regulations. We bought a ticket for Karel, who slung his DSLR around his neck and headed inside to "play tourist" and sneak some footage. Rick, Simon, and I nervously waited with the entire delegation outside. After just a few minutes, Karel walked out the door. "I got kicked off the tour," he shrugged. Nothing could be done.

We regrouped and began filming other sights around Bucharest. A few hours later, as Rick was shooting an on-camera with the Parliament in the distant background, my phone rang.

"I am sorry to say there was a misunderstanding," came the voice of Silvia. "But we have now obtained permission, and you may go film at the Parliament."

We didn't buy it. Rick was giving me the "don't do it!" gesture. "Are you certain we have official permission to film?"

"Yes."

"With our big camera?"

"Yes."

"And with our tripod?"

"Yes."

"Complete access?" Now I was just pressing my luck.

"Yes, of course."

"Do we have to join a tour?"

"No, you may go wherever you like. They will provide you with your own guide. In fact, do not go to the tourist entrance. Go to the parliamentarians' entrance."

Still skeptical, we hopped a taxi back to the Parliament. And there, at the special entrance reserved for members of the Romanian government and visiting dignitaries, we were warmly greeted by a literal red carpet and a press secretary. Sure enough, we had the run of the place, hours after being ejected.

Well into the process, we learned that there was much concern within the Ministry of Tourism about our filming plans. Apparently, a different travel TV personality had filmed a show in Romania a few years earlier. It did not go well. We were told that the presenter—known for his snark and his sharp tongue—grew exasperated with bureaucratic snafus and took it out on Romania, portraying the country as a backwards wasteland. The tourist authority was terrified that we, too, would show Romania in an unflattering light. And so—as if to guarantee the very thing they feared—they exerted heavy-handed control. And their paranoia bred paranoia in us.

Another point of consternation, we learned, was our intention to include a segment on Romania's sizable Roma population. Anyone who drives through Romania sees Roma living in shantytowns on the "other side of the tracks" from many towns and villages. Our goal was to present a balanced view of the Roma experience—not limited to that stereotype of poverty, but also getting to know some Roma people and hearing about their lives.

During my scouting trip, my repeated requests to establish contact with representatives of the Roma community invariably came up short. Meetings were (purportedly) arranged, then "fell through" at the last minute, with a shrug of "Well, that's Gypsies for ya!" (The third time Cristofor told me that one of these meetings was cancelled, I couldn't resist pointing out that, apparently, not *everything* is possible.)

Fortunately, one of our local guides recognized that the Roma community is more than a shameful blemish on the nation's reputation. He brought us to meet Emil, the kind and well-spoken paterfamilias of a Roma family living on the outskirts of a workaday Transylvanian village. Emil's family earns a living through the traditional Roma craft of metalworking. As we spent the morning getting to know the family, filming their lives, and hearing about their experience in their own words, we got choked up at having this opportunity to humanize an often-misunderstood population to our American viewers.

Some of our best footage came from the rugged northwestern fringe of Romania: Maramureş, unquestionably the most authentic traditional culture in Europe. Many people here still live much as their medieval ancestors did. We dropped in on a family of weavers, and the daughter greeted us warmly and demonstrated her loom. As we set up the camera, she disappeared for a few moments, then reappeared wearing a pristine, starched, traditional costume. We politely asked if she'd mind changing back into the skirt and sweatshirt she'd been wearing when we met her. She agreed, and that's why the segment feels real—which it was—rather than staged.

We survived the shoot and returned home with a hard drive loaded up with all that hard work. That's when Steve Cammarano takes over. Steve has edited every single one of the more than one hundred episodes of *Rick Steves' Europe*.

In the field, Simon and Karel always have Steve's concerns in mind, providing him with footage that can be cut together logically. At the beginning of each shot, Karel verbally "slates" what he's about to film: "Hey Steve, this is an establishing shot for that communist statue." "Hey Steve, another angle on that statue." "Steve, a close-up of the two main figures."

Steve also gets a copy of the (semi-) final script, which has been tweaked and polished throughout the shoot—a process we call "scrubbing the script." This is the arduous process of reading through the script, again and again, making each word earn its keep. Part of the scrub is knowing which footage worked—and which didn't—and tailoring the words to what's in the can.

Steve uses the script, the verbal slates, and a rough "scratch track" of Rick's voice-over to stitch together the episode. Like the rest of the process, editing TV is equal parts science and art: Steve has a clear framework, but he employs his own vision.

It's also tedious. Steve has to rewind each snippet and rewatch it, again and again and again, to cut it just right. I used to work in an office adjoining Steve's, and I could hear this mind-numbing repetition through the wall: a two-second audio clip—say, a Swiss cowbell clanging, or a Norwegian girls' choir singing a Christmas carol, or Rick shouting "Freeeedooom!" in the Scottish Highlands—20 or 30 times in a row. How Steve maintains his sanity, I'll never know.

Once Steve finishes the rough cut, Rick and Simon watch it and weigh in with notes. If the show comes in a little long—or a lot long (as in Romania, which was nearly four and a half minutes over)—we decide what to trim. Some cuts are obvious; others come down to a no-win pick-'em between bits that equally deserve to be in the show. But at the end of the day, each episode gets exactly 24 minutes and 16 seconds (once you subtract the open, credits, and underwriting).

Once the final cuts are made, Steve sends the footage to be color-corrected, evening out filming variations and making the show feel visually cohesive. Meanwhile, Rick and Simon watch the final cut one more time—the final "scrub"—and make a few last-minute wording tweaks. Then Rick records the final voice track, a sound mixer appends it to the color-corrected final cut and "sweetens the sound" . . . and the show is finished.

From time to time, I go back and watch that Romania episode with a mix of pride and PTSD. What's striking to me is—contrary to the worst fears of our contacts—how *normal* it all seems. All the chaos of scouting and production are nowhere to be found. If anything, it's pedestrian in showing Romania on equal footing with the rest of Europe.

Which I consider a smashing success. Despite my frustrations with the place, in the end I feel affection for Romania. It's a beautiful country. And it's not exactly a pity that it's inhabited—its inhabitants just need some stability and TLC. The Romanians I met, and came to be friends with, are doing their best with their Sisyphean existence. Each time I leave Romania, it's with a sense of cheering them on . . . and, to be honest, relief.

Fernando told me why their
Columbian coffee was better than
other coffee. Banana trees are grown
among the coffee trees to shade the
coffee trees, which are kept low enough
so the berries can be easily reached and
picked one at a time as they ripen,
rather than stripping off all the berries
at once.

—Mildred C. Scott,
  Jams Are Fun

PART FIVE

Meaningful Hedonism

*T*he more you know about something, the more you like it. This is one of those travel clichés that also happens to be entirely true. And it goes double for things that are purely enjoyable to begin with.

"Hedonism" is a dirty word in some travel circles. It conjures sleazy, singles-only resorts advertised on late-night 1980s TV. But it simply means pleasure, enjoyment, self-indulgence. Even for buttoned-down travelers, hedonism adds more colors to the palette you use to paint your memories.

There's another reason that hedonism gets a bad rap: The mainstream travel industry often seems designed to swap out meaning for hedonism. While the traveler is distracted, they do an Indiana Jones-style switcheroo, replacing the golden idol with a bag of sand.

I believe hedonism and meaning don't have to be mutually exclusive. For the temporary European, the challenge is keeping them in balance. Finding meaning in hedonism is the difference between being an enthusiast and being an aficionado—and aficionados have more fun.

To illustrate this, consider a style of travel synonymous with hedonism: cruising. In 2010, Rick had the brainstorm to produce a guidebook for cruise passengers. Throughout Europe, anytime he was in a popular port city, he'd be approached by adventurous travelers who were using his book while on a cruise. Why not help them by tailoring our coverage for their experience?

In the halls of our office, this idea was met with confusion, even hostility. We are travelers at heart, and many considered "cruisers" as something separate from "travelers"—occupying the lowest rung of the tourism ladder, unclean, deluded, and lost in the wilderness.

Having met many "good cruisers" myself, I saw the wisdom of Rick's idea. When he asked me to go on several cruises to research and write the book, I was thrilled.

Although I was on assignment, I was also trapped on a ship every evening—constraining my instincts to work non-stop. So I dabbled in shipboard hedonism: nursing a drink on the top deck, looking to the horizon as we chased down a sun that was determined to extinguish itself in the glittering Aegean.

As expected, on board those ships, I encountered some passengers I might (snobbishly) consider "not real travelers." One night at dinner, I asked the people at the next table what they'd done that day in Santorini. "Oh, we stayed on the ship!" they proudly reported. "It looked pretty much like the other islands we've seen, so we just hung out at the pool."

(It bears noting that Santorini is the inhabited, half-submerged lip of a flooded volcano caldera. It's one of those mind-bending places that resemble nowhere else on earth. But I digress.)

I also encountered a surprising number of great travelers on board. One young American couple, just married and stationed in Germany, told me this was the only way they could afford to see the Greek Islands. The three of us were the first people off the ship each morning, and the last people back on at "all aboard." Unless the crew was visibly anxious by the time we reached the gangplank home, we weren't doing it right.

In addition to researching the ports—sorting out the public-transit options for getting into town, finding the nearest ATMs and Wi-Fi hotspots, and so on—I loved deconstructing how the cruise industry operates.

I had a fascinating meeting with one ship's hotel manager, a fan of our books who was candid and generous with insights. For example, why do many cruise lines charge extra for "specialty" restaurants? Simply to limit the number of people who will be interested. It's not to defray their costs, but to defray disappointment.

I went on a behind-the-scenes tour of a ship, descending into a hectic labyrinth of sub-waterline galleys. On the wall were large photographs of each dish served on board. Many of the cooks come from non-American/European cultures, and without the photographs they might not know what the food they prepared was supposed to look like.

For me, the most important question was this: Why are cruise lines so inept at informing independent travelers how to spend their time off the ship? The answer: It's a designed ineptitude. Every minute you're ashore, they lose a captive customer, so they certainly aren't in the business of making you a better traveler. The last thing they want is to have you out walking the city walls of Dubrovnik, when you could be downing a few cocktails, then hitting the slots. (I call switcheroo!)

In the end, I went on three different Mediterranean cruises, and then, the next summer, three more cruises to research a guidebook on Scandinavian cruise ports. These books continue to sell strongly, having cornered a market that most travel companies underestimate: the meaningful hedonist.

The next few chapters delve into some "fun" aspects of Europe: Italian gelato; hiking through the Swiss Alps; the thermal baths of Budapest; and eerie "ghost walks" and other scary legends in Britain. In each case, I hope you'll spot the difference between pure enjoyment, and what's gained by going beyond pure enjoyment.

Florence, Italy

Pistachio Gelato Never Lies

O n a visit to Florence, I mention to my friend Virginia that I've always wanted to learn more about gelato. "*Certo!* Of course!" she says. "Let's go."

As we tiptoe between Renaissance balustrades and double-parked *motorini*, Virginia explains that a close friend of hers once opened his own *gelateria*—so she has insight into the business side of gelato, along with the culinary side. It seems I've found the perfect teacher.

I ask Virginia something that I'd never fully understood: How does gelato differ from American ice cream? "Ice cream has a higher butterfat content," Virginia says. "That makes the texture rich and sultry. However, the butterfat coats your tongue. Some people say that gelato has stronger flavors. Not quite—rather, your taste buds are better able to perceive those flavors. Gelato is also churned differently, incorporating less air. That makes it harder, more concentrated."

Strolling through the urban core of Florence on Via dei Calzaiuoli toward the main square, we pass a row of seemingly interchangeable *gelaterie*. So, how do you know which one is best? "Most gelato places use the same powdered or paste-like mixes," Virginia says. "You want a place that makes all of their gelato fresh, on the premises, ideally that same day. That's why you should look

for words like *artigianale*—artisanal; or *fatto in casa*—homemade. But be careful, eh? Some places advertise these words even though they use the same mixes as everyone else. Let me show you how to know for sure."

Pausing at a display case with mountains of colorful gelato, Virginia whispers, "See there? That is not good gelato. The big piles and the bright colors are designed to attract children. At the best *gelaterie*, you don't actually see the gelato—you read a list of the flavors. The gelato is kept in stainless-steel covered tubs, until someone orders it. It's fresh, and they want to keep it that way."

"Another sign of good gelato is muted colors. If you see a color that does not occur in nature, it's artificial. Think about it: What color is the part of the banana that you eat? Not neon-yellow. It's sort of off-white, with a hint of yellow. So a good, artisanal banana gelato will be closer to white than to yellow."

We step into Florence's majestic Piazza della Signoria. Late in the afternoon, it feels like the city's living room. We linger in a quiet corner of the square, peering over at a high-profile *gelateria*.

"Eh, these glitzy *gelaterie* are so sleazy," Virginia says. "When a tourist asks for a cone of gelato, the vendor picks the most expensive, chocolate-and-candy-dipped waffle cone, piles it with five or six scoops, and charges them fifteen euros. Be specific. When I order, I say something like, 'a three-euro cone with two flavors.' Of course, you don't need to be so paranoid at friendly neighborhood places—just the touristy ones."

As if to punctuate this tip, just then a pack of *ragazzi* kicks their soccer ball against the peeling plaster wall next to us. They're gearing up for a game . . . and we are in the way. We surrender the pitch and carry on across the Ponte Vecchio. The languid evening light drapes the famous bridge in a gauzy glow.

As we leave the bridge behind and make our way up a sleepy Oltrarno back street, Virginia explains the business end of making gelato: "A *gelateria* has many flavors, but only a few machines. Every gelato begins with the same, neutral, sweet-cream base, *fior di latte*. As they work through their batches, they make progressively more complex flavors, with darker colors. The last batch of the day is dark chocolate. That's why, if someone has a nut allergy, they should be careful when ordering a darker-colored gelato. Some shops clean their machines properly between batches, but not all do."

Finally we come upon a *gelateria* that passes Virginia's protocol: *gelato artigianale*, from covered metal bins, with muted colors. "But even then," she says "the only way to know for sure is to taste."

Surveying our options, Virginia says, "While Americans like to combine whichever flavors strike their fancy, Italians know that some flavors go together better than others. It's like pairing wine and food: You want a combination that's mutually enhancing. In fact, if a *gelateria* takes its craft very seriously, they might politely refuse to pair certain flavors. If you ask for chocolate and lemon, you might get a funny look—'Are you sure?' Or even a shake of the head and a click of the tongue. For Italians, mixing lemon and chocolate gelato is like putting cheese on seafood, or drinking milk after lunchtime."

"If you are adventurous," Virginia continues, "you can put yourself in the expert's hands and ask them what marries well. Sometimes they can suggest some surprising and delicious pairings." I try this approach, and the clerk tops one of my favorites, *cannella* (cinnamon), with *pera* (pear). *Delizioso!*

Virginia orders pistachio. As we lick our cones, she says, "My choice of flavor is strategic. If you really want to gauge the quality of a *gelateria*, you try the pistachio. Here's why: Did you ever notice that every gelato flavor costs the same to buy? But, of course, they cost differently to produce. There's a huge profit margin for *fior di latte, crema, vaniglia,* and other basic flavors. Meanwhile, the most expensive flavor to make—if it's done correctly, with real nuts—is pistachio."

She gives the cone another judgmental lick. "Only the rare *gelateria* uses real pistachios. Places that are cutting corners will make almond or sunflower-seed gelato, then mix in artificial pistachio flavoring and green food coloring. But if the pistachio is real pistachio, it's a very good sign that the *gelateria* owner is committed to making quality gelato, even at the expense of potential profits."

Licking once more, Virginia concludes, "Mmmm. This one is real pistachio. You can taste the difference."

Unfortunately, the Italians' artisanal approach to food isn't quite universal. As anywhere, some proprietors are more interested in profit than quality. But with local insights, you can learn to tell the difference and survey your options with confidence. And it goes to show that—wherever you travel—when it comes to food, doing a little homework pays off.

Making Hay While the Sun Shines

I wasn't planning on doing a three-hour hike when I rode the funicular from Mürren up to Allmendhubel. But it's glorious out. The white snowcapped peaks pop against a deep blue sky. And in a matter of days, perhaps hours, summer will give way to fall. So off I go, following the North Face Trail to Gimmelwald. Such is the allure of the Alps.

I gingerly let myself through an electrified cattle gate—buzzing like an angry beehive—and head down into Blumental, the "Valley of Flowers." In the early summer, this meadow bursts with wildflowers. But on this mid-September day, those blooms have long since withered, the cows have chewed the grass to the nub, and the air has a pre-autumn crispness.

Crossing Blumental, I reach the hut called Suppenalp—a primitive wooden barn that stands like a lone tombstone at the edge of the meadow. It could accurately be described as "shiplap," but that sounds far too trendy. Attached to one side is a muddy paddock where cows are contentedly munching and mooing.

Suppenalp is a true and proper "alp": a high-mountain meadow where cows graze. Cowhands spend about a hundred days at huts

like Suppenalp each summer, rising seven days a week at five o'clock to milk the cows and take them out to pasture, and then bringing them back to milk again each afternoon. And, to avoid the tedious chore of hauling heavy cans of fresh milk down the mountain, they make the Swiss mountain cheese right here. For the cowhands, it's a high-altitude summer sabbatical at 6,000 feet, working hard while ensconced in alpine splendor.

Cheesemaking operations like this hut are funded by the Swiss government, which provides farmers with nearly 60 percent of their income. Let that sink in: Swiss taxpayers subsidize an antique dairy operation, high up in the middle of nowhere. They do it gladly, because they believe traditions are worth investing in. And it works. In many rural communities, parents fret over the next generation leaving for the glitz of big cities. But in the Swiss Alps, kids fight over who gets to take over the family herd. These policies also protect land use for the cows, preserving virgin slopes like the ones I'm exploring today—unblemished and practically glowing with bright-green grass.

The Suppenalp hut is closed today so the cowhands can take a break: *Montag und Dienstag Ruhetage*, says the chalkboard. No cheese samples for me . . . yet.

From the hut, I head up a steep, rocky path, curving around the midsection of a ridge. Above my head, a packed-to-the-seams cable car silently floats up toward the mountaintop called the Schilthorn. Looking up at all those sweaty faces pressed against the windows, selfie-sticks glancing off scratched and smeary glass, I realize there are far more people in that cable car than along this entire hiking path.

I rode up to the Schilthorn—one of Switzerland's top viewpoints—earlier today. The panoramas are as spectacular as ever. But these days, I find it hard not to feel cynical about the crass attempt to squeeze every last drop from the James Bond movie filmed at the Schilthorn 50 years ago. This theming—once a kitschy footnote—has gotten out of hand. The cable car is emblazoned with a hot-pink 007 logo, the observation deck is scattered with George Lazenby cut-outs to pose with, and "Bond Girl" silhouettes shimmy seductively on the bathroom stalls.

Feeling fortunate to be here rather than there, I pass through a brief stretch of alpine forest. I emerge at another pristine pasture, which stretches like an infinity pool toward the sheer gray cliffs of the Eiger, Mönch, and Jungfrau on the far side of the valley.

Crossing this alp, at what feels like the top of the world, I make my way down to a gathering of huts called Schiltalp. This is where most of Gimmelwald's cows spend their summers. But summer is nearly over, and very soon the cowhands will strap big ceremonial bells around the cows' necks, bedeck them with wildflowers, and parade them back down through the village to their barns for the winter. You never know exactly when the cows will come down—it's dictated by the weather—but I was lucky enough to see this spectacle years ago. It remains one of my all-time favorite Swiss memories: an impromptu folk-life parade where the bovine grand marshals were cheered like returning war heroes.

Schiltalp's cows haven't gone down yet. I can tell even before I see any, because those giant bells still hang from the eaves of the biggest hut. The hut has a self-service fridge, where hikers can buy a drink or a wedge of alpine cheese. The outdoor tables are enjoying some late-afternoon sun, and the only people sitting there are four rough and grizzled locals nursing beers, giving me suspicious looks. Clearly, I've crashed a local party.

To break the tension, I attempt the local *Schwyzerdütsch* greeting: *"Grüezi!"* After more than 20 years of traveling in Switzerland, I'm still trying to master it: "GREWT-see!" In Swiss cities, that does the trick. But in the countryside, singsongy Swiss German grows singsongier. And up here, each village—or even each farmhouse—gives the phrase its own color.

As usual, the four old-timers respond with four entirely different ways of saying the same word:

"GRÜÜÜÜÜ-zeh!"

"Khhruh-suh!"

"Grut." Pause. Pause. Pause. *"Si!"*

"Khhhhrew-tzee!"

They return to their beers, making it clear that our conversation is now complete.

I drop a few coins in the jar and help myself to a wedge of mountain cheese. It has a pungent aroma, but it's still soft: not quite fresh, not quite aged, and speckled with tiny bubbles. I saw a small chunk off the slab, mount it on a skinny slice of full-grain bread, and take a bite. The texture is smooth and creamy; the flavor is sharp and searing—filling my mouth with the taste of hay and wildflowers and a tannic kick and deep, deep Swiss tradition. It marries perfectly with the aroma of fresh-cut hay and day-old manure. It's easily the best cheese of my trip, if not my life.

I slowly work my way through the wedge, savoring each bite. When it's gone, craving one last taste, I whittle a final, crumbly curl off the rind and pop it in my mouth . . . the dairy equivalent of sucking the meat off the bones. The flavor will linger on my palate for hours.

Recharged, I bid the gang a cheery *Adieu!* (that one's easy) and head on down the path. Within moments, I'm immersed in a "hills-are-alive" landscape of grassy slopes, wooden barns, and mooing cows.

And then, in the distance, I hear cowhands hooting and whistling. The mooing becomes more agitated. The cows are on the move.

The cowhands crest the hill and come into view. It's a family—dad, mom, and a couple of kids—working together to drive their herd in for the night. They're dressed in shorts, T-shirts, and trucker hats, but they enact a timeless ritual of human and beast: moving a fleet of giant animals, many times their own size, armed only with insistent yelps and a big stick.

And then, I'm surrounded. Cows on all sides of me; cowhands behind them, trying to move them up the gravel road I've just come down. A bit frightened by the thousands of pounds of impatient beef plodding my way, I stand still—a rock in a stream of livestock.

Once the cows have passed, I carry on down the path, leaving the slow-motion stampede behind me. I'm buzzing from the moment I just experienced—one of those beautiful serendipities where it feels like every decision I made today conspired to put me in the perfect place, at the perfect time.

Continuing on down the path, I pass through yet another alp settlement—Spilbodenalp—where the cowhand is wrapping up a busy day's work while a few lazy cows doze in the front yard. From here, I make my way steeply down on a switchbacked trail through a thick forest that smells like Christmas. I reach precarious steps

carved into a cliff and follow them—with my heart thumping in my ears—to slip behind a thundering waterfall. Grasping for dear life to the metal cable drilled into the cliff, I climb back up the slippery stone steps on the other side, then make my way up through more thick forest.

Finally, I emerge at the top of a near-vertical meadow. Narrow ruts, barely wider than my scuffed and muddy shoes, cut down through the lush grass to the rooftops of Gimmelwald. This shingle-clad Swiss-mountain village sits on a meadow-draped granite shelf above the Lauterbrunnen Valley. It's a sleepy time warp . . . most of the time. But today it's a hive of activity.

Crossing a concrete path high above town, I dodge out of the way of a tractor, racing to wrap up chores before they lose the sun. The fields around me are alive with farmers, harvesting the hay they'll use to feed those cows all winter long. A visit to Gimmelwald just before the cows come back teaches you what they mean when they say, "Make hay while the sun shines." It occurs to me that this adage applies to travelers, too.

At the top end of town stands Hotel Mittaghorn—better known as "Walter's," for the Swiss senior citizen who has run the place since, I have to assume, the last Ice Age carved out the Lauterbrunnen Valley. Nothing ever changes at Walter's—he makes darn sure of that. If it was good enough 30 or 40 years ago, it's good enough today.

Many, many years ago, Rick Steves tours stayed at this dusty firetrap of a hotel. The only way we could fit was to squeeze six couples—that's 12 paying adults, about half the group—into one big sleeping loft in the attic. They shared a toilet and a coin-op shower, not just down the hall, but down the stairs. (Our tour guides mastered the art of identifying which dozen people were best equipped to tolerate, or even enjoy, this experience.) Understandably, our tour members grew to expect a higher level of comfort, and about two decades ago we stopped using Walter's. But, I swear to you, the tour members who stayed here adored the experience.

Out on the hotel's front porch sits perhaps the only relaxed person in Gimmelwald: Tim, the Englishman who's been Walter's trusty right-hand-man for years. I sit and chat with Tim for a while, getting all the village gossip. Tim says that Walter, now 95 years old, opens his hotel only three months each summer—when Tim can be here to essentially run the place for him. In a few days, Gimmelwald's cows will be back in their barns, and Tim will be on his way back to England.

While Tim and I chat, the bleating of goats in a pen next door intensifies. One of the goats finally jumps the fence and starts wandering around in the road. Tim, the good neighbor, hops up to herd the goat back home.

"Those two goats are sick," Tim explains. "That's why they keep them down here while they take the rest of the herd to the upper meadows during the day." He explains that local families keep goats to provide milk through the summer, when the cows are away. Sure enough, a few minutes later, our conversation is interrupted by a chorus of bleating and tinny, off-key bells. A couple of village kids drive several more goats down the path to join their ailing friends in the pen.

Before I move along, I head into the hotel kitchen to say hello to Walter—still with that same twinkle in his eye, all these years later. I bid Godspeed to both of them and head into town.

Across the street from Walter's, steps lead down into the heart of Gimmelwald: an intersection of paved cow paths with overly enthusiastic directional signs pointing every which way, two modest guesthouses, and the youth hostel and cable-car station just around the corner. I go for a lazy lap through town, following the main street past busy barns, log-cabin homes, perpetually flowing faucets that fill carved-tree-trunk cow troughs, lovingly tended flower boxes, and bazillion-dollar views. I fantasize about living in a cliff-hanging cabin. And I pause here and there to enjoy the serene sight of meticulously stacked firewood.

At one point, as I'm lost in the glorious mountain views across the valley, a towheaded, cherry-cheeked teenager emerges from the bottom of the steep incline in front of me. Laboriously, he pulls a giant tarp filled with freshly scythed grass up the hill and dumps it by the front door of his house. He pulls a handkerchief out of his back pocket, wipes his brow, then grabs the empty tarp and heads back down for another load. If Norman Rockwell were Swiss, he'd paint what I just saw.

I circle back through town, filling my bottle at the dugout fountain and dodging a couple more speeding tractors on my way to the cable-car station. I get there just in time for the lift's arrival from the Schilthorn high above. Dozens of day-trippers pour out and cross the platform—blowing right through this sweet village—in their oblivious rush to the connecting cable car back down to the valley floor, and their awaiting tour buses.

I get on the cable car they just got off, which will take me back up to Mürren and my hotel. Waiting for the ride to begin, I'm lost in thought—already daydreaming about those entirely unpopulated high-alpine meadows, those stunning mountain views savored all alone, and the feeling of being the only non-Swiss human being out on a vast and lonesome alp.

And then I'm swept up in another memory: On one of my earliest visits to Gimmelwald, in the springtime of 2001 or so, I came to catch a cable car at this very station and saw a small herd of five or six cows. Farmhands were leading them into the cable car, whose glass walls had been lined with old mattresses. The cows resisted, but finally they relented, the doors hissed shut behind them, and in seconds they shot down the mountain to the valley below.

Puzzled by all of this, I asked a villager to explain. "Oh, yes," he said. "They do this before they take the cows up to the high pastures. They evaluate the herd. If there are any sickly ones who will be difficult to keep healthy in the high alps, they take them down to the valley to meet the butcher."

It's striking how Switzerland leverages modern technologies to carry on centuries-old customs. Everything in Switzerland has its place, like it or not. And that includes preserving space for the old ways alongside the new. You put your money where your priorities are, and Swiss money is all-in on the traditional mountain culture I've been savoring today. Gimmelwald isn't a Swiss Norman Rockwell fantasy. It's a reality, funded by the Swiss electorate.

The cable-car door closing jolts me awake, and I look down as I fly over the rooftops of Gimmelwald and the steeply switch-backed trail that tethers it to Mürren. I catch one last glimpse of Walter's rooftop just before I'm swallowed up by the Mürren cable-car station.

Up to My Earlobes
in Hot Water

$\mathcal{S}$zéchenyi Gyógyfürdő is a palace of thermal bathing in the heart of Budapest's sprawling City Park. Architecturally, the bath complex is grand, with imperial colonnades and stone nymphs and copper domes. And hedonistically, it's the most purely enjoyable of the city's two dozen spas. As I near the end of an intensely busy day in Budapest, the sun hanging heavy in the sky, the soreness in my feet, and the trickle of sweat down my back are all nudging me toward Széchenyi.

Inside the lavish lobby, next to the ticket desk, hangs a three-foot-long menu of services, variations, and caveats: cheaper before noon or after 7, more on weekends, changing cabin or locker, a dizzying array of massages and pedicures and other treatments, and so on. Ignoring all of this and marching up to the cashier, I tell them I want a swimming pool ticket with a cabin. And before I know it, I'm in my swim trunks and up to my earlobes in hot water.

Out in the canary-colored courtyard, bobbing in the hottest of the three big pools, I squint around through the haze. Not long ago, Széchenyi felt local. On this visit, it's reached a tipping point where I can identify as many tourists as Budapesters.

But the people-watching remains unsurpassed: Nearby, a trio of Frenchmen—cheap liquor oozing from their pores—dare each other to hit on bathing beauties. A Canadian choir group bobs in a circle and practices pitchy harmonies. And over in the corner, a vigorously affectionate middle-aged couple appear to have completed foreplay.

Discreetly paddling to the far end of the pool, I find a pocket of Budapesters. Speedo-clad old men display bulbous potbellies that hang precipitously over skinny legs, as if determined to defy the laws of physics. In a timeless scene, four white-haired elder statesmen—submerged to their nipples—huddle around a chessboard, cheering and jeering as they wage their attacks.

Beginning to sweat, I climb out of the pool. Instantly chilled by the twilight air, I scurry, soggy and barefoot, to the opposite end of the courtyard. I shiver as I pass the long lap pool, where skullcapped swimmers cut sharp V's through Széchenyi's coolest waters. Along the pool's edge, statues observe the swimmers' progress, while overhead looms an empty grandstand.

At the opposite end of the courtyard is Széchenyi's third outdoor pool. It's like Goldilocks' Baby Bear: not too hot, not too cold, juuust right. This is also the liveliest pool, with jets, cascades, and an area where miniature bubbles seltzer from grates underfoot, tickling their way up your legs.

In the center of this pool, a tiled whirlpool spins and spins. Once sucked into its steady flow, it's hard to escape. Some people try to paddle against the current, but I enjoy going limp and bumping my way around, like a rag doll in an angry eddy. Drifting close to the outside wall comes with a boost of extra propulsion from the jets that keep it spinning. And then, suddenly, the whirlpool goes still. Across the rippling water, I hear jets and cascades elsewhere spurt to life. In a diplomatic spa tradition, the various water features take turns operating.

I'm finished with the whirlpool anyway. Braving the cool air once more, my waterlogged legs wobble me back to the warmest pool. I find a small yet thundering waterfall and park myself directly beneath it. Feeling the steaming cascade pound and pound and pound against my shoulders, I slip into a meditative trance, losing all track of time and place. It's the opposite of water torture . . . it's water bliss.

Feeling as relaxed as I have in days, maybe weeks, I contemplate my lifelong love affair with this city. Some places you "click" with and appreciate instantly, on a primal level. (For me, that's Slovenia.) Some places you struggle to connect with and sometimes, ultimately, fail. (For me, that's Spain.) And then there are special cases like Budapest.

I often name Budapest as my favorite city in Europe. But that comes with an asterisk. My affinity for Budapest feels less like affection and more like obsession. If it weren't for these baths, and the amazing food scene, I'm not sure I could even say that I "enjoy" spending time here. Budapest is complex and enigmatic, and it gets under my skin.

I first came to Budapest on my big 1999 backpacking trip. Passing through on the way from Slovakia to Vienna, I hopped off the train and spent several hours just wandering around, exploring without an agenda, or even a guidebook.

From the rusted and tattered train station hall, all the way through the city, Budapest seemed massive, imposing, grandiose, but on terribly hard times—only just starting to recover from the brutality of communism. It made me feel extremely small, and a little scared, but mostly intrigued. I found Budapest intensely beautiful and jarringly ugly. It was the ugliest, most beautiful place I had ever seen.

I walked along the Danube embankment—tripping over weeds that sprouted through cracks in the concrete—to the towering red dome and skeletal steeples of the Hungarian Parliament. It rose from the murky river, proclaiming the greatness of a long-since-toppled Magyar empire. The delicate Neo-Gothic details were caked in soot and grime; I imagined someone spending years filling in all that white stone with a charcoal pencil. The Parliament—and all of Budapest—was as grand as Oz, yet as shabby as a refugee camp. More specifically, it was Oz a decade after the Wizard was deposed, when the Munchkins learned that governance is harder than revolution.

Everywhere else I visited on that trip, I left with a kernel of insight. But Budapest provided no easy impressions. I couldn't slot it in my "good" or "bad" columns; it stood alone under "not

enough information to make a determination." The one thing I knew was that I had to go back.

When I did, two years later, I was training to become a tour guide. And over the next few years, I returned to Budapest several times. With each visit, the city had its act slightly more together. I felt the momentum of recovery. And with each visit, I liked it more.

But I saw our tour members struggle as I had. The better travelers were intrigued but left wanting more. The less experienced ones simply didn't get it; they left shaking their heads and wondering what on earth *that* was all about. Snobbishly, I came to use Budapest as my barometer for judging fellow travelers: The better the traveler, the better they liked the city.

Looking at the steamy hubbub around me, I think how even this, Budapest's most pleasurable experience, comes with an unusually high barrier to entry. As a tour guide, I learned that no matter how much I talked up the thermal baths, almost nobody went on their own. So during our free time, I'd arrange an optional, guided visit to Széchenyi. Virtually everyone showed up. I'd march them right through the front entrance, help each one navigate that dizzying menu of ticket options, and lead them to their changing cabins. Once through that gauntlet and floating in the hot water, the experience invariably became a tour highlight. I've seen the grouchiest of tour members transformed into giddy kids, splashing in the baths. Széchenyi gave them permission to be youngsters at the neighborhood pool all over again . . . but with a dash of *fin de siècle* class.

I faced this challenge again when I wrote a chapter on Budapest in our new Eastern Europe guidebook in 2003, and yet again when I turned that chapter into a complete Budapest guidebook a few years later. Introducing a destination in print is always tricky. But most places—even big, complex cities like Berlin, Barcelona, or Istanbul—have an easy "hook," or a few. Budapest doesn't, or maybe it has too many, or maybe they're too much of the "trust me, it's great" variety. There's no guidebook copy I've written more precisely, or rewritten more frequently, than Budapest's. And yet, every time I reread it, I'm mortified by how incomplete it seems.

Over so many visits to Budapest, I've become a connoisseur of the weirdest things. I get giddy disappearing into the grimy underpasses that sprawl beneath major intersections. Each one is a thriving delta of infrastructure where the Metró system flows up broken escalators into snarls of trams, buses, and cars. Standing still in the rush of commuters, I'm surrounded by meager food stalls, panhandlers, and confusing signage—a happy ant in a busy anthill. Inhaling a pungent mix of sweet pastries, diesel-tinged subway exhaust, and stale urine makes me feel *alive* in a way that only travel can.

For better or for worse, Budapest's beauty has become incrementally more apparent as time goes on. The recovery I sensed around the time I began guiding soon accelerated dramatically. Buildings have been scrubbed clean and shiny; plazas have been resurfaced; parks have been replanted; traffic-clogged streets have been pedestrianized. It no longer requires imagination to see the beauty and majesty in Budapest. The city has even made an asset of its few surviving pockets of ramshackleness, innovating a hot new category of nightspot called "ruin pubs" that fill street-art-slathered courtyards with secondhand furniture under twinkle lights.

But nothing is simple in Budapest, and even these welcome changes came with an asterisk. The city's beautification was driven largely by Fidesz, the nativist political party of Viktor Orbán that took power in Hungary in 2010. Orbán grew notorious for his penchant for whitewashing history, recasting heroes and villains and vice-versa in his efforts to downplay the complicity of the Hungarian government in the Holocaust. He loved a tidy city and big, beautifully renovated squares upon which to stage faux-historic "changing of the guard" ceremonies. His efforts to restore

Kossuth tér, the square behind the Parliament, included the overnight disappearance of a beloved monument to Imre Nagy, the great communist reformer who stood up to Soviet authority in 1956. (Ironically, Orbán first rose to prominence, as a young man, by delivering a speech honoring Nagy's memory.)

The big question, of course, is this: What's so special about Budapest? Why is this place, of all places, the one that I can't shake?

Maybe it's the unique heritage of the Hungarians. Their ancestors, the Magyars, were nomads from the steppes of Central Asia who arrived in the Carpathian Basin in the late ninth century. After a century or so of terrorizing Europe, they decided to become Christians and settle down. From there, Hungary's story was one of integration, of becoming European. And yet, they've retained many aspects of their Asian roots—including their language. On that first visit, Hungarian intimidated me with unexpected pronunciations, long words speckled with accents and umlauts, and even mysterious elongated umlauts. As a lover of languages, I felt like I'd just stepped out of algebra class and stumbled into a seminar on advanced calculus.

Maybe it's because Budapest is the crossroads of Central Europe, a region I adore. When Hungary found itself as Europe's front line of defense against the Ottomans, Budapest emerged as a leading city in the region—a status that was cemented when it became the co-capital of the Austro-Hungarian Empire in 1867. The city was, and is, a melting pot of people from throughout the realm. Many of my Hungarian friends have surnames with vaguely German, or Polish, or Slovak, or Croatian roots. Like American "mutts," they might not even know where that name came from. But it doesn't matter to them, because today they are Hungarian.

Maybe it's the city's rebellious spirit. Budapest gained its stature with Vienna precisely because it was willing to fight for the rights of Hungarians. And during the Cold War, Budapest was the Eastern Bloc's "Sin City," where people from around the Soviet sphere of influence traveled great distances to buy Adidas sneakers and Big Macs and bootleg cassettes by Western bands.

And, to consider all options, maybe it simply comes down to these thermal baths. Before I wrote my Budapest guidebook, I was nervous. Frankly, I was unsure of my ability to do this city justice. I reached out to my Czech friend Honza—a fellow guidebook author and Budapest aficionado—for advice on how to parse the city. "Good luck," he wrote back. "Maybe an old man, clad in a loincloth, will whisper the secret of Budapest in some darkened thermal bathing hall."

I thought Honza was blowing me off. In retrospect, he was handing me the answer I sought. These baths embody the addictive peculiarity of Budapest: They're enjoyable, yet challenging. They're elegant, yet primal. They are the product of a complicated history, of Romans and Magyars and Ottomans and Austrians, and yet they suit our modern world perfectly.

And another thing about the baths: They are for everyone—at least, anyone willing to grapple with idiosyncrasies. Looking around at my fellow bathers, I see Hungarians and foreigners. I see tall people and short people. I see fat people and skinny people. I see pink people and brown people. All being baptized in the essence of Budapest.

There was a time, in my unenlightened younger days, when I might giggle at the giant Hungarians squeezed into their miniscule swimsuits. But in our age of body positivity and acceptance, I see the baths through a new lens: as a celebration of what makes each one of us, us. People have bodies. Those bodies look different. But the joy of soaking in hot water is universal.

To delicate American sensibilities, the Széchenyi Baths may sound unseemly . . . earthy . . . lurid, even. And maybe it is. But it's also so very human. Széchenyi is a place where people come to check their inhibitions at the door and simply have fun together.

Budapest's baths also remind me that, like driving in Sicily, challenges are best met not with rigidity, but by staying loose. This city is like Széchenyi's whirlpool: Once sucked in, don't fight the current. Just go limp, swirl around, and see where it takes you.

From under my waterfall, I glance up at the illuminated clock on the wall. The baths close in a half-hour. The sky has faded from purple to inky black. And I'm determined to stop by my favorite restaurant for a late dinner on the way to my hotel.

Back in my claustrophobic cabin, I change into my street clothes, wrestling grubby socks onto moist feet. I know I'm about to suffer a jarring re-entry to the real world. It's been a very long day, and a very long trip. But an evening spent in this water is just what I needed to recharge for my journey's next leg. And, best of all, I know I'll be back again. And again. And again.

Ghosts and Skeptics

*E*very traveler experiences them: Those moments where you check in to a creaky hotel room and something doesn't feel right. As you unpack, you can't shake the sensation that you are not alone. Someone, something, is there. Watching you. In the night, you awake with a start and feel unsettled. Perhaps you catch a mysterious movement out of the corner of your eye or hear a creak or a bump. By morning, you are more than ready to move on.

I'm not saying that I believe in ghosts, or that I have ever seen one. However, I put a lot of effort into making sure I never do. And when traveling—especially around Britain—I find myself constantly wavering between believer and skeptic.

Several years ago, I visited a half-timbered guildhall from the time of King Henry VI, in what little survives of the historic town center of Coventry, England. As I explored the vast, echoey space, the two museum attendants sat at a table listening to a recording of white noise. On my way out the door, I asked, "What's that?"

The attendants—a young man and a middle-aged woman—exchanged a knowing glance. She took a breath. "Look, you will probably not believe us, but this place is extremely haunted. So every night we set up this recorder to log the creaks and bumps. See?" She showed me a long, handwritten list of times and types of noises. Just then, a loud clapping sound—like a chair tipped over onto a wooden floor—erupted from the recorder. "Ah. There's another one," she said, adding it to the list.

I probed farther. "So, you two have actually experienced this?"

Another knowing glance. "Oh, constantly. Every day, we hear some bump or knock."

They proceeded to tell me stories that curled my toes: Normally it was just a strange sound coming from a room they knew to be empty. But other things had happened. Strange things. People on the overnight cleaning crew kept quitting abruptly, refusing to cite a reason. And one time, when the two attendants were certain they were alone in the building, one last patron arrived to look around. As she left, she filled out a comment card. When they read it later, it said, "Fascinating old space. But that man dressed like a monk in the back room was very rude. He refused to talk to me."

I asked if they'd personally seen anything strange. Both of them had—usually just flashes of light or inexplicable shadows. But the young man described one particularly harrowing experience. One evening, he was all alone in the building, closing up. He went up to the minstrel's gallery to carry out his duties. When he turned back toward the stairs—the *only* stairs—he found a ghostly figure blocking his path. Terrified, and with no other options, he pushed his way through the phantom and quickly left the building.

"What did it feel like?" I asked.

"Cold," he said. "Very, very cold."

"That's terrifying! How do you spend so much time here?"

They shrugged. "It's not so bad, really. You get used to it. It's become routine—just part of the job. And we're never in danger. We're not so much frightened, but curious. That's why we record the noises. Try to see if there's any pattern."

Maybe I'm a total sucker. Maybe they sit there with their recording all day, waiting for a live one to nibble at the bait. But I don't think so. They seemed like decent, honest people. They didn't breathe a word of the hauntings until I asked them about it, and even then, they were reluctant. I think they really believe these stories. Whatever was happening in that guildhall—explainable or not—was happening a lot.

A few years later, in the historic Scottish town of Stirling, I joined one of those nighttime "haunted walks" that are so popular around Britain. An actor, dressed as "the ghost of the hangman," led us through the creepy old kirkyard on the hill. As we tiptoed between tombstones, hearing the moody clang of the church bells, he recited a carefully composed litany of ghost tales from the city's history.

After the show, he broke character, and we chatted on the walk back down into town. Turns out he's a serious historian who's written two books about Stirling.

We passed the heavily grilled top window of the old tollbooth building, which during his spiel he'd described as the place where the condemned would await execution. Pointing it out again now, he said, "That was actually my office for four years. I didn't even

realize that there was anything odd about it until one day, I mentioned the space to a friend, and he said, 'Don't you know that's the most haunted place in town?'"

I asked him if he'd ever experienced anything strange himself. "I've had plenty of strange encounters in this town," he said. "But none of them were paranormal."

It turns out that the person who has devoted the last two decades to studying, researching, and writing about paranormal activity in Stirling is a skeptic. In fact, he sometimes accompanies "paranormal investigators" into the kirkyard and around town, seeking scientific facts to debunk unusual findings.

He described an example. One of the town's historic pubs took down an old bit of paneling, revealing a hidden compartment. Suddenly, the workers were overcome. They couldn't breathe and felt distressed. The only items in the enclosure were some empty cans and a faded old black-and-white picture of a priest.

Paranormal investigators came in to investigate. And while they were doing that, our "ghost hangman" did some actual historical research. He found a watermark on the back of the photograph and conferred with a local museum curator. It turns out, in Victorian times, the pub was owned by the town's portrait photographer. At some point, his darkroom was abandoned and boarded up, with all those nasty chemicals inside, evaporated and trapped for over a century . . . until modern-day workers unsealed the space and inhaled them.

Some might say that debunking ghost stories takes away the fun. Much as I enjoy being scared, I like even better the feeling of getting to the bottom of a mystery. In the light of day, I'm confident in my skepticism. But after all these years of traveling, and all of those antique European hotel rooms, I still get creeped out sometimes . . . late at night, when a floorboard creaks or a strange shadow twitches in the corner. Maybe someday I'll find a definitive answer as to how "real" it all is. But I certainly hope not.

Jams Are Fun

A Rough Day on the North Sea

After that big supper we prepared for bed, and through the
loudspeaker, piped into each cabin, we were told, "If you are
inclined to be seasick, take one of your Dramamine pills. We
will be sailing soon." I didn't think I was inclined to be seasick
so didn't take a pill. Later I was sicker than I think I had ever
been in my whole life. I felt like my body would break in two.
But I didn't lose that big supper until morning.
—Mildred C. Scott, *Jams Are Fun*

As I write this, my cruise ship is rocking violently to and fro. In
addition to the slight but persistent list to port, with the occasional, violent bob to starboard, every ten minutes or so the ship
shudders as if the captain just accelerated over a speed bump.

I went to bed last night as we cruised out of the Sognefjord.
Next stop: Norway's other top fjord, Geirangerfjord. But I awoke
to news that, due to extremely high winds, they were cancelling
the stop.

As we retreated from the turgid surf of the Geirangerfjord,
the screaming winds momentarily cleared out some of the cloud
cover we've been huddled under since entering Norwegian waters.
The brief sun break illuminated wicked whitecaps all around us.
It also teased us with idyllic Norwegian views of green forest, red
cottages, and chalky gray cliffs. It was a Norway we would not

actually visit, nor one we would see again for the rest of the day. Instead, this would be, in the parlance of the cruise industry, an unplanned and very turbulent "day at sea."

As we navigated out of the fjord and into the North Sea, conditions deteriorated. Throughout the ship, subtle indicators hinted that we were in for an even bumpier ride: Racks of small plastic bags discreetly appeared in the hallways. The water was drained from one swimming pool, then the other. Precautions were being taken.

This was the first time I can recall being on truly rough seas. And I was relieved at how well I was handling it. Preparing for this trip, I read horror stories about people who signed on for multi-week cruises without realizing that they were prone to violent motion sickness. Maybe my 25 percent Norwegian DNA equipped me with the iron stomach of a cod fisherman.

In a delicious bit of serendipity, the afternoon's scheduled entertainment was—and I am not making this up—a troupe of Chinese acrobats. Now, I would pay any amount of money to see acrobats perform in these conditions. But this show? This show was free. As the time of the performance drew near, morbid curiosity drew me down to the theater. But a polite notice explained that the show was postponed. Wise move, Chinese acrobats.

Seeking other entertainment, I walked around the ship to survey the damage. At this point, we'd left "rough" and entered "rodeo." People were either green in the face or, like me, immune and chuckling at the absurdity of it all. Everyone—even seasoned crew—walked with the same gait: first leaning a bit and plodding slowly to the right, then rushing with sudden urgency to the left, then slowly again to the right, and so on. I sat looking out a window for a while, watching through the firehose spray the mesmerizing rhythm of the railing as it teeter-tottered dramatically waaaay above, then waaaay below the horizon.

Curious, I made my way up to the top deck, and was surprised to find the door unlocked. I stepped outside and went for a brief, wet walk—one hand in a death grip on the railing, the other in a death grip on my camera. I felt like the only human being on this giant ship. Somewhere in the control room, I imagined someone watching surveillance feed of this idiot wandering around outside, taking bets on when he'd be blown overboard.

As dinnertime approached, I wondered whether, like the Chinese acrobats, the main dining room staff would have come to their senses and called the whole thing off. But dinner, much to my delight, was on. I knew I was in for a memorable evening when I walked past a Dutch teenager whose eyes grew wide as she suddenly—and, apparently, with as much surprise to herself as to me—vomited a little bit into her hands.

Stumbling and careening to my table, I noticed that at least a third of my fellow diners had decided to skip it tonight. The server hustled awkwardly toward me—propelled by an unwanted inertia and briefly overshooting his target—to drop off the menu.

I'm sure there was a good reason for the ship designers to locate the main dining room at the bottom-rear of the ship, directly above the engines. But on a rough night like this, it seemed like a cruel prank. Things were dramatically worse down here than in my stateroom up on the eighth deck. The entire dining room tilted violently this way, then that. The curtains slid themselves open and shut, as if by an occult hand. At one point, a precarious angle sent plates and glasses cascading off tables. And periodically there was a deep, reverberating hum—like the engines had been lifted out of contact with the sea—immediately followed by a sickening thud that rattled the wineglasses.

And then there were the diners. Those of us who had showed up tonight were, no mistaking it, there *on purpose*. We were not about to let this thing get the best of us. And yet, some of us must fall. At the next table, the Italian *nonna* who has this funny habit of staring off into space, which happens to be directly at me, began fanning herself with her menu. The sweet French lady who sits at another table got up after the first course and never came back.

Having grown up watching the movie *Stand By Me*, I kept envisioning a Lardass-at-the-pie-eating-contest chain reaction. Looking around, I tried to guess: Who would be the first to suffer, in the parlance of competitive eaters, a reversal of fortune? Would it be the balding fellow who lifted his napkin to his lips for a suspiciously lingering moment after each bite? The young woman who kept coughing loudly, then swallowing and rolling her eyes? The girl resting her head on the table? Or maybe . . . the American smart aleck at table 103, deriving smug satisfaction from the suffering of others?

Suddenly I found it next to impossible to swallow. I told myself I wasn't sick—just tired of proving I wasn't. I decided that a violently swaying room pregnant with potential for upchuckery was not a smart place to be. And so, like many diners before me, I politely excused myself.

Still hungry, I wandered up to forage at the 24-hour shipboard pizzeria. Unfortunately, their lone variety tonight was topped with a less-than-appetizing combination of tuna fish, capers, and onions.

Oh, well—it's bedtime anyway. If I don't get physically tossed out of my bed, I'll wake up tomorrow in Bergen . . . and, hopefully, better weather. And if I'm lucky, maybe they'll reschedule those Chinese acrobats.

(P.S. They did. And they were spectacular.)

The Merry Band of Travelers

The Cult of Rick Steves

*A*s you drive north from Seattle on Interstate 5, the sparkling skyscrapers and leafy hills of the Emerald City give way to suburban sprawl. A few miles out of downtown, towering evergreen trees—mind-bogglingly tall to anyone not from the Pacific Northwest—rise up on either side of the freeway. Turning off at exit 177, you coast along State Route 104 westward through suburbs and strip malls, past pot dispensaries and lawnmower repair shops, through an intersection flanked by two different Starbucks, and under the boughs of more colossal trees.

Finally, cresting a rise, you turn a corner and head downhill into the "Edmonds Bowl." Here open up spectacular views of Puget Sound: Cruise liners and green-and-white ferry boats ply cold waters, peninsulas and islands break up the swirling shimmer of aquatic light, snowcapped Mount Baker rises from the distant horizon—nearly indistinguishable from puffy clouds—and everything is fringed by yet more of those happy Bob Ross pine trees.

Edmonds, Washington, is the hometown of Rick Steves, and it's home to the headquarters of Rick Steves' Europe. Since I first met Rick, I've spent about one-quarter of my life in Europe. The other three-quarters, you'll find me here. My office shares a wall with Rick's. When he gets a text message, I hear the *ding-ding! ding-ding!* And when he's in a good mood, he whistles at his desk.

It's odd to devote a chapter of a travel book to an office, I realize. But this is no run-of-the-mill office. It's a merry band of travelers, led by a pied piper, who've collectively grown into one of the most respected travel authorities in North America. The stories in this book follow me around as I make my European rounds. But I can only do what I do because a hundred colleagues back in Edmonds are doing their jobs, too.

If you've no interest in what I refer to, tongue in cheek, as the "Cult of Rick Steves," then by all means, skip this chapter. But if you're intrigued by the unlikely tale of a gangly, Lutheran history buff from near Seattle who became a travel guru—or if you're a "Ricknik" yourself—read on.

When I first sent Rick Steves that fan letter back in 1999, I think he sensed a kindred spirit. After working together for more than 20 years, it's clear that Rick and I share a primal, borderline-abnormal passion for Europe. We geek out about the same historical factoids; we love most of the same places and we hate most of the same places; and we're equally driven to learn and teach about our favorite continent. Sometimes, especially in Europe, I'm mistaken for Rick, or people think I'm his son.

And yet, we complement each other in critical ways. One longtime colleague has observed that I "have the other half of Rick's brain." (She intended this as a compliment, and that's how I've chosen to take it.) And that qualifies me as well as anyone to answer an often-asked question: What is Rick Steves really like?

The gee-whiz, borderline-goofy Rick Steves persona you see on TV is real. The unbridled love of travel; the evangelical zeal for history and art; the strange cocktail of enthusiasm, awkwardness, and stealth charisma—that's all 100 percent Rick. Like any public figure, he dials up those qualities for the camera, even as he dials down others. He's perfected the "lovable nerd" character because, deep down, he is one.

Like a Southern preacher or a natural politician, Rick commands the attention of an audience. When he's on stage, you glimpse more of the "real Rick"—unscripted, he reveals the

natural flow of his intelligence and wit. I've seen audiences in the thousands held in rapture by an unprepossessing man, in a frumpy sport coat and jeans, dissecting the pros and cons of rail passes. They're anxious about an upcoming trip, they have questions, and before them stands someone with the answers. And he's entertaining, to boot.

Rick is a born salesman. Hustle flows through his veins. When not in Europe, Rick travels around the United States to sidekick pledge drives on public television affiliates. Frequently, the host of the show just holds on for dear life as Rick commandeers the telecast and gets those phones ringing off the hook.

In person—when it's just you and him—Rick is mellower. He still speaks with that wholesome, vaguely Canadian-Scandinavian-Upper Midwest cadence that he inherited from his mom. But it's subdued. And you get more of the wicked, subversive sense of humor that he doles out cautiously for the cameras.

Rick is the quickest wit in the room. He's what the Brits would call "clever," in a holistic sense. Whether in casual conversation, on stage, or in his writing, Rick comes up with the most bizarre, yet perfect, metaphor for any situation—pithy, surprising, and profound. When training new arrivals to edit Rick's writing, our biggest challenge is convincing them not to iron out his quirky asides. They're features, not bugs.

Intellectually, it's rare that Rick isn't several steps ahead of whoever he's talking with. Rick's active mind hops to the end of a complex argument before you've even finished a sentence; frequently, someone leaves his office with a solution that hadn't begun to cross their mind when they went in.

But this doesn't mean Rick can't be reasoned with. In fact, he relishes when someone is willing to climb in the ring with him and engage in heated debate. One (unfortunate) way he attempts to lure people into battle is by making bold assertions that he doesn't necessarily believe. This befuddles those who assume Rick has just one constant belief on a given topic rather than a fluid range of ideas that he's always trying on and tinkering with. He's a creature of instinct, and instinct is unpredictable and inconsistent.

Watching Rick on TV, you might imagine him the ultimate rule-follower. But he has a rebellious streak—a disruptiveness that can sneak out when you least expect it. He's gotten in arguments with our property manager about not wanting to paint lines in the parking lot. Several staffers spend most of our working hours attempting to corral his creative spirit. In writing, it often falls to me to temper Rick's full-blast instincts with thoughtfulness, pragmatism, and what Rick once described as "an Alan Alda sensitivity." (Here again, he meant this as a compliment—I think—and that's how I've chosen to take it.)

Rick's paternal grandfather was a Norwegian ski jumper who was famous for his explosive temper and his death wish on the slopes. While his family lore casts that ancestor as a "black sheep," Rick feels an affinity for his disgraced gramps.

Rick savors being a nonconformist CEO, doing everything in a way that should, by any rational assessment, fail miserably. It's this contra-conventional approach that, I believe, is key to his success: Rick is willing to buck the strictures of the mainstream travel industry, which taps him into a huge audience of travelers who crave more depth and meaning in their travels.

These wild ideas work partly because he *makes* them work— sometimes by sheer force of will. I believe that Rick, in a moment of honest self-reflection, would acknowledge that he likes to be in control. His devotion to the purity of his vision can lead to an idiosyncratic understanding of "consensus" and "collaboration." But his advisors find ways to navigate our way to a satisfying outcome.

Rick also likes to "*kontroll*" things in a Germanic sense—that is, randomly check in on progress. On my first guidebook research assignment, in Amsterdam, I visited a B&B run by a mother-daughter team who were old friends of Rick's. When I came down the creaky stairs from inspecting the room, they were sitting awkwardly on the couch, with a pile of pillows between them, and instructed me to sit facing them to ask my questions. As we spoke, they giggled awkwardly, like alphas at a slumber party playing a practical joke on the new kid. At one point their weight shifted and the receiver of a telephone poked out from the pile of pillows. I suddenly realized that Rick had told them I was coming and asked them to call so he could listen in. (I never told Rick that I knew he was spying on me that day. But I'm still here, so apparently my questioning was on point.)

Rick is obsessed with stapling. He geeks out about centering the staple on a packet of papers just right, diagonally across the corner, with a millimeter of clearance on each side. His pet peeve is when he asks a hotel receptionist to print out the latest draft of a TV script, then discovers that they've stapled it sloppily, or—worse!—not at all. Through our shared office wall, I often hear Rick's little printer spit out his latest project, followed by the decisive *KA-CHUNK!* of a stapler, and a satisfied sigh. (Bosnians would identify stapling as Rick's *ćejf*.)

Rick describes himself as a "workaholic." That's putting it mildly. I've rarely known someone so driven by a job they love. Speaking as a friend, I worry that this comes at a cost. While he tries to carve out time for loved ones, he's atrocious at simply *relaxing*. Going to the movies, lingering over a leisurely dinner, watching a baseball game on TV—Rick sees these as demerits in a zero-sum game that only he is playing. (Early in the pandemic, Rick called me with an urgent question: How, exactly, does one "binge" a TV show?)

At a stage in life when most successful people are courting retirement, Rick insists he has no intention of slowing down. "I may think about retirement in ten years or so" is something he's been saying, on an annual basis, for about ten years now.

Despite being America's most famous traveler, Rick is very much a creature of habit. He still lives in the town where he grew up; from his house on a slope just above downtown, he walks to the office most days. And then, around ten o'clock, he strolls through Edmonds to get his morning latte, greeting members of his community (and the occasional star-struck visitor) along the way.

Rick eats lunch every day at the same Mexican restaurant, ordering the same meal, sitting at the same window booth. Comparing notes about our lunch meetings with Rick, my colleagues and I have discovered that we've had identical experiences: First, you and Rick both scan the menu in a masquerade of choice. Then, when precisely enough time has passed for this not to seem forced—but not long enough to have committed to any dish in particular—Rick says, "Do you like chicken tostada? How's about we split one?" Before you can answer, he waves down the owner. "Miguel! One chicken tostada, two plates, Cherry Coke." Then he turns to you, almost as an afterthought, and asks, "Do you want a Cherry Coke, too? Or just water?"

From his office window, Rick looks up the street at his junior high school—now a municipal arts center that he bankrolls to ensure a steady flow of culture into the town that created him. This is just one of many ways that Rick's generous nature shines through. Rick has also invested heavily in building community centers in and near Edmonds; buying, then donating, an apartment building to house mothers and kids who are experiencing homelessness; investing $2 million (and counting) in climate smart projects in the developing world; and generously supporting—with money and time—many other causes near and dear to him, from ending global hunger to legalizing marijuana.

While you could view Rick's philanthropy through the lens of flower child/kumbaya idealism, I believe it's largely driven by his Lutheranism. While being religious is often seen as corny and old-fashioned these days—especially in the secular Pacific Northwest—Rick is a true-blue Christian who goes to church every Sunday and tries to walk the walk the rest of the week. When he's not traveling, he plays bongo drums with the church band at the contemporary worship service and acts as an agent of modernization within his largely traditional congregation. As he's gotten older, Rick has become preoccupied with the notion of "travel as a spiritual act"—pondering how his faith informs his travels, and vice-versa.

During polarizing times, Rick has written sweeping (and, frankly, condescending) generalizations about "small-town, white, American Christians." Each time I gently remind him that he is, himself, a small-town, white, American Christian. It's yet another one of the paradoxes of Rick Steves.

It seems impossible—even to me, the "other half of his brain"—to reconcile these many Ricks into one. In my first week on the job, one of Rick's longtime colleagues described him, perfectly, as "mercurial." One moment, he's the goofy jokester, then he's a bleeding-heart philanthropist. Minutes later, the puppy-dog cheerleader metamorphoses into the shrewd businessman, with a hint of the hot-tempered ski-jumper. But at his core is a kind heart, a creative soul, a mind at work, a healthy ego, and a born traveler who has inspired countless Americans to, as he likes to say, fit in a little better with the other 96 percent of humanity.

The town of Edmonds is best known to Seattleites as the place from which the ferry departs every 50 minutes or so to the Kitsap Peninsula. "Deadmonds" is also thought of as a low-energy retirement community. In my first few weeks on the job, I enthused to a co-worker about how scenic Edmonds was. He rolled his eyes. "Beautiful, yes. But that sign on the way into town says it all: 'Reduced speed ahead.'"

To be fair, Edmonds has grown more youthful and diverse in recent years. The annual Halloween party fills the downtown with hundreds of costumed kids. Youthful microbrew pubs and tapas restaurants are now shuffled in among the hearing aid clinics, antique malls, and soup-and-salad diners. The Edmonds Theater—a single-screen movie house where tickets are a third cheaper than the multiplexes—offers just-for-fun screenings for film buffs. And on Saturday mornings, the theater hosts European travel classes taught by the staff from the business just around the corner.

The Rick Steves' Europe Travel Center, a few doors up Fourth Avenue North from Main Street, is a handsome, boxy, red-brick building that flies a European flag. If you didn't look closely, you'd miss the Notre Dame gargoyles and a winking Mona Lisa carved in stone. This is the home office of the team that keeps our guidebooks, tours, TV series, radio show, online presence, and philanthropy humming.

I showed up here for my first day of work on St. Patrick's Day in 2000. I was a Travel Advisor—helping travelers plan their trips, answering phones and emails, and selling guidebooks, backpacks, and rail passes to walk-in customers. I was immediately impressed by how each and every co-worker had a passion for Europe and a knack for sharing it. So much so, it struck me as a nonprofit masquerading as a for-profit company.

My co-workers spoke reverently about "our mission" and "our travelers." Despite working in front-line retail, I was given no sales quotas, and in fact, I was expressly trained *not* to upsell customers needlessly. Rather, my job was to equip travelers with exactly what they needed for the best possible experience in Europe—no more, no less.

While much has changed over the last 20-some years, this ethos has not. Rick Steves' Europe was a "mission-driven organization" long before that was trendy. And the mission has never been, specifically, to sell guidebooks or tours, but to create vivid European experiences. Rick frequently reminds us that he measures success not by gross revenue, but by "gross travel happiness created."

While this may seem a dangerously naive business model, it works remarkably well. Customers intuit when they're dealing with something genuine and substantial. When you preach good travel and back it up with quality content, the money will follow.

We are a merry band of travelers. And travelers are a special breed: adventurous, free-spirited, curious, gregarious, and restless. In those early days, our motley crew included three general groups: The "old guard" created the business with Rick, going back to the 1990s. "Refugees" from more traditional corporate backgrounds, escaping dress codes and buttoned-down workplaces, imported their expertise from what we called "the real world." And "converts" like me had learned firsthand how the company's mission could make trips better.

In recent years, many members of the "old guard" have retired, handing the reins to the next generation—including many of us who began on the front lines selling backpacks and rail passes. But that idiosyncratic culture, mission, and esprit d'corps remain intact.

You'd sense this immediately if you wandered through our offices. Visitors enter through the Travel Center, which is less a store than a space purpose-built for planning a trip. Clocks on the wall indicate the local time in all three European time zones (UK, Central Europe, Greece and Russia); big canvas prints show off lush European scenery; next to the fireplace is a cowbell with Edelweiss embroidered on its strap, plus a pair of easy chairs; and ringing the room are bookshelves stacked with hundreds of travel books.

A few years ago, the Travel Center team suggested erecting a life-size cardboard cutout of Rick for fans who wanted photo evidence of their pilgrimage to Edmonds. I love watching excited travelers posing with cardboard Rick, only to see the real one walk through the front door with his morning latte.

From here, hallways lead to desks piled with paperwork, photos of happy families, and personal bric-a-brac. The desk decor takes on a distinctly European flavor: magnets shaped like Amsterdam gables; stacking Russian dolls; Lego models of Big Ben and Neuschwanstein; miniature Norwegian trolls; little wooden tubes of Bulgarian rose water; annual backpack patches from our tours, dating back to (at least) 1993; wee bottles of Baileys, Ballantine's, and Becherovka; erasers shaped like Eurostar trains; matchbox cars of Fiat 500s, Mini Coopers, VW Beetles, and East German Trabants; and *Keep on travelin'!* coffee mugs.

Upstairs is a marketing bullpen that faces a closet filled with a paper chronicle of the company's early days: each and every *Europe Through the Back Door Budget Travel Newsletter*, starting with issue #1, from 1982. Through the 1990s, Rick and his marketing partner, Rich Sorensen, would huddle over a desk late at night, tweezing and pasting tiny scraps of copy into this free travel fanzine. The newsletter was where they pioneered the unique mix that still characterizes our brand: loads of free, insightful, inspiring, practical content with gentle sales nudges to related books and tours.

It's at this corner of the building that Rick and I have our offices. Surrounding our doorjambs and windows are yet more nostalgic odds and ends: exuberant photographs of travelers sending their thanks for a wonderful trip; yellowed newspaper clippings that mentioned Rick before he was famous; an email sent by an irate former customer (chastising Rick for "advancing your liberal agenda"); and a photocopy of the letter that Walter, that antique Swiss hotelier from Gimmelwald, mailed to Rick in 1981, suggesting he come check out Hotel Mittaghorn for the guidebook.

The clutter continues into Rick's office: a foot-tall, metal sculpture of Martin Luther hammering his 95 Theses to the Wittenberg church door; posters from the Washington State marijuana legalization campaign of 2012; a sun-faded Norwegian flag from some long-ago Syttende Mai parade; a miniature bus from Heidebloem, the Belgian company that drives for most of our tours; a fresco Rick created with his own hands at an artisan class in Florence; a ratty old chair, which Rick mysteriously loves, with wicker backing pulling out of its wooden frame; and a high school-era photo of his kids, Andy and Jackie.

From the upstairs of the "new building"—opened in 2000—four steps lead down into the adjacent "old building." Twisting through a musty hallway, you pass the "Wall of Shame"—an improvised collection of 40 or so faded and curled-edged photographs showing staffers in their awkward adolescent years. At this point, you begin to hear the sound of Rick's voice spitting out the same sound bites, again and again and again. You're passing the tiny room where Steve Cammarano edits our TV shows. If Simon's in town, you'll find him in there, too, squeezed into an even smaller broom closet with a window over Fourth Ave.

The hallway carries on to our kitchen/break room, where—until a recent remodel—the cabinets and countertops still bore some of the scratches and gouges of the time when this was Rick's family apartment.

At the end of the hall, you hear Rick's voice again. This time it's the radio studio, where Tim Tattan and his team cram into a former bedroom—walls plastered with soundproofing foam—as they crank out our weekly national public radio show. When our guides are in town for the annual meetings, they record hours of interviews back-to-back in that studio, banking months' worth of content. Guides mill around in the kitchen, sipping coffee and trading notes about their home countries, as they wait for their turn on the air. (Sometimes I find eavesdropping on those conversations even more interesting than the recorded ones.)

Our guidebook team works in an old blue house across the street. Adorably nicknamed "Book Haus," it's a warren of desks where editors and cartographers work among piles of manuscripts. I love the thought that North America's bestselling guidebooks aren't created in some skyscraper in Manhattan or San Francisco, but in a small town at the northwest corner of the USA—in an unassuming house with a temperamental furnace, stained carpets over creaky floorboards, and mousetraps in the kitchen.

It's hard to believe I've been working at this same office for more than 20 years. From the Travel Center, I moved into our guidebook department. But Rick kept pulling me into more and more side projects until it became time for a more expansive role. For the last several years, I've kept an eye on the brand to ensure we remain true to our mission, and I've traveled more than ever to create and perfect our content. As the "other half of Rick's brain," I try to channel Rick when he's not around, and complement him when he is.

We've expanded over time, from about 40 people when I started to over 100, plus more than 150 freelance guides who are mostly based in Europe. "Managed growth" is a recurring theme: How do we stay true to our roots, providing quality experiences that live up to our customers' expectations and our own exacting standards? The answer usually involves putting the brakes on growing too fast. (It also answers one often-asked question: Why doesn't Rick do guidebooks to the USA, or Asia, or Latin America? Because we're determined to do just one thing, and do it well.)

But our merry band of travelers isn't just co-workers—it's the people whose trips we touch. On the road, "Rick Steves travelers" are a roving, like-minded community of people who are curious, respectful, and fun. When doing guidebook research, I hear plenty of complaints from Europeans about ill-behaved tourists. But anytime the subject turns to our guidebook readers and tour members, people rave: "We love Rick Steves travelers! They're our favorite. When we see that someone found us through Rick Steves, we know that they will be an excellent guest."

This all may sound Pollyannaish. But believe me, I have a remarkable capacity for cynicism. (Have you heard my thoughts on *The Sound of Music*?) And the fact is, the Cult of Rick Steves comes with a unique sense of community and unified purpose that goes well beyond one travel guru: We love to travel, we want to travel well, and we do.

Before the era of jet travel, I flew across
the Swiss Alps. They were beautiful and
it seemed like we could almost reach
out the window and pick up a handful
of snow. A year or two later I crossed
them again in a jet. That time we flew
so high we couldn't see so much, and
"Zip!"—we were over them.

—Mildred C. Scott,
  Jams Are Fun

PART SIX

Changes and Challenges

*T*he enduring wisdom of Aunt Mildred illustrates how travelers share a timeless kinship. And yet, there's no doubt that Mildred and I would see certain things very differently (salami sandwiches, for starters).

This question of generational change is a rare point of disagreement between Rick Steves and me. As an optimistic Baby Boomer, Rick believes that travelers are travelers are travelers—if something "works" for a traveler born in 1940 or 1960, it'll be just as good for one born in 1980 or 2000. As a cynical denizen of Generation X, I'm not convinced; I believe travelers' tastes evolve over time.

When I was a backpacker, printed guidebooks were the dominant source of travel information. Online resources gradually eclipsed print, and crowdsourced sites became the go-to way to research and book a trip. And now social media influencers have emerged as the new travel gurus. But do changing technologies actually impact that fundamental spirit of travel?

I'm old enough now—in my mid-forties—to be blossoming into full curmudgeonhood. That makes it easy for me to dismiss the Instagram-obsessed as "not real travelers." But that's unhelpful, and it's incomplete. I think my real concern—reasonable or not—is that seeing Europe through the frame of a six-inch-by-three-inch smartphone screen makes it too easy to miss those moments of simply slowing down to enjoy the church bells.

To Rick's point, though, maybe the "how" is a distraction. The key is tapping into the essence of good travel. When I read *Jams Are Fun,* some of Aunt Mildred's stories seem hopelessly old-fashioned. But then I turn the page, and I can imagine myself doing exactly what she describes, in exactly the same way.

In the end, I suspect Rick and I are both correct. There is something unchangeable about travelers. But the way that passion is expressed can vary, depending on each traveler's lived experience. For example, I believe that, in general, people my age seek to integrate food in their travels more than people Rick's age. (That's certainly true of Rick and me, at least.) This doesn't make us better or worse travelers—just different.

Change is relentless, and it can have unexpected results. Sometimes I get nostalgic for my earlier travels. On my semester abroad in Spain, my mom would snail-mail me football scores clipped from the sports page of the *Columbus Dispatch*. On my first backpacking trip across Europe, I'd buy cheap scratch-off phone cards and call home from sweaty, urine-perfumed phone booths. And when I was first traveling for work, my wife would record my favorite shows on a stack of VHS tapes for me to binge when I came home. (Avoiding spoilers was much easier then.) Today I can watch anything and talk to anyone, anywhere, anytime, virtually for free.

Sometimes I wonder whether this is truly "progress." Easier is not necessarily better. Speaking only for myself, there's no question I was more present in Europe 10 or 20 years ago than I am today. Being more connected with home is comforting and convenient; it takes the edge off homesickness and culture shock. But homesickness and culture shock can be, in retrospect, hallmarks of a great trip. Adversity builds character. And jams make great travelers.

Traveling to Europe has become easier and cheaper—more democratized, no longer the pastime of wealthy elites (or, in the case of Mildred, fortunate inheritors). That's a good thing. But it also translates into more crowds. Increasingly, "overtourism" has become an overriding concern in European travel. To the extent that too much travel can become a problem, as someone whose job is encouraging people to travel, I'm part of that problem. I've nibbled around the edges of these challenges so far. In the following pages, I confront them head-on.

In Italy's once-sleepy Cinque Terre, I consider the peculiarities of a tiny, tight-knit community, and what happens when it becomes a tourism superstar. On a train platform in Zagreb, I bump into some Syrian migrants who put a face on the "refugee crisis." Traveling through South England during the Brexit negotiations illustrates how "current" events—whatever and wherever they may be—have roots that go back centuries. And in Hallstatt, a lovely alpine village in Austria's Lake District, I get nostalgic and ponder how tourism can erode the specialness of a place, and what that means for the people rooted in that place.

Finally, this book's Epilogue brings us up to date, considering the impact of the coronavirus pandemic—which brought the biggest, fastest changes and challenges in the era of modern travel—and what might come next.

Cinque Terre, Italy

The Sublime and
the Ridiculous

*I*n all of Europe, there is one place from which guidebook researchers return and say, "If you need someone to do that chapter again in the future . . . thanks but no thanks." Strangely, it also happens to be one of our readers' most beloved destinations: Italy's Cinque Terre.

Cinque Terre means "Five Lands": five seaside villages, on the Italian Riviera between Genoa and La Spezia, strung together by a rail line. Each village has a harbor bobbing with fishing boats protected by a chunky breakwater; a canyon filled with tall, ram-shackle homes, built of stone and painted in cracked and faded pastels; and, on the green-and-white slopes overhead, a community cemetery and cascades of dry-stone wine terraces. Between the villages, the Ligurian Sea churns, while high on the hill, a vertiginous hiking trail lets you walk from the first town to the fifth in a matter of hours. Monterosso, Vernazza, Corniglia, Manarola, and Riomaggiore . . . for many travelers, these names trigger gauzy memories.

A generation or two ago, the Cinque Terre was a poor back-water with virtually no tourism. As a young vagabond, Rick Steves stumbled upon the five towns and filed them away in his mental rolodex. When he began building his network of "Back Doors"—underappreciated, out-of-the-way corners of Europe—the Cinque Terre topped the list. It became a favorite getaway for his North American readers.

But from a guidebook researcher's perspective, the Cinque Terre is a minefield of allegiances, grievances, and temper tantrums. A few years ago, we were striking out on finding someone willing to take it on. I had done it once already, and had the scars to prove it. But I felt a sense of duty. So I volunteered. And it was precisely as glorious and as tortuous as I expected. The Cinque Terre constantly, recklessly teeters between the sublime and the ridiculous.

My plane arrives in a stiff wind, and Genoa's airport provides a hard landing—both on the runway, and out at the curb, where I cram into an overstuffed bus for the trip to the train station. Despite the jet lag, I somehow find my way onto the right train. Tossing my bag on the overhead rack, I notice that everyone in the three-facing-three compartment is toting the same teal-and-gold guidebook. The Cinque Terre truly is Rick Steves country.

At the Monterosso train station, I step out into invigorating sunshine and follow the beachfront promenade to the Old Town and my hotel. It's only April, but people are already out at the beach, luxuriating on fine pebbles. A few kids are even brave enough to go for a swim.

Checked in and showered, I stroll through Monterosso. Local *ragazzi* are playing soccer on the piazza in front of the church, kicking the ball against the wall hard enough to send puffs of disintegrating plaster into the air. As if saying "ouch," the off-key church bells begin to clang. It's evening, and the waterfront restaurants are starting to fill up (even though at this time of year, you can't see the sunset from here). Sore-kneed hikers—with

their shorts-and-boots ensembles, sporty backpacks, and trekking poles—are trickling down the steep steps from the clifftop trail, having just hiked over the bluff from Vernazza. Periodically, a train rockets through town on the elevated tracks, briefly—but only briefly—shattering the serenity.

I survey the options along "restaurant row," inhaling a deep breath of shellfish and pesto and humid sea air. Taking my pick without a reservation (a perk of shoulder-season travel), I settle in for a meal of all the Cinque Terre classics: anchovies prepared a dozen different ways (but, frankly, none of them really delicious). A puffy piece of focaccia, encrusted with nuggets of sea salt. A big dish of *trofie*—dense, chewy pasta twists—with gaudy-green pesto. And for dessert, biscotti dunked in the sweet local wine, Sciacchetrà.

As I enjoy the meal, it sinks in that, like it or not, I'll spend the next week enjoying these same flavors and views as I explore the five lands, hike those trails, hop on those trains, and reconnect with a colorful cast of small-town characters—living a lifestyle I think of as *La Vita Cinqueterre*. I must admit, it's good to be back. And I'm enjoying the anonymity; as soon as word gets out that the Rick Steves researcher is in town, my mellow mood will come to an abrupt end.

In tiny, tight-knit communities, people are, in a word, strange. Or perhaps it's just harder to hide their strangeness with so few numbers. The Cinque Terre may be just five teensy villages, with a few hundred residents each. But in each one, generational grudges age like fine wines. When everybody is everybody's cousin, it requires diplomatic acrobatics to get the latest gossip about which restaurant is going downhill and which accommodations are overcharging. Each town has its own quirks and mini-mafias. It's my job to suss out exactly how people line up, without stepping on too many toes.

Over the years, we've cultivated a network of allies: smart, sensible locals who, for whatever reason, are able to transcend the pettiness and corruption. I think of them as spies for the cause. In Monterosso, it's Matteo, who runs two of the town's best hotels and somehow tiptoes the line between insider and complicit. I can ask him any question, and he knows just who to call. He pulls out his phone, dials some mysterious locals-only hotline, chatters for a few minutes in Italian, and gives me the most elusive thing in the Cinque Terre: a definitive answer.

Especially here in the Cinque Terre—but also throughout Europe—I find that expats are the best source of reliable insights. This is a person who loves a place so much that they chose to make it their home, and have been part of the community for years or decades. In every way that matters, they are a local. And yet, an expat remains tethered to "our" reality, making them ideal cultural translators.

My top spy in the Cinque Terre is Ruth Manfredi. Many years ago, on a visit to Vernazza, Ruth was having trouble pulling herself away from this stunning place and missed her train. Killing time on the breakwater, she found herself chatting with a local man. She wound up marrying him, and now they're raising two kids here. After a devastating flood in 2011, Ruth and some other expat women started a nonprofit called "Save Vernazza," which drew attention and funding to restore a town that had been nearly wiped off the map by a downhill tsunami of mud.

Ruth is also my savior in Vernazza. With each visit, I meet up with her to go over my questions. Often my notes have become so tied in knots with conflicting reports and pointless side-quests that I can't even formulate my questions. But Ruth has a knack for unraveling the confusion. And usually her answer involves "Cinque Terre logic" that is anything but logical to me.

Complicating matters is that the Cinque Terre is a moving target. It makes the rest of Italy feel like a paragon of order and predictability. In 1999, as the region's popularity surged, Italy designated the Cinque Terre as a national park. This could have been an opportunity to introduce protections and efficiencies. It wasn't.

The trails, ticketing, and other logistics of Cinque Terre National Park are managed by career bureaucrats who are big on talk but slow on action. Each one promises a bold new master plan to revolutionize the park experience: Elevators to connect train stations with clifftop neighborhoods! A combo-ticket that includes boats! Information kiosks and free public bathrooms in each town! Timed entry tickets for the trails!

But then . . . none of it materializes. Throughout the Cinque Terre, hikers trudge past half-built, boarded-up bathrooms and elevators that ran for a few weeks, a decade ago, and have never run since. And then, every so often—I imagine to foster the illusion that something is actually being accomplished—park authorities suddenly decide to change all of the trail numbers, rendering any prior maps or trail guides (or guidebooks) hopelessly misleading.

All of this creates a worst-case scenario for updating a guide-book. Every guidebook captures a moment in time. In most cases, real-world changes are gradual, so a book updated in the previous year or two is mostly accurate. But writing a guidebook on the Cinque Terre is like predicting the weather next July 15 based on what's happening on November 23. I scramble around the five towns, working every relationship we have in the region, and then toil over precise explanations. I double-check it all a few weeks later, before turning it in to our editors, only to find it's all differ-ent. The editors double-check details a few weeks after that, and make yet more revisions. And no matter how diligently we all do our jobs, it's all embarrassingly out of date the moment it rolls off the press.

Another challenge: Doing guidebook rounds here is physically demanding. Most of the accommodations are tiny one-off B&Bs: a person who rents two rooms on this side of the harbor, two others across the harbor, another one behind the station . . . and lives three towns away. Sometimes that person works afternoons at the wine bar or the pizzeria, so you can just drop by. But for most, you have to call ahead. I spend a lot of time crouched in doorways, hid-ing from the blazing sun or pouring rain, dialing the next person on my list. Sometimes they're nearby and can meet me in 10 minutes. Other times, they're in the next town and want to make plans to meet here tomorrow . . . when I'll be in the next town.

In Vernazza, my cell phone has service only when I'm standing out on the breakwater, bouncing my signal off the Ligurian Sea. But it goes dead anytime I actually enter the town. Meanwhile, many of our accommodations hide in the steep medieval lanes (called *caruggi*) up at the very top of town—more than a hundred stone stairs above the harbor. After updating one B&B, I walk a few doors down and spot the sign for the next B&B. Nobody's home—nobody is ever home—so I run down to the breakwater and call them. "Sure, meet me up there in five minutes!" Back up I go. And then back down. And then back up. And so on, all day long.

Being listed in a Rick Steves guidebook can have a big impact on a business. The smaller the town, the bigger the impact—and the more carefully the business tracks what we're saying about them. For one edition, our editors reorganized the sleeping sections. The following year, our researcher returned and discovered that those "minor" changes had ripped through each one of the tiny towns like an atom bomb. Each time she contacted a B&B host to update their details, she was met with confusion, pointed questions, and arm-waving fury. One woman screamed at her on the main street: "I was listed seventh last year, and now I'm listed ninth! What a disaster! My life is ruined! How dare you do this to me!" (That researcher never went back.)

Local residents often wage aggressive campaigns to get listed in the book (or to get someone else un-listed). If a Rick Steves researcher begins at the top of town, once she hits the middle of town, everybody knows she's there. And by the time she reaches the bottom of town, a line of people brandishing business cards is trailing her like kids following the pied piper. One morning I slept in, then caught up on some writing. When I finally left my room around eleven o'clock, two people were waiting for me out on the stoop to pitch me their businesses. I believe they'd been camped out there for hours.

A similar story, but worse, and one I'm not proud of: On that same visit, my B&B host kept showing up to greet me with a friend who had a room to rent. To make things easier for our readers, we only list people who rent multiple rooms, speak English, and can be reserved through email. The friend didn't tick any of these three boxes, so she wasn't going in the book, period. I kept politely turning her down, and she kept showing up.

Finally, one morning, I was passing through a little piazza when she cornered me and demanded, yet again, that I come see her room. Trying to extricate myself, I said, "No, thank you. No. No, I really can't. No. No, I just don't think it's right for the book. Nope. Well, maybe later." She perked up at the word "later" and seemed satisfied to let me on my way.

I spent hours running all over town, and was finally heading back to my B&B when I passed through that same piazza. And there she sat, right where I'd left her. When she saw me coming, she rose triumphantly, smiled with great satisfaction, and said, "OK, now it's later. Can I show you the room?"

A few years ago, I was staying in Vernazza and had scheduled a day to research the next town over, Corniglia. I decided to go there by foot. It was an idyllic commute: The well-tended trail, with just enough rocks and roots to hold your attention, meanders along a green shelf overlooking the frothy Ligurian Sea.

Reaching the outskirts of Corniglia, I came across the first of the hotels I needed to update for the book. I stopped in and asked my questions. Just as I was about to leave, the owner placed a forceful hand on my forearm.

"Listen," he said, conspiratorially. "If you want some gelato, I strongly recommend the first gelato place on the main street." He made severe eye contact. "Not the second one! The *first* one. You understand? *This is important.*"

I left with a noncommittal "*grazie* for the tip" and headed into Corniglia. Sure enough, on the main street, two rival *gelaterie* stood next to each other. I proceeded to update the rest of the town's hotels and guesthouses. As I made my rounds, a few other locals also weighed in—randomly and unsolicited—about which *gelateria* was superior.

Curiosity piqued, I dropped in at the second *gelateria*—the one we recommend in the book. I was warmly greeted by Alberto, who couldn't be more excited by my visit. He showed me a photo of himself with Rick, and a cover shot of our book that he likes

to put in the front window. He forced several samples on me, and dished up a tipsy cone piled comically high with scoops of different flavors.

As I was leaving, Alberto pulled me in close. "Before you go," he said, "can you do me one very big favor? That *gelateria* next door, they put up a picture of your book. But they are not recommended! They are lying! You must do something about this."

I walked past the other shop's window. No Rick Steves sign. Oh, well. But Alberto chased after me. "Aha! They take it down because they know you are here. Please go in and tell them to stop!"

"Look," I said, "if they don't have the sign up when I'm here, then what can I do?" (In fact, there's little I can do in any case. We've seen this from time to time: Once a place recognizes the touristic currency of a Rick Steves endorsement—whether they are actually recommended or not—we can ask them to stop, but we can't effectively police them from 5,000 miles away.)

One thing had become abundantly clear: Somehow, all of this town's frustrations, quarrels, and grievances, dating back generations, had boiled down to these two neighboring *gelaterie*. And I had been enlisted to play Solomon. I managed to escape without any more drama . . . but I could never forget the gelato controversy that gripped little Corniglia.

Flash forward. I'm back in the Cinque Terre, and back in Corniglia. This time, I'm prepared. I arrive in town with my shields up. I will not be drawn into Gelatogate. I will do my work and leave as quickly as possible.

The day goes well. I make my rounds and am ready to head out. I've saved the gelato for last—partly to forestall further conflict, and partly to treat myself before the train ride home. But first, I'm updating one final restaurant. The restaurateur is warm and gregarious. As he talks me through his creative menu, his enthusiasm and pride lull me into a sense of normalcy.

But then, just as I'm turning to leave, like a coiled cobra— he strikes.

"Say . . . did you happen to see the new *gelateria* at the start of town?" he asks me, too eagerly. "It's a very good one. You really should see it." His tone flips from casual to intense, as his laser-beam eyes pierce mine. "You *must* see it."

The next few moments are a blur, as somehow I find myself following him down the street, where he physically plants me inside this new *gelateria*. Aren't two *gelaterie* more than enough for this tiny town? Do they really need a third?

I ask a few probing questions. And finally, they 'fess up that this is, in fact, a second outpost of one of the original *gelaterie*— the one that's *not* recommended in the book.

This new shop is an interloper. But, at some level, I have to admire the gambit. Now there are two clone *gelaterie*, across the street from each other, before you even get to Alberto's. (It also means that Alberto's is, technically, no longer the "second one.")

The list of flavors displays scars from many skirmishes in the gelato wars. Alberto's shop has a delicious honey flavor, which we mention in the book. This shop, too, has a honey flavor. Alberto is very proud of his basil flavor—new for this year. This shop, too, now has a basil flavor. With a JFK-Khrushchev brinksmanship, these rival gelato makers are keeping pace with each other as they slowly, slowly escalate hostilities.

Case made, the restaurateur tries to close the deal. "So then, you will put this *gelateria* in your book?"

I hedge. "Um, I'll think about it."

"*Think* about it!?" He turns sour and confrontational. "What's to think about? It's the best one. The *best one!*" At this point, as weirdness layers on top of weirdness, it occurs to me that—as far as I know—this restaurateur is not the *gelaterie*'s owner. He's just a very, very, *very* concerned citizen.

I try to explain myself. But he won't let me finish. "The last time Rick Steves was here, I took him to this *gelateria*. And it's still not in the book. That was nearly two years ago! What is taking so long?"

I excuse myself and bail out of the shop. I try to ignore the now-furious restaurateur as he hangs his head, Charlie Brown-style, and theatrically sulks back to his own restaurant—stomping his feet like a furious toddler.

Escaping town, I scramble down the 385 steps that connect Corniglia with its seaside train station. Uncomfortable as these interactions are, at least I get to leave and return to the real world. For these poor villagers, this is just the latest salvo in the Gelato Wars of Corniglia.

Perhaps you're wondering whether Alberto's gelato is truly the best. The answer: Yes. How do I know? Because on both trips, I tasted both. And Alberto's wins the taste test, hands down. So if any Corniglia gelato warriors are reading this, now you know: If you want to be in the book, make better gelato.

* * *

Stepping onto the Vernazza train platform around noon, I see hundreds of people milling about, waiting for (delayed) trains in both directions. It's a mob scene. Cruise passengers—easy to spot with their numbered lapel stickers and their whisper-system earbuds—stick close to their guides, in big packs along the platform. Individual travelers, toting heavy backpacks, do their best to weave through the crowds, filling in wherever they find gaps.

All of us are whipped by a sudden horizontal vortex as the train charges through the tunnel. It slows down, brakes squealing at a deafening pitch as it stops along the platform. It's already full. The doors open. Just a few people step off the train. Everybody else wants on. And the scene becomes a disorderly Bosch painting of twisting bodies, human drama, and Mephistophelean chaos.

People pull their travel partners into the tiny alcoves by the doors. I slip in and find a place to stand. I see a tour guide at the door of the train, shouting to his group with exaggerated calm: "Don't worry. Don't worry. Just poosh your way in. Poosh in. I will be the last one." An elderly woman behind me starts howling. "This is scary! I'm getting crushed! I'm getting crushed!"

Finally the last person pooshes their way onto the train, we all suck in our breath, the doors shimmy shut, and we're on our way to Monterosso—where, minutes later, the entire contents of the train disgorge onto the platform, creating yet another logjam. The whole experience feels less like a vacation, and more like a self-imposed refugee crisis.

When I describe this experience to my friends in the Cinque Terre, they tell me that it happens several times a day throughout the summer. They say, "It's only a matter of time before somebody gets pushed onto the tracks and gets hurt, or worse."

Since Rick's first visit here, the Cinque Terre has gone from "undiscovered" to "manageably popular" to "miserably crowded." Locals tell me the turning point came when cruise lines began calling at Genoa and La Spezia, the industrial port cities that flank the Cinque Terre. One cruise ship can dump as many as 6,000 people ashore—each one desperate to wring some Cinque Terre memories out of their few hours on land. At the same time, the region has become popular among Italian day-trippers, especially on busy holiday weekends.

Much as I enjoy complaining about getting sucked into the Gelato Wars of Corniglia, it's only honest for me to reckon with the role that I might have played in escalating them. Even without Rick Steves' attention, this place would likely suffer from a scorched-earth competitiveness. But encouraging travelers—and their money—to come here just throws gasoline on those embers. This begs the question: Is it ethical to promote travel to a fragile place?

On the one hand, I've met countless people—both travelers and people who work in tourism—whose lives are immeasurably better thanks to travel. I've seen how tourism injects much-needed affluence and pride into a community that could use more of both. When managed properly, tourism can subsidize and celebrate endangered vestiges of culture. Without tourism, would the Cinque Terre still be producing Sciacchetrà wine? Would Monterosso celebrate its Lemon Festival? Or would those beautiful hilltop cemeteries become overgrown and neglected as younger people fled to the cities? Locals tell me that more tourism means more demand for local wine, which encourages farmers to restore eroded terraces, which makes the five towns less vulnerable to floods and landslides like the one that nearly wiped out Vernazza.

And yet, in excess, that attention can trample everything that's special about a place. Tourism isn't simply good or bad; there are different degrees and shades of gray—ways that the right kind of tourism can strengthen communities, and the wrong kind can weaken them. And, on the sliding scale of "not enough" to "too much," the Cinque Terre is in the 99th percentile.

The irony is that, by the time many places become "overtour-isted," it's after several years of actively, even aggressively, seeking tourism. For example, on my first trip to Iceland—as that coun-try's global popularity was peaking—Icelander after Icelander told me they were concerned about the onslaught of visitors. But those visitors were there because of a successful advertising campaign funded by the Icelandic government. Then, about a year and a half later, I returned to Iceland. One of the country's budget air-lines had gone bust, and international arrivals had dipped ever so slightly. The tone had changed dramatically. "We are very worried about this decline in tourism," people would tell me, gravely. "We were counting on continued growth. How can we weather this?"

The Cinque Terre went through its own setback, when those 2011 floods wiped out many businesses. They feared they might never bounce back, and they begged visitors to return. Within a few years, tourism had resumed its status as the bane of their exis-tence. And the people of Dubrovnik, who faced a similar crisis with the 1991-1992 siege, desperately wanted tourism to recover—and now seem to have regrets. All of this makes me wonder if there's no such thing as the "right number" of tourists. Perhaps it's always too few, or too many. It's human nature to long for greener grass.

Some travelers like to credit (or blame) Rick Steves for "dis-covering" the Cinque Terre. That's debatable. But he certainly contributed to its fame. Locals tell me that this attention has, on the whole, made life better here—helping a hardscrabble area find firm financial footing. But then other tourism—mass tourism—piggybacked on that popularity, took it to extremes, and corrupted it. Does that mean Rick should have left it undiscovered? Is it Rick's "fault" that what he started metastasized into something malignant?

Sometimes when I rave about an underappreciated corner of Europe, I get dinged by critics: "How dare you! You're just going to attract too many people there. You're going to *ruin* it!"

I imagine that, for these people, a place is pure and pristine only in the absence of tourism. Their dream destination must be untouched and untrampled—a Brigadoon that appears, from time to time, out of the ether—and they are the sole tourist.

The "tourism ruins places" philosophy also smacks of elitism. A place is good and properly touristed when I go there. But if it grows a smidge more popular, it loses that immaculate specialness. In fact, any further visitors should be shamed for contributing to its ruination.

Consider the hypothetical, virgin destination I'll call Schrödingburg-in-der-Kiste. The people who live in Schrödingburg might benefit from tourism, and/or the town could lose some of what makes it special. The only way to find out if tourism is a net gain, or a net loss, is to open Schrödingburg's Box.

But here's the thing: Schrödingburg has some say in the matter. The townspeople can resist greed and make tough decisions that cultivate conscientious tourism—as Siniša is attempting on the Dalmatian island of Hvar.

I'm not willing to write off travel entirely, because I still believe that, fundamentally, travel can be a force for good. But it's important for me to be aware of these challenges, and to find ways to help Schrödingburg emerge from its box with its soul intact. I see my job not as promoting travel indiscriminately, but rather—as with that milk bar in Kraków—presenting each place in a way that helps it attract visitors who will appreciate it and treat it with care. Just to make sure, I constantly probe local complaints to understand what we can do to help, even if it's telling people *not* to go there.

The universal response is: No, we *do* want travelers—just the "right kind" of travelers. That means people who are curious and respectful. And, frankly, those who will leave some money behind. The "wrong kind" of travelers are cruise ship passengers and day trippers, who rush in, congest the already overtaxed infrastructure, then rush out while barely spending a dime. (That's why, in our cruise guidebooks, we actively discourage cruise passengers from going to the Cinque Terre; we don't even cover it in the book, in favor of less fragile alternatives.)

There are no easy solutions. But it begins with each visitor making a point to be the "right kind" of traveler. That means, for starters, empathizing with the people you meet as fellow human beings, not just service providers. It's not easy; you're an underdog in the battle against Big Tourism, which worships the primacy of money at the expense of substance. But if you're mindful, you can patronize locals who are trying to do their work thoughtfully.

If you notice that tourism is overwhelming a place, find creative ways not to personally contribute to that trend. Often you'll find a more rewarding alternative anyway. In the Cinque Terre, if I know cruise arrivals are about to deluge the region, I try to clear out during the busiest time of day. By doing this, I've enjoyed some of my favorite Ligurian memories: Hiking the tranquil, high-altitude vineyard trail between Manarola and Corniglia, instead of the tourist-clogged main route; or bicycling from Levanto to the sleepy seaside village of Benassola. As dusk falls and the cruise ships head on their way, I return to the five towns for a mellow dinner amidst a more relaxed community.

The beauty of the Cinque Terre is sublime; its crowds, its petty politics, its gelato feuds, and its aggressive B&B hosts can be ridiculous. In the grand equation, the two usually even out. At the end of an exhausting week of researching here—which feels like a month—I'm ready to move on. But I'm also confident that someday, I'll be back for another fix of that addictive *Vita Cinqueterre*.

One Day I Met Some Refugees

*I*n 2015, war in Syria left a quarter-million people dead. Throughout that summer and fall, more than one million refugees—about half from Syria, the rest from other failed states—slowly made their way to Europe. These new arrivals came in through Turkey and Greece, then moved up the Balkan Peninsula toward prosperous northern European nations, seeking amnesty.

That summer, watching news clips of migrants stranded at train stations and border checkpoints, I felt pangs of sympathy. But mainly, I'm ashamed to admit, I was worried that my fall research trip might be inconvenienced.

In early September, I arrived in Croatia's capital, Zagreb, during a sunny weekend. The mood was festive and I was enjoying my work. That afternoon, engrossed in my guidebook chores, I stepped into the main train station. All of the international departures on the big timetable were flashing *otkazan*—"cancelled."

And that's when I saw them: eight or nine refugees, including two young children. At this moment, they weren't howling in despair, or running for their lives through wheat fields, or climbing over razor wire, or stuffing themselves through the windows of train cars—like I'd been seeing on TV. They were just standing around. Waiting. Bored.

The refugees were dressed neatly, wearing fanny packs, and glancing at their smartphones. The little boy was tossing a stuffed animal into the air to entertain himself. They had the air of a family who just learned that the last flight out was grounded and now had to figure out another way to get to their destination. They were calm. Perhaps, after whatever they'd been through, simply hanging out in a quiet train station on a sunny Saturday afternoon was a relief.

In the middle of the group was a pair of young Croatians. One smiled broadly, as if determined to project an air of peace and normalcy. The other was a force-of-nature activist with a blond ponytail. She was simultaneously talking with the refugees and making calls on her phone.

Passersby (and the many police officers on duty) were mainly keeping their distance—shooting glances of sympathy or suspicion from across the platform. Occasionally someone would approach to offer them food or water. But they already had overflowing shopping bags, as much as they could carry. One woman tried to hand them a shrink-wrapped flat of eight water bottles. "Thank you," the young man said politely. "We only need two."

I approached the grinning Croatian and asked what I could do to help. Did they need groceries? Water? Money? Cigarettes? *Anything?* Like the others who'd offered, I was told none of this was necessary. "We're just trying to organize a ride to Slovenia," he explained. "The taxi drivers keep trying to rip them off."

Just the day before, I had toured a wrenching museum in Sarajevo about the 1995 massacre at Srebrenica. I was haunted by the final words of the exhibit, that famous quote from Edmund

Burke: "All that is necessary for the triumph of evil is that good men do nothing."

I can't express how helpless I felt on that train platform. I like to think I'm a good man. But there I stood, doing nothing. In that moment, I could no longer view these people as the kind of abstract social problem that causes caring people to shake their heads and mutter, "Such a shame. But really, what can be done?" I was standing face-to-face with human beings in crisis. And my every instinct was screaming that they had to get to where they were going. They couldn't stay here, and they certainly couldn't go back. Any person with a conscience, in that moment, would reach the same conclusion.

After a few minutes, the refugees' Samaritans led them over to the taxi stand, put them in a car, and waved goodbye as they embarked on the next leg of their journey. I went back to my hotel room, called my parents, and sobbed for half an hour about how cruel this world can be. (And I am not a sobber.)

A couple of days later, I followed the refugees' trail north, to the Slovenian capital of Ljubljana. Because the trains still weren't running—and because my endowment of privilege includes a US passport and a Visa card—I effortlessly booked a shared transfer with a van service. We hopped on the expressway, and a half-hour later, we were approaching Slovenia.

The grassy median strip leading up to the border checkpoint was cluttered with dozens of multicolored tents. The refugees, who'd been camping here for days, had finally crossed into Slovenia the night before. Discarded clothes and blankets littered the grass. Sleeping bags hung over fences. A staging area was piled with cardboard boxes of food, bandages, and other supplies. Reporters stood in discussion under their switched-off lighting rigs. Humanitarian aid workers in reflective vests were attempting to tidy up.

For those of us in the van, the border crossing was a non-event: the flash of a passport, and in minutes we were rolling along at 120 kilometers per hour to Ljubljana. I was heartened when I arrived there and found a message spray-painted onto a street sign downtown: "Refugees Welcome!" Of course, I never saw those refugees again, or learned what became of them. But I still think about them frequently.

It's easy to become complacent, jaded, even irritated about migrants and refugees. We see them either as some distant, sad spectacle or as a vaguely sinister threat. That 2015 migrant crisis became a lightning rod for Europe's nativist movements. Hungary's authoritarian leadership, Fidesz, exploited the fear of refugees to shore up their base. And a year later, on my side of the Atlantic, another nativist rode a wave of anti-immigrant paranoia into the White House. Apparently, it's universal for politicians to scream, red-faced, about how some poor person from a faraway corner of the globe is to blame for all of society's problems.

But when I met those refugees in person, the only thing I could see was their humanity. It was painfully obvious: These were not stealth terrorists, or George Soros-funded crisis actors. They were just desperate people in need of compassion.

All refugees and migrants—including my own Norwegian and Polish and Irish ancestors—share the same motivation: to find a safe place to live and raise their families. What could be more understandable? And yet, the original sin of the migrant is being born in the wrong country at the wrong time; their crime is taking action to improve their circumstances; and their sentence is to be political props, scapegoats, and boogeymen.

A year and a half after my encounter in Zagreb, I found an epilogue of sorts in Berlin, the capital of the country where many of those refugees ended up. Throughout 2015, Chancellor Angela Merkel (who, it bears noting, led her country's conservative party) graciously took in more than one million migrants.

The Berliners I talked to acknowledged some growing pains. But they already saw signs of integration and collaboration. One example was a newly opened Syrian bakery that had become a hotspot for Berlin hipsters and foodies seeking authentic honey-soaked sweets from the Middle East. Even Berliners who had some reluctance were confident that the new arrivals would make Germany stronger, not weaker. And they were very clear on one point: Taking in people in need is simply the right thing to do. (A few months later, Merkel was decisively re-elected to her fourth term.)

Back home, I encounter a very different approach to migrant issues. Provocative American "news" outlets describe a Europe that's being plunged into a hellish new reality by these dangerous migrants. They're "ruining" everything that's special about the Old World, we're told. Paris, Oslo, Brussels, London, and so on simply aren't the great cities they once were. I've been asked about this by family friends and relatives, who haven't been to Europe and struggle to reconcile my enthusiasm for the place with the horror stories they're seeing online.

It's nothing short of surreal how different those stories are from the reality I encounter in Europe. With my own eyes, I see how many parts of Europe gracefully and constructively take in new arrivals from non-European backgrounds and make them a vital part of contemporary life.

Those Syrian baklavas in Berlin are just one example. Berlin—which rivals London as Europe's greatest melting pot city—has been *Multikulti* since before it was cool. Soon after World War II, Turkish *Gastarbeiter* ("guest workers") helped rebuild the shattered city, weaving their own strands into the fabric of Berlin. To this day, the Kreuzberg district is at least as much "Turkish" as it is "German" (but actually, it's both at once).

The most enjoyable evening I've spent in Brussels was exploring the Congolese neighborhood of Matongé, where you can buy cassava, batik fabric, and afro-care products just a short subway ride from the *Mannekin-Pis* and the Atomium.

The traveler often connects with this side of European culture most vividly through food. In Oslo's Grünerløkka district, I've had fantastic chicken curry at a Pakistani restaurant. In Amsterdam, some of the most memorable eats include an Indonesian *rijstafel* feast and a crispy Middle Eastern wrap sandwich called a *manoushe*. And throughout Portugal, I seek out restaurants featuring cuisine from far-flung former colonies in South America, Africa, the Indian subcontinent, and Oceania.

Across Europe, migrants become residents become citizens who revitalize a society, adding depth and richness to the culture and fostering a more global outlook that benefits everyone. If this sounds familiar, it's because the United States once prided itself as a melting pot that worked in just this way. *E pluribus unum*, huddled masses yearning to breathe free, and all that.

Europe does have its traditionalists and nativists, of course. And conservative voters in some countries—like Hungary and Poland—have become very cozy with those movements. But for the most part, Europe, whose days of glory and global domination have passed, understands that the only viable path forward is multicultural. They realize that you can preserve treasured traditions while also flexing with a changing world and a changing populace. Culture is not a zero-sum game.

Many of this book's stories are about the hedonistic joys and the cultural epiphanies of travel. But there are moments when travel does even more: It exposes you to raw realities. It assaults your assumptions, confronts your privilege, challenges you to develop empathy in spite of yourself, and teaches you that the more of the world you experience, the less frightening it becomes. It subverts fear by providing real context for the news (and the "news"). And it reminds you that, at the end of the day, we're all human.

Blood, Toil, Tears, Sweat, and Surrendering to Brexit

*H*ave you ever learned a new word—one that you'd swear you never heard before—and then, over the next days and weeks, you hear it again and again?

Sometimes, in the same way, themes emerge in your travels. In the spring of 2019, I spent a few weeks in London and South England. The Brexit referendum—obligating Great Britain to leave the European Union—had passed nearly three years earlier, but Britain was still struggling mightily with how to enact it. And everywhere I turned, this trip seemed determined to provide me with historical context for the moment it now faced.

On my first big backpacking trip, in 1999, I visited some old, dear friends of my parents in Durham, England. Over my first-ever chicken tikka masala at the town's finest curry house, I told them I planned to visit all the different parts of Europe—starting here in England. The awkward silence that ensued made it clear I had said something inappropriate. "Well, yes, but . . . " they finally said, kindly but firmly. "Britain is not Europe."

I am a true believer in the European Union. This inclines me to ignore evidence of the EU's flaws, and to dismiss pro-Brexit rationales. But by forcing myself to travel with an open mind, I've observed how Britain and Europe have always been strange bedfellows.

When planning this trip, nostalgia compelled me to book a ticket on the Eurostar train through the Channel Tunnel from England to Paris. On that first backpacking trip, I "rode the Chunnel," which had been open just five years. Back then it seemed so exciting, optimistic, even futuristic. This was the heyday of European unity: A few years later, eleven European countries would retire their individual currencies in favor of the simplicity of the euro. And a couple of years after that, the European Union would expand far to the east—bringing a wave of Polish and Slovak and Lithuanian workers to British shores.

In retrospect, perhaps that was too much Euro-togetherness, too fast. Today the Chunnel tethers England to a continent a majority of its voters say they want no part of. And at Ashford International train station, it shows.

Ashford International—where I'm hitching my ride through the Chunnel—is sprawling, characterless, and drab. Nobody seems to like it very much. The simple task of returning my rental car here is an ordeal. Circling the station, eyes peeled for a *Hertz* sign that never appears, I keep winding up on the parkway to the adjacent Ashford Designer Outlet. Many times the size of the station, it exerts an inescapable gravity—as if everybody has quietly decided that the shopping mall, and not the station linking Britain to Europe, is what Ashford should be known for.

Like many travelers, I'm a connoisseur of train stations—especially here in Britain, where historic brick, steel, and glass architecture mingles with modern embellishments. But Ashford International has zero personality. It feels like a too-big boondoggle airport in a depressed city, whose developers are currently serving five to ten in a minimum-security prison.

The concourse is a ghost town. In my imagination, tumble-weeds swirl past the shuttered newsstands. There's a pack of loud French teenagers, apparently returning home from a class trip. And at the opposite end of the concourse—keeping their distance—are a few weary-looking Brits, sitting sourly like patients in a backed-up NHS waiting room. All of this is starkly at odds with the many colorful, life-size Mickey Mouse cutouts with the message, "Disneyland is closer than you think!" and encouraging me to "Find all 10 of the hidden Mickeys!" Apparently, the only group still gung-ho about the Chunnel are marketers responsible for luring British families to Disneyland Paris.

While most of the shops in the station are closed, two cafés are open. Comparing the two, I choose the farther one, if only because it's easier than backtracking to the first one. The cashier—casting suspicious glances up the concourse—grumbles about the other café. "It's Saturday!" she hisses. "And on Saturdays, only one of these two cafés is supposed to be open. Today is our turn. But *this* lot"—more accusatory glances up-concourse—"decided to open anyway."

"Um," I say. I noticed, walking by earlier, that the offending café is French-run.

"Don't worry," she says with a satisfied wink. "I've already reported this to the supervisor."

Duly relieved, I slink away with my bitter, burned-tasting latte (a British specialty) and my cheese and ham panino. As I eat, I look out over the heartbreaking mediocrity of the platforms. The gray metal canopies over each track match the overcast sky. I think about how the very name—Ashford International—carries a cheeky optimism. Fancy that! An *in-ter-na-tion-al* train station—in England! This must have seemed thrilling when it opened. But today, I can't shake the sense that the station is the embodiment of a deeply unsatisfying British-French compromise that made nobody happy—and, increasingly, feels like a regrettable albatross.

Looking over those gray tracks, I think back on what have, until now, seemed a random assortment of impressions during this trip. My mind weaves them together as threads of a thousand-year tale of Britain and Europe.

I arrived in London about three weeks ago, which happened to be just before an EU-imposed Brexit deadline. Curiosity drew me to the Houses of Parliament, where Big Ben's tower was entirely covered with scaffolding—howlingly on-the-nose symbolism for Britain's current "work in progress" approach to sensible governance. I arrived just in time to see a smattering of pro-EU protesters, waving flags and hollering. They huddled together and mustered all their energy for a chant: "No Brexit! No Brexit! *NOOOOO BREXIT!*" It seemed like they were just getting warmed up. But then, having said their piece, they dispersed just like that . . . wandering off in every direction, their limp EU flags dragging on the pavement.

A few blocks up Whitehall, I walked past one of my favorite monuments in London, honoring British women who died serving in World War II—many of them on European soil. It stands immediately in front of Downing Street, where, at Number 10, another exemplary British woman's talents were being squandered trying to clean up a mess created by headstrong men. Theresa May already had one foot out the door; the pinnacle of her career, it seemed, was to take the fall for David Cameron's Brexit referendum, then quietly excuse herself for another reckless man to take the reins. (And sure enough, a few months later, Boris Johnson did precisely that.)

Moving on from London, I went on a road trip throughout South England, from Brighton to Dover to Canterbury—the corner of Britain that's closest to the Continent.

Brighton, an hour's train ride south of London, fancies itself Britain's Riviera—a beach break alternative to Mykonos or Dubrovnik or the Costa del Sol. On a warm spring day, the beach's

chunky pebbles were filled with working-class Londoners trying to get comfortable on towels and sling-back chairs. Most people stayed well back from the water, with just a few kids dipping numb toes into frigid surf. This seemed a poor substitute for balmy Adriatic or Aegean beaches. But Britain was, apparently, willing to give up easy access to those and settle for this fully English substitute.

On a walking tour, my guide pointed out the Brighton Dome, where ABBA's "Waterloo" won the Eurovision song contest in 1974. (Am I pushing it too far to note that the song was about Britain's defeat of Napoleon's French forces, thereby containing Continental expansionism? Yes? OK, never mind.) There was a time when Eurovision captivated all of Britain. It was the pop music equivalent of the Olympics or the World Cup, uniting people across countries and cultures. But these days, the Brits have grown cynical. "It's not what it used to be," I've heard many say. "After the Iron Curtain fell, the Eastern Bloc broke into a million little countries that just vote for each other's songs. It's not fair!"

An hour's drive east, in the town of Battle, I trudged through drizzle at the site of the Battle of Hastings—where, in 1066, the Norman (read: French) William the Conqueror defeated the

Anglo-Saxon (read: English) Harold Godwinson with an arrow through the eye. This precipitated centuries of French rule over Britain. While seemingly a loss for Britain, historians credit this battle with bringing the until-then-remote island more fully into the European fold. If not for the Norman Conquest, Britain might still loom on Europe's distant periphery. The English language and culture not only survived, but were enhanced by their French connection. Most English speakers don't realize how many words came into our language from French—including ones for fundamental concepts like art, money, justice, diplomacy, theater, cuisine, and many others.

In Canterbury, I found myself reciting the prologue of Geoffrey Chaucer's 14th-century masterpiece, *Canterbury Tales* (which I was required to memorize in college). A museum docent pointed out that Chaucer's work was so influential, in part, because it was written in vernacular English, at a time when French was still the language of learning and literature. But things were changing. A few decades earlier, the Great Plague had halved England's population—disproportionately killing off French speakers (who tended to live in cities, where disease spread wildly). And Chaucer was writing just as the Hundred Years' War was turning popular opinion against the French. At this pivotal moment, Chaucer asserted the worthiness of English as a literary language; two hundred years later, Shakespeare would cite his influence.

In Dover, peering across the English Channel, I could plainly see France despite the cloudy, drizzly, blustery weather. It's *right there*, after all—just 20 miles away. Up at Dover Castle, I toured the secret tunnels from which British authorities orchestrated the "Miracle of Dunkirk"—rescuing 338,000 British troops who'd become stranded on a broad French beach after being boxed in by Nazi forces in some of the earliest fighting of World War II.

Standing atop a windy white cliff, looking across to France, I recalled the words of Winston Churchill's most famous speech, delivered the day after Dunkirk to rally Britain for the coming winner-take-all war with Germany: "We shall defend our island, whatever the cost may be. We shall fight on the beaches, we shall fight on the landing grounds, we shall fight in the fields and in the streets, we shall fight in the hills; we shall never surrender." Churchill—who knew his Chaucer—made a point to use exclusively words of Anglo-Saxon origin, with just one pointed exception that came from French: "surrender."

Down on Dover's waterfront, I stumbled upon a chilling monument: a panel (donated by Germany in peacetime) where Nazi artillery forces made a note of each one of the 84 shells they lobbed at Dover from their positions on the cliffs of Calais across the English Channel. Imagine: The Nazis were so close to Britain—on French soil—that they didn't even need airplanes or rockets to bomb it.

Finally, leaving Dover, I pulled off the motorway at a quiet park called Samphire Hoe, tucked at the base of Dover's famous white cliffs. This artificial meadowland was created by dumping more than six million cubic yards of chalk excavated during the construction of the Chunnel between 1988 and 1994—a time when, just a few decades removed from Hitler, Britain found itself decisively moving *toward* Europe once again, following the pendulum of history. By the seaside, a poignant plaque listed the names of 11 workers who died during construction—yet more casualties in the ongoing struggle to unite Britain and Europe.

Back at Ashford International, I'm jolted awake by the announcement—first in English, then in French—that it's time to board the train that will take me through that tunnel.

After all this buildup, crossing from Britain to Europe is anticlimactic. The train pulls up, I get on and find my seat, they serve a meal. A few minutes later, while they're pouring coffee, it grows abruptly dark. No "Cheerio, England!" No nothing.

Brexit is complicated. It was driven by economic discontent, especially in the industrialized, depressed North, where resentment festers toward the "Soft South" (as they call London and its sprawl). It was driven by Euroskepticism—by the many Brits who never really bought into the notion of a united Europe. It was driven by xenophobia and a global movement of nativism, stoked by social media and misinformation. And, not unlike the election of Donald Trump in my own country a few months later, Brexit can be seen as a protest vote: disillusioned voters throwing a hand grenade into the halls of government. In the end, though, the roots of Brexit go far deeper than any of those reasons.

Travelers become engrossed in "current events" when visiting a place. What we sometimes miss is that those events are usually just another chapter in a long and messy saga. Britain's struggle to reconcile its relationship with Europe is as old as "British-ness" itself. Now, as ever, Britain can't live with Europe . . . but can't live without it.

Several minutes later, it gets light again, and my phone jingles: "Welcome to France!" (My cell phone company—eager to explain their roaming policy—seems to be the only entity that cares I'm in a new country.) And then, the loudspeaker: *"Mesdames et Messieurs, nous approchons maintenant Paris."*

Hallstatt, Austria

Hallstatt Never Changes...
Except When It Does

uzzing along the glassy surface of a glacial alpine lake, feeling the sun on my face and the wind in my hair, it dawns on me: I'm enjoying my favorite moment of this trip so far.

I'm in—actually, bobbing in a plastic boat just offshore from—the tiny town of Hallstatt, in Austria's Salzkammergut Lake District. Before me, the pointy Protestant church spire stands like the town flag, staking its claim on the narrow ledge of land that Hallstatt occupies. Higher on the hill is the subtler, stubby onion dome of the Catholic church. With sheer granite cliffs on one side, the deep waters of the Hallstättersee on the other, and a waterfall thundering through the heart of town, Hallstatt is one of those places that begs the question: What would possess someone to build a village here?

The answer is simple: salt deposits, buried in the mountain. But today, salt is the farthest thing from my mind. The weather is glorious, and I'm tooling around the lake in a little electric rental boat. It has two speeds: "stop" and "go." The Hallstättersee forbids gas-powered watercraft, so there's no worry about dodging

speedboats and jet skis. It's just me, a few plodding paddleboats shaped like the lake's resident swans, and *Stefanie*, the little ferry that tethers Hallstatt to its train station across the lake.

Back on land, I stroll through wee Hallstatt. It's a 30-second walk from the boat dock to the main square, which feels like a movie set. The square's centerpiece, a gurgling fountain, is surrounded by an amphitheater of cozy, colorful house fronts. They're painted in restrained pastels, draped in climbing ivy that's bushy and green, punctuated with Juliet balconies and colorful window boxes, and topped by heavy wooden beams supporting heavier roofs.

At the bottom corner of the square, a hot-pink house peeks between two bigger buildings, like a kid sister elbowing her way in for the view. This is Gasthof Simony, where I stayed on my seminal 1999 backpacking trip. I'd booked a room at a cheap pension on the hillside above town. But the room didn't meet even my extremely forgiving standards. So I bailed out, walked down the hill, and knocked on the first guesthouse door I came to.

Frau Scheutz answered my knock and warmly offered me a deal on her budget single. Rick described her as "grandmotherly," and sure enough, she helped me feel at home midway through a long journey. Rick also said the hotel was "stocking-feet-tidy." I didn't know exactly what that meant. But once I was checked into my woody room, I distinctly remember enjoying the sensation of taking my shoes off and feeling the floorboards under my stocking feet.

Gasthof Simony is still there, albeit with a flashy new paint job. But Frau Scheutz retired several years back. And, based on my inspection, the hotel is still creaky and traditional, but no longer "grandmotherly" or "stocking-feet-tidy." It's being run as an afterthought by a bigger hotel in town.

Standing in front of the guesthouse, feeling nostalgic, I'm recognized by a fellow traveler who's seen my picture on Rick's website and books. (This does not happen often.) He and his mother are on an epic journey through Central Europe—pausing for the night in Hallstatt on their way between Český Krumlov and Slovenia's Lake Bled. He says that, like me, he stood on this very spot 20 years ago. And he's struck by how similar things still look. "Except there used to be cars parked all along this square," he says.

Bidding farewell to my one and only fan, I think about how Hallstatt hasn't changed, and how it has. Yes, on the surface it's still the same wonderful old place. But I sense a creeping corporatization.

Updating my guidebook, I learn that three of the classic old hotels on this square have been purchased and remodeled by big-city investors. And at another hotel, I'm told that jolly old Herr Zauner—who "wears lederhosen like pants were never invented," as Rick wrote—has passed day-to-day management duties to his son. The rooms have been modernized, and the prices have increased. But the receptionist reassures me: "Oh, don't worry, Herr Zauner still hangs out at dinnertime. And he still loves telling all of his old mountaineering stories."

I'm glad Herr Zauner still makes an occasional appearance. And he's certainly earned his retirement. But the glamification of Hallstatt concerns me. Yes, the town's rehabbed hotels are more efficient and modern. For most travelers—the ones who demand reliable plumbing, speedy Wi-Fi, and room service—that's a good thing. But to me, it's at least as much a loss as a gain. Hallstatt no longer a locally owned community of quirky villagers who run creaky old guest houses on the side. It's a tourism machine with a veneer of quaintness.

People-watching on the square for a few minutes, I notice two different types of tourists. One is Chinese tour groups, sticking close together as they rush through town. In southern China, a mining company built a replica of Hallstatt's main square and pointy Protestant church on a lake near the city of Huizhou. This grew the fame of the original, and the Chinese bucket list when traveling to Europe now includes Hallstatt West.

I also spot an inordinate number of American kids, some wearing Elsa or Kristoff costumes. Disney's megahit *Frozen* takes place in some imaginary, vaguely Nordic land on a mystical fjord. But animators drew inspiration from images of Hallstatt. And so now, the world's children have joined the hordes of people flocking to Hallstatt—in their case, seeking Arendelle.

It troubles me that neither of these reasons have anything to do with Hallstatt itself, beyond its superficial appearance. So I go on a desperate scavenger hunt for the Hallstatt of yore, heading to the far end of town. Soon I'm lost in a rustic world of wooden lakefront houses. This part of Hallstatt has a special smell: damp, moss-covered rocks, and heavy timbers. Like summer camp.

My olfactory flashback ends abruptly as I pop out at Hallstatt's postcard viewpoint: a gap between houses offering views back on the town and its mammoth mountain backdrop. A mob of people stands in line, waiting to re-create the prefect Hallstatt snapshot they've seen on Instagram.

Dejected, I head back toward town, detouring to the Catholic church up on the ridge. Here it's quiet, save for the clang of bells every quarter-hour. The small, fenced plateau next to the church is home to a cemetery, its simple graves bedecked with fresh flowers. Hallstatt has only so much space for burial, so after a designated period of time, the dead are "evicted" and their bones neatly stacked in a chapel. Stepping into this charnel house, I'm greeted by neat rows of skulls, each yellowed forehead lovingly painted with the name of the person who once filled it.

Surveying the macabre but strangely touching scene, I notice clusters of shared family names: Steiner. Kierchschlager. Heuschober. Binder. All still together, beyond death. (Hope you like your in-laws.) It's a poignant—and eerily tangible—chronicle of a tight-knit community that's changing faster than these people could have imagined.

Stepping outside, I see a crew digging a fresh grave at a centuries-old headstone. Surveying the changeable nameplates—like postmortem dry-erase boards—I notice several death dates in the last few years. With a start, I wonder whether some of the Hallstatters I met back on that first visit might be permanent residents here now.

I've been doing this work long enough that people I once enjoyed visiting on the road are no longer alive. Walter, the ageless Swiss curmudgeon who ran a firetrap hotel in Gimmelwald,

passed away just months after the visit I described in these pages; he died peacefully in his hotel kitchen around New Year's Day, 2020. Dear friends of mine in Dubrovnik and Budapest have lost close relatives to cancer in the last couple of years. And that Croatian restaurant where my tour group was subjected to the hottest dinner of their lives? One of the owners was among Croatia's very first COVID-19 casualties.

Thinking back on those Hallstatters who made such an impression on me, and imagining them now in this cemetery, makes me sad at first. But then, looking at the sweeping views over the church steeple, the glassy lake, and the glorious Alps, I realize that if that's the case, then that's exactly as it should be.

Change though Hallstatt may, traditions die hard. And— tourists and Viennese investors be damned—the people of Hallstatt will always belong to the soil of their village, enjoying this gorgeous panorama for eternity . . . or at least until they're dug up and stacked on a shelf to make way for the next generation.

It's easy to view our experiences, even over what feels like a "long time," as definitive. But I try to remember that my lifetime as a traveler is just a blip in the story of Europe. This is a lesson I've learned from Roberto de Lorenzo, the Dubrovnik tour guide.

In recent years, Roberto's hometown has grown in popularity even faster than Hallstatt has. But Roberto reminds me that Dubrovnik has always been a gathering place—a trading post of sailors, merchants, and pirates from throughout the Mediterranean, Asia Minor, and North Africa. Sitting out on Dubrovnik's main drag, sipping a coffee as we people-watch, Roberto challenges me to mentally erase the flip-flops, tank tops, and sunglasses and see passersby simply as people, reenacting the timeless practice of going someplace new.

Romantics "discovered" Hallstatt during the Grand Tour days of European travel. A century later, "Rickniks" descended on the

town. Today, it's Chinese tourists and Disney pilgrims. The story is the same; only the people are different.

For the sake of those old Hallstatters, we can only hope that the next generation of both caretakers and visitors find something special here, too. The little girl dressed as Princess Elsa, or the tourist from Guangdong Province, appear to have very different life experiences from my own. But who knows? Today's "superficial" tourist may turn out to be tomorrow's temporary European.

Aunt Mildred could never have imagined that her great-great-niece—whom she knew only as a cheerful toddler—would marry someone who'd find such meaning in her memoir. And when Rick Steves received a long letter from that kid in Ohio, he couldn't have guessed it would blossom into such a long and fruitful collaboration. And yet today, I carry on their legacy of exploring the world. Mildred just had to tell her travel tales, and so does Rick, and so do I. When you love something that much, you just can't keep it in. And I hope that someday, someone I'd never expect will pick up that baton from me.

Jams Are Fun

In Rome, You Can Never Get a Taxi When It Rains

The airport clerk had directed the taxi driver in Spanish to call for me at eight o'clock in the morning. The driver was there right Johnny-on-the-spot. He was a good driver, taking me through Caracas and back to the airport. I couldn't thank him in Spanish, but I had a little English-Spanish dictionary, so I pointed to "good" and to "drive." He beamed with a broad smile.
—Mildred C. Scott, *Jams Are Fun*

Visitors (and even Romans) often describe Rome in terms of chaos. That strikes me as a little unfair, because I so often experience great hospitality and kindness in the Eternal City.

But then it rains, and everything goes straight to hell.

I'm finally going home, after a six-week journey through Europe. It's been a great trip, but I'm ready for a rest. On the morning of my departure, I pack up my bag and head downstairs to hop in a cab to the airport. It's Saturday morning, about nine o'clock.

When I tell the receptionist I need a taxi, a flash of quickly suppressed panic crosses his face. Feigning competence like a champ, he promptly gets on his computer and requests a cab for me. "It'll just be a moment. Once they confirm, I can give you the name and the time of arrival."

A few minutes pass. I'm relaxed, but he's growing agitated. Finally, he tries calling and is put immediately on hold.

Enough time goes by for me to recall how, just yesterday, I overheard a fellow guest ask to order a taxi for today. They were assured it was not necessary—"Just tell us when you're ready to leave, and we'll call one. It will be here in five, ten minutes maximum. No problem."

Last night, I double-checked and got exactly the same response: "Five, ten minutes, no problem."

But this morning—a mere ten hours later—the receptionist's quest to order a taxi is entering its eighth minute.

He looks at me apologetically and says, "In Rome, when it rains, it becomes very hard to get a taxi." He shrugs.

I glance outside, at bright sunshine gleaming off wet cobbles. "But . . . it's . . . not raining."

"Huh. Well, yes, *now*. But thirty minutes ago . . . ." Big shrug.

He glances over at the bellhop, who smiles and returns the big shrug.

We stand there, waiting, serenaded by the taxi dispatcher's schmaltzy hold music. The receptionist clicks feverishly on his keyboard. Finally, after about 12 minutes, the phone muzak is abruptly disconnected.

"Well," he says, "it seems that we may not be able to get you a taxi." Big shrug.

"But," I say. "I was told that it wasn't necessary to order one ahead. That you could just call one."

"Huh, yes. Well, *normally*," he shrugs. "But it's raining, so you understand, there are no taxis available." He repositions his computer screen toward me, so I can see for myself that his online request, too, has twice been declined.

"Don't you think, maybe, you could have told me that when I asked about this yesterday? You could have said, 'It's no problem *unless it rains*, in which case you need more time'?"

This idea is preposterous. He explodes with laughter. "Ha! Well, sir, of course you can't expect us to *predict the weather*, now can you?" He laughs heartily at his own zinger and glances over to the bellhop for backup. The bellhop looks up from what he's doing to return a generous chuckle, with a side of shrug.

It takes the bellhop a moment to respond because—and I swear I am not making this up—at this precise moment, he is talking to a rather unpleasant American guest who has been loudly complaining about the weather. To egg her on, he is showing her the many rainclouds in the weather app on his phone.

Also—and not to belabor the point—it's not like we're in the Gobi Desert here. It rains in Rome. It has rained four of the last five days in Rome. In Rome, it rains, on average, something like 70 days every year. If you work at a Roman hotel, and it's a rainy week, and you are aware that it's impossible to get a taxi in the rain, don't you think you might furnish this information to guests who ask about it?

It dawns on me that perhaps this maddening duo assumes my taxi trip is an optional one. Maybe it's just, you know, a passing fancy. A joyride. Skippable. "Oh well, no matter. I could use the brisk walk anyway!" But I have a 5,000-mile journey ahead of me. And the first step of that journey is *getting to the friggin' airport.*

"So then," I say. "What do you suggest? Am I supposed to *walk* to the airport?"

The receptionist gives me an "Oh you're still here?" look, then theatrically shrugs three times—the first, presumably, for the Father, the second for the Son, and the third for the Holy Spirit.

"Well, there is a taxi stand. It's next to the Zara, across the piazza and to the left." He gestures with an exquisitely unhelpful vagueness toward the front door.

The bellhop nods vigorously as if to say, "Yeah, yeah, taxi stand, yeah."

"But if you can't call a taxi, why should I expect that there will be one just sitting there, waiting for me?"

Trapped in an impenetrable cage of logic, our antagonist can only offer a big shrug in response. "Well, we only work with certain companies. But there are many companies. So . . . maybe . . . one of the *other* companies . . . has taxis there?" While he's grasping for reassurance, it's clear that he's making this up as he goes, and he achieves exactly the opposite.

This guy may not have been the star of his hospitality school class, but I've gotta hand it to him: He's the living embodiment of ¯_(ツ)_/¯. I have seen a lot in my travels, but I have never had a hotel flatly refuse to help me find a taxi. I predict a 90 percent chance of downgrades in the next edition of our guidebook.

I know when I've been beat, so I sigh theatrically—the only meaningful response to the Roman Shrug—and try to get more precise directions to the (quite possibly hypothetical) taxi stand across the piazza. The bellhop halfheartedly offers to accompany me there, but at this point it will be a tremendous relief to simply cut ties with the crack staff of the Grand Hotel Shrug.

I trudge through brilliant sunshine across the piazza and make my way to Zara. The taxi stand has but one taxi. But one is all I need. Friendly Fabrizio hops out, loads my bag in the trunk, and rattles my fillings as he mounts the curb to catch a yellow light—getting me to Da Vinci Airport in record time. *Grazie*, Fabrizio!

As for the security line at the Rome airport . . . well, that's another story, for another day.

Epilogue

After the World Changed, a New Hope for Travel
Or: Shutterbugs Miss the Lion

We were stopped beside a pond one day and a lioness dashed across to the other side, trying to catch a zebra. Our guide yelled, "The lion!" I saw it, but the shutterbugs were so busy trying to get their cameras poised that I think most of them missed the lion.
—Mildred C. Scott, *Jams Are Fun*

In September of 2019, I flew to Europe for about the fortieth time. Over the next six weeks, I enjoyed a productive guidebook-research trip in Iceland, Switzerland, Provence, and Slovenia—experiencing some of the events described in this book.

But it was a strange time for travel. A few months earlier, I had huddled with the rest of our Leadership Team—Rick's inner circle of advisors and department heads—to grapple with challenges we saw on the horizon. Our focus was managing growth smartly and dealing with the crush of crowds descending on Europe.

If travel in 2019 had a theme, it was "overtourism." Over the previous decade or so, the growing middle classes in China and India had reached a tipping point of affluence, and their travel appetites had extended to Europe. Layering entire new demographics of visitors onto an already overtaxed infrastructure came with serious growing pains.

On that visit to Switzerland, formerly sleepy cities and mountaintops were noticeably crowded. I kept getting an earful from people I knew to be stoic and patient and good-hearted. But they had reached a breaking point, and now they were doing an uncanny impression of xenophobes and racists. "Those Chinese are such a scourge! Enough!" one hotelier grumbled. Another said: "When you go up to the Jungfraujoch, all you smell is Indian food. The cafeteria that used to sell *Bratwurst* and *Rösti* has been turned into a 'Restaurant Bollywood' with curry and samosas."

These sentiments may well have been tinged with racism. But that alone was not behind them. The Swiss were reacting to the culture clash of people from opposite corners of the globe, who had different understandings of appropriate behavior, thrust together in massive numbers. Traveling across Europe, observing the melee that erupted at each major museum, iconic landmark, and lift station—places that had once been regimented and controlled—I could see this friction firsthand.

It struck me that these Chinese visitors were at a very specific moment in their touristic evolution: Travel was suddenly possible and exciting. Naturally, they packed in everything they could, without much regard for the impact they were having on the places they visited. It reminded me of American travelers in 1950s and 1960s Europe, when the stereotype of the "Ugly American" was born. In the decades since, I believe Rick Steves—with his encouragement to travel as a temporary European—has done more to civilize American travelers than anyone else. And China hasn't yet found its Rick Steves.

At the same time, Instagram had become a driving force in travel. Increasingly, people traveled to capture a carefully staged "ephemeral" moment for their friends and followers.

Everywhere I went that fall, I saw people striving to re-create scenes from their social media feeds. In the Swiss mountain village of Mürren, on the way from the train station into town, there's a tree stump at the edge a cliff, with the panorama of the Eiger, Mönch, and Jungfrau just behind. Every time I walked past that stump, hordes of people were lined up for that influencer-endorsed photo op, ignoring the exact same (and entirely crowd-free) view 50 yards up the road. And then they'd walk on, faces buried in their phones, getting in the way of local farmers and ignoring the alpine majesty all around them.

I wondered whether this could be sustainable. That's not quite true: I knew it was not sustainable. Europe was at a boiling point. And as the world economy chugged ahead, these trends showed no sign of relenting, barring some external force grinding travel entirely to a halt.

On a personal note, the last day of that trip was one of my most frustrating in years. I'd arranged a 36-hour layover in London on my way home, to treat myself to a full day in one of my favorite cities at the end of a very busy year of travels.

However, everything was off-kilter. My flight into London was several hours late. The next day, I woke to cold and rain. I had a list of neighborhoods I wanted to explore, just for fun, but it was anything but fun. My one day in London—my last day in Europe before the world changed—was the very embodiment of *not* living in the moment.

I decided to attend a matinee at Shakespeare's Globe and spent the morning incessantly checking for last-minute tickets on my phone. I finally found one, 45 minutes before show time, and stood in the doorway of a café to mooch their Wi-Fi long enough to book it. Then I raced to the Tube stop—abruptly ending my exploration of a neighborhood I'd long been curious to see—and made it to the theater just in time.

On the way to the theater, I saw that Bill Bryson—a writer I've long admired—was speaking in Oxford that evening. And so I spent the entire first half of the play distracted with trying to figure out whether I could make it there in time. I spent the intermission on the phone to book a last-minute ticket, standing in the wooden stairwell as I read my credit-card number into a choppy connection. I returned to my seat under the thatched roof a few minutes after the play had resumed—yes, I was the clod stepping over a row of people while the actors were performing. And, once seated, I spent the remainder of the show praying it would end early enough to catch my train.

I made it to Oxford and greatly enjoyed Bill Bryson's presentation. During the Q&A, he confessed that he was going to take a break—perhaps a permanent break. After many prolific years, he was tired of researching. Tired of writing. Tired of letting his passion get in the way of time with his family. He was, simply, tired.

After narrowly missing a train back to London, then sitting on the pitch-black platform for 45 minutes waiting for the next one, I got to my B&B after midnight. Early the next morning, I packed my bag for the flight home. I reached Victoria Station with plenty of time to spare, but the platform was eerily quiet. At the turnstiles, a British Rail attendant cheerfully informed me that the Gatwick Express wasn't running today.

I was, instantly, in a panic. "What! How am I supposed to get to my flight?"

"Hmm, well, yes. That's a tricky one. You can ride the Tube to Westminster, then change to the Jubilee line to London Bridge station. From there Thameslink trains go to Gatwick."

"Great, thanks," I said sarcastically, ignoring him as he trailed off: " . . . but those aren't express . . . "

With six weeks' worth of accumulated nonsense strapped to my back, my aching, too-old-for-this-shit legs sprinted through the station to the Tube. Then I sprinted through tunnel-like concourses to change trains at Westminster. Then I sprinted through

London Bridge Station and hopped on the Thameslink train seconds before the doors hissed shut. And finally, I sprinted through Gatwick, and made it onto my flight just in time for final boarding.

I was furious, for some reason, *at London*. But it wasn't London's fault. It was mine. I had gotten ahead of myself in pursuit of magic, forgetting that magic only happens when you're not forcing it. I'd lost my ability to find the fun in the jams.

During my journey to Gatwick, the famous Samuel Johnson quote echoed in my mind: "When a man is tired of London, he is tired of life."

Quite right. Like Bill Bryson, I was tired. And I think Europe was tired. We all needed a break. And we were about to get one.

A few months later, I was planning for a very busy 2020: Guidebook research in Amsterdam, Berlin, Budapest, and the Norwegian fjords. Filming new TV shows that I'd scripted in Poland and Iceland. And in the fall, I'd be coming out of tour-guide retirement to lead our first-ever Poland tour, an itinerary I'd helped design.

Around New Year's Day, I saw a news item about a mysterious new illness afflicting people in Wuhan, China.

A few weeks later, I went to a drugstore to buy some hand sanitizer and surgical masks. They were out of stock.

Around that time, the first US case of the novel coronavirus was diagnosed in Snohomish County, Washington. The patient was treated at a hospital a 30-minute drive north of Rick Steves' Europe headquarters.

Also just then, my office hosted our annual guides' gathering, a busy week of hugging and kissing cheeks and sharing food with people from across Europe and the USA. I invited two dozen Eastern Europeans into my home for a convivial dinner. We did the "Chicken Dance" together in my living room. Several of the guides arrived sick, as they always do. Several of them left sick, as they always do.

Over the next few weeks, as the virus—now called COVID-19—continued its spread, we quietly prepared for the possibility of working from home. At that point, I still believed I'd be taking off for Amsterdam on May 11. I was already booking flights and hotel rooms.

The turning point came in March. It became clear that travel—something I'd built my life around—was now guilty of accelerating the worst global pandemic in a century. That culture clash I'd observed on the mountaintops of Switzerland was a practice run for what was happening now, on a microbiological scale, in Wuhan and New York City and Bergamo and Snohomish County's nursing homes.

On March 11, our Leadership Team gathered, furiously rubbing our hands with sanitizer, to consider next steps. Mid-meeting, we paused to watch our governor, Jay Inslee, soberly lay out the risks and precautions to keep our community safe. And we knew it was time to close down.

The next afternoon, Rick gathered the troops. We stood outside in the backyard of Book Haus, doing our best to get our heads around this new concept of "social distancing." It was sunny and warm—one of the first nice days of the year, with a promise of spring renewal drifting ironically in the breeze. Rick explained that we were about to begin working from home. And, despite the uncertainty before us, he remained militantly optimistic. As a company, we'd been through several once-a-decade crises: Gulf War, 9/11, Great Recession. Each time, we persevered and emerged stronger on the other side. The pent-up desire to travel never goes away, it only builds. And during hard times, our responsibility is to survive so we're ready when travelers are ready to get back to what they love.

As that meeting broke up, I looked around at one hundred scared but momentarily soothed faces, and I grew very sad. I feared that some of those faces might not be here on the other end of this

crisis. As it turns out, nobody on our team contracted a fatal case of COVID-19. But my fears were realized in a different way.

By early summer, Rick wisely realized that we needed to hunker down for the long haul, which meant keeping as many people employed as possible, and sharing the sacrifice in the form of partial furloughs. Several people, quite reasonably, left for other jobs with full pay and more promising near-term prospects. And a few members of the "old guard" realized that the way they could best serve the company they helped build was to retire ahead of schedule.

For the next several months, I worked from my dining room table. I hung a "Keep Calm and Carry On" tea towel in my front window to rally my neighbors through our version of the Blitz. Not long after that outdoor meeting, I cancelled plans for my spring trip to Europe. Then my summer trip. Then my fall trip. Weeks passed. Months passed.

On a couple of occasions, I went to sit with Rick on his big deck overlooking Puget Sound. Normally we'd be watching cruise ships sail toward Alaskan adventures. But like us, they were taking an unplanned gap year. Squinting in the Seattle summer sun—something both Rick and I often miss, as we're usually in Europe—we daydreamed about the day when we could get back to traveling. We reminisced about favorite travel memories, compared notes about what each of us had heard from our favorite Europeans, and made vague, unkeepable promises about the post-pandemic future of travel.

Meanwhile, we worried for our many European friends: freelance tour guides, local guides, hoteliers, restaurateurs, and many others whom you've met in these pages. Some were trapped in tiny urban apartments, allowed outside only once or twice a week to get groceries and take out garbage. (One friend, in Rome, would go to the rooftop of her apartment building and walk in tight circles for hours, listening to American pop hits from the 1980s.) Others escaped to the countryside, finally having the time to become avid hikers or even farmers.

From Slovenia, Tina Hiti sent me updates about her dad and her boys, who were furious about not being able to play hockey for the first time in their lives. When I wrote to Roberto de Lorenzo, he wrote back: "Many regards from Dubrovnik, a city that remains hopeful and holds its heart open."

All of our European friends faced at least a year without income. These kind-hearted people, who open up their hearts to the world, were locked down and unemployed. As each side of the Atlantic settled into our respective quarantines, isolation set in. I'd spent months each year hanging out with Europeans non-stop. And now I was going cold turkey. As time wore on, I found myself growing increasingly, unaccountably cranky. It took me months to realize that I was desperately missing Europe, and more important, Europeans. Much as I lean into my introversion, at the end of the day, perhaps I'm a Euro-extrovert after all.

* * *

During that interminable year, in an attempt to make good use of my unplanned hiatus from travel, I dedicated many months of quarantine to writing this book. Around the time I began working full-time on the project, news began to trickle out of successful vaccine trials and FDA approvals. As I write this, nationwide vaccination is underway, as is the rise of troubling variants. After months of false starts, I'm cultivating a cautious hope that—for the first time since that wasted opportunity to enjoy a day in London—I'll be back in Europe before too long. By the time you read this, the outcome of all this will be ancient history . . . it may even seem quaint, if you were fortunate enough to emerge relatively unscathed.

What have I learned from the last year? And, with the benefit of ample time for retrospection, what have I learned from 2019, with its distractions from good travel?

As I worked through the material that became this book, I found a consistent theme hiding away on every page. This subtext is, I'll admit, painfully obvious. But I can't escape its simple wisdom: The best moments arrive when you forget about your itinerary, stow your guidebook and phone, and simply be present in Europe. (Aunt Mildred could've saved me 20 years, if I'd read her book earlier.)

I've devoted my career to guidebooks. I believe in them, and I use them anywhere I go. But when I design one, I don't want it to be "indispensable." I want it to get you to the point where you can put it away and enjoy yourself.

The best travel tip—now more than ever—is this: Slow down. Sit on a bench. Take a breath. Listen to the birds chirping and the waves lapping the shore and the hubbub of a life you'll never live, except for right now, except for in this moment. Notice details you've always missed. Forget about where you're going

next—focus on where you are now. Believe me, with my endless to-do lists, there's nobody who has a harder task of this than I do. But somehow—not always, but just enough—I manage. And I'll redouble my efforts when I hit the road again.

On my earliest trips, travel humbled me. It taught me that the world is a big and beautiful and fascinating place, and I am but a speck in it. Reading Aunt Mildred's book, I'm amazed by the sheer effort travel demanded back then. Mildred had to earn every mile and every moment. And she savored each one. Things were much easier for me when I first started to travel, and had become easier still by the time I finished, for a while at least, in 2020.

Before the world changed, we'd come to take travel for granted. "Travel" for many had become ticking items off a list—bundling experiences into a tidy package for consumption on social media. On my last day on the road, I had a full, unstructured day in London, one of the world's great cities. And I wasted it by doing too much and not slowing down to appreciate any of it. As Aunt Mildred might point out, shutterbugs miss the lion.

Europe is so many things, as you've seen in these pages. It's beautiful, and complicated, and delicious, and confusing, and filled with kind and fascinating and aggravating people. I'm aching to get back there. The Impressionist painting that is Europe, in my mind, still isn't finished—and never will be—but I'm always eager to add more brushstrokes. That's the beauty of travel, and even more, it's the wonder of ever-so-gradually becoming a temporary European.

I am hopeful that, as the world begins anew, travelers won't just dive in headfirst, but wade in slowly. If ever there was a time to renew our dedication to more thoughtful travel—to travel on purpose—it's now. We may be busy and, at times, stressed. But we should never forget, or squander, the privilege of living at a time when the planet is ours to explore. Travel can be more than hedonism and distraction. It can be an opportunity for meaning, humility, and grace. But only if you take a moment out of your busy day to stand still and listen to those church bells.

For much of the planet, 2020 was frightening and frustrating and tragic. But even during the most hopeless of times, I found myself falling back on a muscle memory I've been developing, without realizing it, over a lifetime of travel: When plans go sideways, you take a deep breath, regroup, and find your way. Whether you're trying to get to the airport in London, or you lose an entire productive year to a pandemic, you get to choose how to respond.

During those interminable days of the pandemic—with very little changing other than the death toll—I often imagined Sisyphus, the arrogant, disgraced king of Greek myth who was sentenced to an eternity of pushing a giant rock up a hill. Each time Sisyphus reaches the top of the hill, the rock rolls back down to the bottom, and he must begin again.

I can never think about Sisyphus for too long; that sense of infinite futility makes my brain ache, like I'm inhaling some noxious chemical. I have to turn away. Through history, though, others have been willing to confront the plight of Sisyphus head-on. Some have tried to rationalize away his misery: Perhaps, one scholar suggests, Sisyphus brings a small stone from the top of the mountain to the bottom with each trip, eventually leveling the terrain and easing his task. But that's a cheat; you don't get to ignore a difficult reality. You have to face it.

In 1942, the French existentialist Albert Camus came up with the most elegant solution for relieving Sisyphus. When you exhaust all other alternatives—denial, anger, bargaining, a *Shawshank Redemption*-like effort to remove the mountain—you're left with only one viable option: acceptance. Like the traveler whose itinerary has been blown to smithereens, the only sane response is to find a way to be present in the chaos. As Camus reasons, "One must imagine Sisyphus happy."

Or, as Aunt Mildred put it: Jams are fun.

Lumpensammler

Favorites (and Least Favorites)

When my parents lived in Switzerland, the final tram of the night—which picked up all manner of drunks, weirdos, and ne'er-do-wells as it passed through town—was nicknamed the *Lumpensammler*, or "collector of dirty rags." I always thought that would be a perfect alternative to an "Appendix": the loose odds and ends that get swept up just before the final pages.

My *Lumpensammler* is a list of my favorite places and experiences in Europe, providing a sort of roundup of the journey we've taken together. It also helps answer one of the questions I'm most frequently asked: What are your favorite places? (In other words, where should I go on my next trip?)

Any list like this is arbitrary and cheeky to the point of fool-hardiness. It's admittedly subjective; your mileage will vary. If you wonder "why?" for any of these, in many cases, you can divine the answers from this book's travel tales.

Favorite Country: Slovenia, followed by any one of a half-dozen countries I've been to most recently (Great Britain, Hungary, Italy, Norway, Poland, Iceland . . .)

Countries I've Visited Briefly and Would Love to Know Better: Ireland, Portugal, Estonia, Serbia

Countries I've Had Enough of for the Time Being, Thanks All the Same: Spain, Romania, Slovakia, Austria

Most Misunderstood Countries: France, Hungary, Poland

Most Perplexing Country: Russia

Most Perplexing Non-Russian City: Budapest

Favorite Big Cities: Budapest, London, Berlin

Favorite Small Cities: Ljubljana, Slovenia; Gdańsk, Poland; Sarajevo, Bosnia-Herzegovina

Favorite Towns: Sarlat, France; Eger, Hungary; Canterbury, England; Nafplio, Greece

Most Underappreciated Cities: Oslo, Norway; Salamanca, Spain; Sofia, Bulgaria; Antwerp, Belgium; Bern, Switzerland; Erfurt, Germany; Porto, Portugal; Olomouc, Czech Republic

Most Overrated Cities: Salzburg, Austria; Milan, Italy; Vienna, Austria

Least Favorite Cities: Bucharest, Romania; Catania, Sicily; Bratislava, Slovakia

Cities that Initially Seemed Meh, but Have Gotten Under My Skin: Warsaw, Poland; Palermo, Sicily; Reykjavík, Iceland

Favorite Hipster Neighborhoods: Prenzlauer Berg, Berlin; Psyrri, Athens; Brick Lane/Spitalfields, London; Seventh District, Budapest; Monti, Rome; Chiado, Lisbon

Favorite Natural Areas: Val d'Orcia (Tuscany), Italy; Julian Alps, Slovenia; Mývatn geothermal area, North Iceland; Dalmatian Coast, Croatia; Sognefjord and Lustrafjord, Norway

Favorite Road Trips: Iceland's Ring Road; Slovenia's Vršič Pass and Soča Valley; pretty much anywhere in the British countryside (especially North Wales, Dartmoor, and the Cotswolds)

Favorite Seaside Escapes: Rovinj and Dubrovnik, Croatia; Salema, Portugal; Collioure, France; Kardamyli, Greece

Favorite and Least Favorite Seaside Escape: Italy's Cinque Terre

Most Dramatically Situated Towns: Reine, Norway; Veliko Tarnovo, Bulgaria; Santorini, Greece; Ronda, Spain

Most Overrated Dramatically Situated Town: Taormina, Sicily

Favorite Hedonistic Activity: Thermal baths (Hungary or Iceland)

Favorite Food Experiences: Pasta-making class at Cretaiole, Tuscany; browsing London's street markets; truffle pasta in Istria, Croatia

Favorite Castles and Palaces: Alhambra (Granada, Spain); Peleş Castle (Romania); Château de Chillon (Lake Geneva, Switzerland); Hermitage (St. Petersburg, Russia); Konopiště Castle (Czech Republic)

Favorite Houses of Worship: Gaudí's Sagrada Família (Barcelona, Spain); Church of the Savior on Spilled Blood (St. Petersburg, Russia); Mezquita (Córdoba, Spain); Hopperstad Stave Church (Vik, Norway); Hagia Sophia (Istanbul, Turkey); Viscri Church (Transylvania, Romania)

Favorite (Lesser-Known) Museums and Sights: Vigeland Park (Oslo, Norway); Zlatyu Boyadzhiev Museum (Plovdiv, Bulgaria); frescoes at Monte Oliveto Maggiore (Tuscany, Italy); European Solidarity Center (Gdańsk, Poland); Herring Era Museum (Siglufjörður, Iceland)

Favorite Places to Feel Far from Civilization: Norway's Lofoten Islands, Iceland's Westfjords, Romania's Maramureş, rural Bosnia-Herzegovina, Orkney (Scotland)

Weirdest Places I've Been: Chernobyl, Ukraine, followed by the places listed above

Favorite US Escapes: Central Oregon Coast; Kaua'i, Hawai'i

Favorite International Destination Beyond Europe: New Zealand

To answer that overarching question, there's a special place in my heart for underrated gems—places that I'm confident any traveler would fall in love with, if given a chance. Topping that list is Slovenia. I've never met someone who went to Slovenia and didn't adore the place, and come home kicking themselves that they didn't allow more time there.

The many people zipping to Iceland for a 48-hour "layover" really should consider extending that by a week or two; impressive as Iceland is on a short visit, it's even better on a long one.

And I believe that anyone interested in historical, beautiful northern European cities would fall in love with Gdańsk, Poland, as I have.

In general, I'm a fan of what I call Europe's "third-rate" towns. These aren't the top-tier cities (London, Paris, Rome), or even the "next most popular" destinations (York, Nice, Milan). They're the ones much farther down the list. Several of these appear on the list above; others include Dresden or Freiburg, Germany; Albi, Honfleur, or Colmar, France; Delft or Leiden, the Netherlands; and so on. Even if you're determined to hit some of the biggies, mix in a few of these lesser-known gems.

Acknowledgments

I thank my many European friends, especially the ones mentioned in this book: Alma, Ermin, and Jaz Elezović; Tina, Gorazd, and Breda Hiti, and Sašo, Anže, and Tomaž Golub (Private Guide Slovenia); Andrzej Durman (a.k.a. "Cousin Andrew"); Pero Carević, Pero Paviša, Ivana and Anita Raič, Jadranka Benussi, Roberto de Lorenzo, Marija Tiberi, Pepo Klaić, and Siniša Matković-Mikulčić (Secret Hvar); Roberto Bechi, Adamo Pallecchi (Cantina Contucci), Cesare Mazzetti (Rinomata Rameria Mazzetti), Giulio Ciolfi (Osteria dell'Acquacheta), and Nicola Sgarbi (Buon Gusto Gelateria); Vincenzo Pauciullo (Mondo Tours); Marco Romeo (Streaty Tours); Tomasz Klimek; Mathilde Ploix (Taste of Provence); Lovey and Sigmund Thesen and Mo and John West; Isabella, Carlo, Luciano, and Liliana Moricciani (Cretaiole); la Família Dominguez-Bravo; the many wonderful Romanians (names changed to protect the innocent) who did their best to help our TV shoot; Virginia Agostinelli; Walter Mittler and trusty Tim (Hotel Mittaghorn); the whole blessed city of Budapest (especially Péter, Andrea, Elemér, George, and Eszter); David Kinnaird (Stirling GhostWalk); Ruth Manfredi and her fellow spies of the Cinque Terre; and Frau Scheutz, Herr Zauner, and Hallstatt's other old-timers. And yes, I even thank the cranky ticket-seller at the *Last Supper*, the motorists of Sicily, and the crack staff at the Grand Hotel Shrug—all of whom conspired to create some of my favorite jams.

Acknowledgments

Rick Steves took a chance on this ballsy kid from Ohio and gave me opportunity after opportunity to share my passion with our travelers. Thank you, Rick. I've never stopped learning from America's favorite travel teacher, and who knows? Maybe I've taught him a trick or two along the way.

Much as I love to travel for a living, I consider myself even more fortunate to have found a family of wonderful colleagues in Edmonds. Thanks to all of the co-workers—too many to name—who've woven their way, often unseen, through these pages. Amy Duncan offered both advice and encouragement as I created the blog that eventually became this book. Thanks to Craig Davidson and Teresa Miller for their support in taking time for this project (not to mention, for keeping our company alive through a once-a-century pandemic). And special thanks to the many talented tour guides I've learned from (including Rick Garman, Ian Watson, and Honza Vihan) and to our TV production team extraordinaire: Simon Griffith, Karel Bauer, and Steve Cammarano.

Dave Hoerlein was Rick Steves' first-ever hire and hand-drew all of our maps for years. Thanks, Dave, for this book's map. And thanks to my fellow guidebook co-authors: Gene Openshaw, Steve Smith, and Pat O'Connor. The four of you have been my friends, my mentors, and my inspiration since I first arrived in Edmonds.

Risa Laib deserves as much credit as anyone (and, frankly, probably more) for creating America's most trusted guidebook series; along the way, she taught me just about everything she knows. I thank her, along with the many other "Bookies" I've worked with and learned from—especially Jennifer Madison Davis, who carries on Risa's legacy of both excellence and kindness.

Ben Curtis—my fellow Slavophile—read an (embarrassingly) early version of this manuscript, and his keen insights focused my energies to make it immeasurably better. I also received impactful feedback along the way from Nikki Ioakimedes, Rachel Allen, Amy Duncan, and above all, Shawna.

And I thank Bill Newlin, Larry Habegger, James O'Reilly, and Tiffany Hawk for believing in this book and helping it find a path to publication.

Thanks to Mildred C. Scott for her inspiration, and to the Scott clan, who took me in as one of their own . . . and even allowed me to appropriate their auntie and family lore in my writings.

Aunt Mildred is a stand-in for the many strong, smart, funny, compassionate, courageous, exemplary Ohio women who shaped my most formative years: Di Huston, Syd Schnaars, Helen Andersson, Tracey Scott, Mo Kissner, Louise Scott, Erika Hewitt, Courtney Scott, Bonnie Cozze, and so many others. And even though they're not Buckeyes, that list includes my beloved grandmas, Lillian and Pearl. I believe they and Mildred would've been fast friends.

Speaking of which, three close friends have been with me on various stages of this journey: Aaron Cook was there in Madrid the moment I first set foot in Europe; Trevor Holmes lured me to Eastern Europe and met me on Kraków's main square; and Andy Snyder almost talked me into lugging his Russian textbook to Trevor in Slovakia. You guys can't know how much you've impacted my travels, and my life.

Above all, I thank Mom and Dad, Fawn and Kempton Hewitt, for teaching me that this world is a beautiful and fascinating place; for equipping me to appreciate it once I finally experienced it; and for emboldening me to go out and discover it—even if that meant physically planting me in an airplane seat and strapping me down.

And, of course, I thank Shawna, my high school sweetheart, best friend, and favorite travel partner. You're a "travel widow" one-quarter of our lives and unfailingly patient and supportive year-round. This book is just the tip of the iceberg; nothing in my life, in Europe or at home, would be possible without you.

About the Author

Cameron Hewitt was born in Denver, grew up in Central Ohio, and moved to Seattle in 2000 to help Rick Steves research and write America's bestselling guidebooks. Since then, Cameron has spent about 100 days in Europe each year. He has traveled to and written about more than 35 European countries and has co-authored guidebooks on Croatia, Budapest, Iceland, Scotland, Greece, Berlin, and more. Cameron also guides Rick Steves tours in Europe; contributes to Rick's television series and radio program; presents travel talks; and blogs about his travels at www.cameronhewitt.com. Cameron married his high school sweetheart and favorite travel partner, Shawna; they live in the Phinney Ridge neighborhood of Seattle, Washington.

A SELECTION OF TRAVELERS' TALES BOOKS

Travel Literature

The Best Travel Writing, Soul of a Great Traveler, Deer Hunting in Paris, Fire Never Dies, Ghost Dance in Berlin, Guidebook Experiment, Kin to the Wind, Kite Strings of the Southern Cross, Last Trout in Venice, Marco Polo Didn't Go There, Rivers Ran East, Royal Road to Romance, A Sense of Place, Shopping for Buddhas, Soul of Place, Storm, Sword of Heaven, Take Me With You, Unbeaten Tracks in Japan, Way of Wanderlust, Wings, Coast to Coast, Mother Tongue, Baboons for Lunch, Strange Tales of World Travel, The Girl Who Said No, French Like Moi, End of the World Notwithstanding

Women's Travel

100 Places Every Woman Should Go, 100 Places in Italy Every Woman Should Go, 100 Places in France Every Woman Should Go, 100 Places in Greece Every Woman Should Go, 100 Places in the USA Every Woman Should Go, 100 Places in Cuba Every Woman Should Go, 50 Places in Rome, Florence, & Venice Every Woman Should Go, Best Women's Travel Writing, Gutsy Women, Mother's World, Safety and Security for Women Who Travel, Wild with Child, Woman's Asia, Woman's Europe, Woman's Path, Woman's World, Woman's World Again, Women in the Wild

Body & Soul

Food, How to Eat Around the World, A Mile in Her Boots, Pilgrimage, Road Within

Country and Regional Guides

30 Days in Italy, 30 Days in the South Pacific, America, Antarctica, Australia, Brazil, Central America, China, Cuba, France, Greece, India, Ireland, Italy, Japan, Mexico, Nepal, Spain, Thailand, Tibet, Turkey; Alaska, American Southwest, Grand Canyon, Hawai'i, Hong Kong, Middle East, Paris, Prague, Provence, San Francisco, South Pacific, Tuscany

Special Interest

Danger!, Gift of Birds, Gift of Rivers, Gift of Travel, How to Shit Around the World, Hyenas Laughed at Me, Leave the Lipstick, Take the Iguana, More Sand in My Bra, Mousejunkies!, Not So Funny When It Happened, Sand in My Bra, Testosterone Planet, There's No Toilet Paper on the Road Less Traveled, Thong Also Rises, What Color Is Your Jockstrap?, Wake Up and Smell the Shit, The World Is a Kitchen, Writing Away, China Option, La Dolce Vita University